Revised Edition

The Private Voice Studio Handbook

A Practical Guide to All Aspects of Teaching

by Joan Frey Boytim

ISBN 978-0-634-04738-1

HAL•LEONARD®
CORPORATION

7777 W. BLUEMOUND RD. P.O. BOX 13819 MILWAUKEE, WI 53213

Visit Hal Leonard Online at
www.halleonard.com

First printing of revised edition, 2014

Printed in the United States of America

Library of Congress Control Number 2003103048

ISBN 978-0-634-04738-1

Joan Frey Boytim is nationally known in the field of voice instruction. In her workshops and presentations at many events over the years, especially at the conventions of the National Association of Teachers of Singing, she has shared her expertise with thousands of other voice teachers. Through her ability to articulate to other teachers the special issues in guiding young singers, Mrs. Boytim has become the most recognized American expert in training the young voice.

For over fifty-five years Mrs. Boytim has taught voice in her private studio in Carlisle, Pennsylvania. It is unusual that a teacher of Mrs. Boytim's caliber has devoted herself almost exclusively to teaching teenagers to sing, which has been her passion.

Joan Boytim is the compiler of the twelve-book G. Schirmer series *The First Book of Solos*, *The First Book of Solos Part II*, and *The Second Book of Solos*. She also is compiler of the four-book Hal Leonard series *The First Book of Broadway Solos*, among other publications, and is the author of the widely-used bibliography *Solo Vocal Repertoire for Young Singers*, published by the National Association of Teachers of Singing.

Mrs. Boytim was educated at Indiana University of Pennsylvania where she received a Bachelor of Science degree in Music Education and a Master of Education in Music Education. Her continuing education included 30 graduate credits in Voice and Vocal Pedagogy at Indiana University in Bloomington and a year's study at the Staatliche Hochschule für Musik in Munich, Germany.

OTHER PUBLICATIONS BY JOAN FREY BOYTIM
Compiler and Editor

G. Schirmer publications (distributed by Hal Leonard Corporation):

Easy Songs for the Beginning Soprano
Easy Songs for the Beginning Mezzo-Soprano/Alto
Easy Songs for the Beginning Tenor
Easy Songs for the Beginning Baritone/Bass

The First Book of Soprano Solos
The First Book of Mezzo-Soprano/Alto Solos
The First Book of Tenor Solos
The First Book of Baritone/Bass Solos

The First Book of Soprano Solos Part II
The First Book of Mezzo-Soprano/Alto Solos Part II
The First Book of Tenor Solos Part II
The First Book of Baritone/Bass Solos Part II

The First Book of Soprano Solos Part III
The First Book of Mezzo-Soprano/Alto Solos Part III
The First Book of Tenor Solos Part III
The First Book of Baritone/Bass Solos Part III

The Second Book of Soprano Solos
The Second Book of Mezzo-Soprano/Alto Solos
The Second Book of Tenor Solos
The Second Book of Baritone/Bass Solos

The Second Book of Soprano Solos Part II
The Second Book of Mezzo-Soprano/Alto Solos Part II
The Second Book of Tenor Solos Part II
The Second Book of Baritone/Bass Solos Part II

The First Book of Soprano Solos – Complete Parts I, II, and III
The First Book of Mezzo-Soprano/Alto Solos – Complete Parts I, II, and III
The First Book of Tenor Solos – Complete Parts I, II, and III
The First Book of Baritone/Bass Solos – Complete Parts I, II, and III

Hal Leonard publications:

36 Solos for Young Singers

36 More Solos for Young Singers

Christmas Solos for All Ages
 High Voice
 Medium Voice
 Low Voice

Daffodils, Violets and Snowflakes
 High Voice
 Low Voice

The First Book of Broadway Solos
(in four volumes)
 Soprano
 Mezzo-Soprano/Alto
 Tenor
 Baritone/Bass

The First Book of Broadway Solos Part II
(in four volumes)
 Soprano
 Mezzo-Soprano/Alto
 Tenor
 Baritone/Bass

Lovers, Lasses and Spring
 Soprano

Roses, Laughter and Lullabies
 Mezzo-Soprano

Sacred Solos for All Ages
 High Voice
 Medium Voice
 Low Voice

Young Ladies, Shipmates and Journeys
 Tenor
 Baritone/Bass

Easy Classical Duets

Traditional Sacred Duets

To my husband Jim, for his assistance in editing this book and his support of all my musical activities and those of my students, young and old, throughout the years.

CONTENTS

INTRODUCTION
TO THE REVISED EDITION

I have been told by many teachers and students that the original edition of this handbook has been a great help to young college students beginning to plan to have a part-time or full-time career of teaching voice, and established teachers wanting to be more business-like in their approach to their established studios.

This new edition tries to address many of the changes in our lives during the last eleven years. Before you continue, it would be advantageous for you to completely read the *Introduction from the Original 2003 Edition* (page xiii) so that you have a basic understanding of the purpose of this volume.

Eleven years ago we knew nothing about smart phones and iPads as well as all the other amazing electronic devices available to us now. Television shows have changed with so many reality shows like *American Idol*, popular style singing competitions, and *Glee*. During the Johnny Carson era, one often heard classical musicians and new famous opera singers on his show. This is completely missing from current late night TV shows. The Metropolitan Opera *Live in HD* broadcasts are a very significant addition to our culture, bringing great opera to movie theaters. We have YouTube to thank for providing many quality examples for our young people to view at will. "Junior" musicals are now widely used in our middle/junior high schools and community theaters. Contemporary Commercial Music has become a big part of vocal training in many studios.

With the demise of some music stores even in large cities, and the elimination of much music in single sheet form, anthologies are the basis of most lesson literature. There are Internet sites where one can still purchase single copies, however.

The lives of the teen students are so very busy these days because the students and their parents want them to be in so many activities to increase their chances to get in the best colleges. Learning to balance all they do is a major job and can at times become overwhelming. Years ago I could schedule duets and trios in my recitals, but at present getting two or three together to rehearse is a major undertaking. Having a strong policy statement and conducting the lessons in a very organized way can help the student feel a sense of achievement instead of frustration. Quality performances in twice-yearly recitals give students and parents a sense of a true budding achievement and not just a trophy for sitting "on the bench."

In this revision, many chapters are expanded with more case studies and updated information. New anthologies and more discussion about teaching voice, especially to children, are added to appropriate chapters. Also added is a chart of 50 ways to say "very good" to vary your vocabulary, and more thoughts about students who may have "reading problems" with "Scotopic Sensitivity Syndrome." In addition, the Syllable Sheets have been made more user friendly to read. The largest section is Appendix VII, which contains a listing of 53 publications for which I am compiler, and the complete Table of Contents for each book. Some of the true rewards that come with this profession are actual written letters like those included in the last chapter. All teachers are truly appreciated at some times in their lives, so start collecting your file of similar thank you notes from current and former students.

To Joel Boyd, I express my deep appreciation for giving all of my additions and deletions of material in each chapter his upbeat professional attention.

When my editor, Richard Walters, said, "Joan, we need to revise this book," I did not believe that at my age I would have the energy to take on this major challenge. I resisted for three years and finally realized that with his help, I could make this book a much more up-to-date and more valuable guide for all those new and potential voice teachers graduating each year from college wanting to make voice teaching a career like I have done. Rick has been my guiding force in the realization of this book. Our friendship has strengthened over the years and I am forever grateful for his encouragement. I truly believe that this edition is so much more helpful even to those who own the previous book.

My husband, Jim, kept prodding me to take on this revision. He has been my inspiring guide and consultant even through his health challenges. Now at age 81 with 58 years of teaching experience in public schools, college and privately with a continuing studio of 30 teens and adults, I am proud to present the revised edition.

INTRODUCTION
from the Original 2003 Edition

At the Seattle National Association of Teachers of Singing Convention in 1995, while on a boat trip to Tillicum Island, I was asked by Julie Fortney, editor of *InterNos*, a NATS periodical for members, to write a column about the "grass roots" private voice studio. By this time some members were familiar with *Solo Vocal Repertoire for Young Singers*, an annotated bibliography which I edited for NATS in 1980, and many were using my published compilations of songs. Teachers were also familiar with my workshop and convention sessions on "Vocal Repertoire for Young Singers" and "Marketing and Management of the Voice Studio." After much discussion, I finally agreed to take on this *InterNos* assignment.

Together, Julie and I decided to call the column "A Private View." I distinctly remember Julie stressing that this was to be a practical column. She said, "We want to know what *you* do!" As a result of this directive, I decided to use an informal style and share my experiences as they have unfolded in a lifetime of studio teaching.

I developed a format that began each column with questions from "Nancy," followed by a response written as a long letter to a younger teacher who is just establishing herself as an independent studio teacher of voice. During the life of the column, which ran for five years in fifteen issues of *InterNos*, several readers inquired about "Nancy." Let me tell you about her.

Some thirty years ago, Nancy, a former high school private student of mine, went to college and graduate school and became a voice teacher. She wrote me great letters with all kinds of questions about teaching and repertoire selection. In fact, here are selected quotes from her letters, which I have shared in many workshops:

Dear Mrs. B.,

My students are all beginners with *no* experience. I'm having a hard time choosing English songs that aren't trite but are still easy to sing. I don't particularly care to have my students all sing the same songs. Can you suggest any anthologies and collections that are particularly good? There are no good music stores here. Everything must be ordered—one cannot browse. The college library is not too good—mostly opera and Lieder.

Dear Mrs. B.,

I remember asking you before about books for students and you wrote a very informative letter which I still have. I am wondering if you have found any *new terrific* books for beginners. I am still disappointed with the available collections. I want a book for beginners with a limited range (medium voice), with good songs in English, contemporary, Old English, good folk songs, Italian, easy German, American and all for $5.00 [this was many years ago].

Dear Mrs. B.,

Thank you 100 times for your lists of repertoire and thanks for sending programs. I am still collecting music...

Dear Mrs. B.,

I've found myself in need of good contralto literature. I know the Bach Cantatas and oratorio in general go low, but what else?

Dear Mrs. B.,

  I am *still* looking for a collection of good English and American songs for the beginner. Do you know of anything—all in English (not translations), from Dowland to Rorem, for example? That's what I'd like. Why don't you edit one and publish it? Something like Glenn & Spouse but for older, more mature students.

Dear Mrs. B.,

  You wouldn't believe how often I dig out your old programs, repertoire lists, etc. I have a file called 'Boytim' to get ideas for programming or whatever. Whenever you have extra stuff left over from conventions and workshops, remember me.

Dear Mrs. B.,

  …In general, I believe there should be more emphasis given in college preparing teachers on high school level literature.

When I started the columns, Nancy, the real person in my life, was transformed into a fictitious, generalized "Nancy," in part, because ideas for the columns came from a variety of sources.

When the executive board of NATS decided to change the format of *InterNos* to include only association business, "A Private View" and other similar columns were discontinued. At this point, my editor at Hal Leonard Corporation, Richard Walters, encouraged me to revise these fifteen columns (for which I had retained publishing rights) into chapters and write additional material that could lead to a handbook that would be useful to studio voice teachers and those preparing for this profession. After a couple of years of massaging the concept and content, the book you hold in your hands is the result.

As a bonus, I believe this book allows me to honor the many requests that I have received over the years for a copy of my five syllable sheets that I always use with beginning and transfer students. By including them in the book, I hope that teachers will use this concept to improve music reading ability, increase accuracy in singing, instill well-placed tone quality, and develop the capacity for independent learning in all of their students.

This handbook is a direct result of all that I have learned from each of my students over the past forty-five years. My fellow teachers, through conversations, letters, and telephone calls, have shared so many ideas over the years, some of which I have tried to incorporate into this book.

The focus of *The Private Voice Studio Handbook* is in the practical, day-to-day matters that might face a typical teacher. Those private teachers in large cities able to charge high fees to work only with the most elite singers don't need a handbook! Most of us in this profession work with the average to modestly talented students in our communities for a gigantic proportion of our studio work. We have an important role to play teaching teenagers, children and interested adults. We may have the good fortune to sometimes have the opportunity to work with highly accomplished professional classical singers, but to be honest, most of us cannot make a living as a private studio voice teacher if we specialize only with this type of student. This book uniquely and primarily addresses the teaching of teenagers and community adults, which reflects my own teaching career. Because these topics have rarely, if ever, been written about, particularly in a book, perhaps others will find this point of view valuable. Our colleagues who work in a more conventional faculty situation at a college or university have their own unique priorities and approaches. Many of the ideas in this book, however, will be adaptable to these faculty studios. This book may also be useful in teaching vocal pedagogy, preparing students to consider broad aspects of voice teaching as a future profession.

Standard art song, opera and oratorio literature is beyond the scope of this book. Such topics are widely addressed in our standard classical vocal education, and in many other sources. Though I use standard repertoire in my teaching, I did not feel that when and how I incorporate it was a necessary topic to address.

I have been humbled and so thrilled to have the opportunity to write what may be the first book ever published that is devoted to the honorable and unique profession of the private studio voice teacher. While *The Private Voice Studio Handbook* could be viewed as instruction for the beginning teacher, it is my hope that veteran teachers in the field also will find ideas to incorporate into their teaching.

My editor, Richard Walters, from the beginning of our work together, has been so trusting of an unknown "grass roots" teacher from a little town of 20,000. His apprehensive concern over my choice of repertoire for teens was replaced with faith when our first collections of songs (*The First Book of Solos* series) sold more copies than he had ever imagined. He has heard my lectures, he sees my student recital programs, and has reviewed many performances of my students on tape. Above all, Rick has been a firm but fair negotiator in the projects we have shared. Together we have developed a genuine mutual respect that has resulted in a unique collaboration and friendship. I thank him for his vision and encouragement that enabled me to complete this general guide for both seasoned and beginning teachers of singing.

My husband, Jim, deserves so much credit for the countless hours he devoted to serious editing, rewriting, and making suggestions of material to include that were relevant to the text. Without his genuine love and continual support of my teaching and my students, this project could never have been completed. Together we hope this book helps you avoid many of the mistakes I made before I had my studio fully established as a real business, which became the center of a lifetime career.

THE
PRIVATE
VOICE STUDIO
HANDBOOK

CHAPTER 1
GETTING STARTED

The Transition from Singer to Professional Voice Teacher, The Mission Statement, New Teaching Location

---

Dear Mrs. B.,

Since I received my master's degree in voice, I have been teaching a few students from my church and my immediate neighborhood, in addition to working part-time as a waitress and a church choir director. I really would like to move to a new area and develop a full-time private voice studio. I am interested in hearing any business and teaching ideas you may have to help me start, develop and maintain such a studio. I am eager for any insights you can provide.

Sincerely,
Nancy

Dear Nancy,

Let me applaud you for wishing to develop the private voice studio as your major vocation. It can be rewarding emotionally, yet it may take years to make it a financially secure occupation. Perhaps some of my ideas and viewpoints will help you to achieve your goal. Today, I would like to address your mission statement and things to consider when moving to a new geographical area.

Sincerely,
Mrs. B.

THE TRANSITION FROM SINGER TO PROFESSIONAL VOICE TEACHER

Every year, a group of freshly minted graduates of music departments, schools and conservatories embark on careers as musicians, as performers or teachers, or often, as both. Many of these are singers who found pleasure and satisfaction in the vocal arts through their lives, and elected to study voice in college, and also in graduate school in some cases. At some point, either immediately upon graduation or some years later, many will want to open a private studio and become professional voice teachers as part of their musical identity, either as a full-time or part-time pursuit. These Nancys and Neds are often long on enthusiasm but short on experience. They may say to themselves, "I know what I want to do, and I know I want to be the best I can be, but what do I need to know and do to be successful as a voice teacher?" Even veteran teachers may pick up some fresh ideas in reading this book.

THE MISSION STATEMENT

It is very important for each private voice teacher, if you have not previously done so, to formulate a statement that explains exactly what your philosophy is as a teacher of voice students. This takes a great deal of soul-searching, for you must explore what your goals are, what type of students you wish to teach, and how you want to meet your individual needs while serving the profession in general. Your statement should be condensed into a paragraph and finally reduced to one or two sentences.

One needs to evaluate if you have an interest in working with young children (ages 6-12), teenagers, college students, community adults, beginning professionals, advanced professionals, or mature adults. Your academic preparation, musical expertise, and performance experience, as well as your personality, local opportunities and competition, will be determining factors of how you will develop your studio.

The influence and place of a private studio voice teacher in today's society needs to be considered. Are we training young people primarily to get leading roles in school musicals, to become finalists in local pageants, to perfect three audition selections for the college of choice, or to become soloists of church choirs, community choral groups, or musical theater companies? Because of the drastic music personnel cuts, and in some places, the "dumbing down" of a substantial portion of music education in our public schools, are we now assuming some of the basic music reading training that in days gone by were the domain of the public school music teacher? Are we teaching music appreciation when we expose our students to new repertoire with which they have never been acquainted? Are we challenging our students by continually, yet carefully, increasing the difficulty of the formal vocalise studies and songs we present to them? Are we adequately preparing our young people for excellence in college as music majors or as participants in demanding music ensembles, musical theater, and opera productions?

In our private studios, do we expect to teach only students of the quality of college voice majors or professional classical singers? How many of us have the realistic chance to make a living teaching only the highest level of singers, given that most of our students have never before had a private voice lesson?

Are we providing a vocal education experience for those many community adults who, for the first time in their lives, have a chance to develop latent talent that was never explored due to lack of opportunity, lack of money, time restraints due to early career and family obligations, or the unavailability of adequately trained vocal instructors? Who will serve the ever growing aging population?

As our population is aging well into the sixties, seventies, eighties and nineties, are we exploring possibilities of vocal training for mature singers? Lung capacity does decrease with age; however, people who learn proper breathing for singing and continue to sing even as a hobby can lead more healthy lives. Are there opportunities to work with singers in residential retirement homes, senior centers, or community groups?

Are there ways that, as private studio teachers, we can make ourselves accessible to area colleges where voice lesson options for non-majors (or even majors) are reduced or no longer exist because of budget and staff cutbacks? Have we checked the possibility of teaching in music stores and community music schools, or even some sort of inventive affiliation with a public or private high school? Have we approached area non-profit organizations, continuing education programs, and local libraries to be part of their outreach programs?

The questions I have posed are intended to challenge you to think of other ways to find and serve potential students and ultimately expand the possibilities of the private teacher's profession. Perhaps other music teachers in your area will have additional suggestions for your consideration.

Based on my work as a private teacher since 1956, I have developed a personal philosophy particular to my situation that I would like to share with you.

> As a private voice teacher in a small community I feel that my responsibilities are to prepare young students for college music departments and choral groups both as majors and non-majors; to develop appreciation for all styles of vocal music; to provide musical challenges, a musical education and performance opportunities for those many adults who are busy in their individual careers but who have an intense interest and latent talent in singing; and for the students who are active in church music, to develop a church soloist dedication and experience that will insure a solid foundation in church choirs for years to come.

I recently condensed this into the following mission statement: "I am providing for my students the opportunity to learn as much as I can teach them, including the tools to help them teach themselves, in the amount of time they study with me."

You may ask, why is philosophy important? It defines who you are, it provides a focus for your thinking, it defines a service that you can market, and it gives you a legitimate reason for calling what you do a profession as well as a business.

NEW TEACHING LOCATION

In deciding to move to a new area to develop your studio, you must decide what type of community meets your needs while allowing your business to flourish.

Are you interested in relocating to the suburbs of a large city, a smaller community near a medium sized city, or a small town in a rural area? In any case, it would be a good idea for you to research the area by contacting school music teachers, church choir directors, area colleagues, and music stores to find out how many private voice teachers are now actively teaching there. It is ideal to locate in a geographical area where there are limited opportunities to study with qualified voice teachers. It is extremely difficult to move to a large city and expect to have a full studio unless you have made a name for yourself as a performer or as a college or university based teacher of renown.

You should also take into account any other work opportunities you might find while you begin building your studio. If your qualifications are such that you can also teach beginning piano or other instruments, you can usually get students almost immediately since there are needs for private teachers in these fields in most communities. As the number of voice students increase, you can gradually decrease the number of piano and instrumental students you teach. You need to have patience because this may take more time than you expect unless you have a built-in referral system established. Good luck to you!

CHAPTER 2
FINDING MY SPACE
and
WHO AM I, ANYWAY?

The Teaching Space, The Next Step: Teaching in Your Home, Letter of Introduction

---

Dear Mrs. B.,

Since I last wrote to you, I have recently moved to a town of 20,000, near a city located 30 miles away. I chose this area in part because no voice teachers are serving this population. I have found an apartment and my piano is being moved from my parents' home very soon. Within a year or two, I expect to rent or make a down payment on a house in this area. Meanwhile, I have a part-time job where I will work 25 hours each week. Do you have any suggestions for starting my studio?

Sincerely,
Nancy

Dear Nancy,

It was great to hear about your new location. Let me offer some suggestions for teaching while you are in your new apartment and some thoughts about choosing the future location of your house. In addition, I believe you should formulate a letter of introduction to send to selected people. Let me hear from you after you have begun to teach several students.

Sincerely,
Mrs. B.

THE TEACHING SPACE

If you wish to teach in the apartment where you are living, you will need to research the rules for the building, the acoustical design and the attitude of the neighbors. Unless there is a precedent for teaching, as in some large city aprtment complexes, it would be wise for you to establish a studio elsewhere. Stronger voices can be problematic in less soundproof structures. When I started teaching, it was in an apartment located over six garages, so my lessons did not cause problems for my neighbors.

Very often music stores provide small studios for local music teachers for a nominal fee. These stores usually keep referral lists of teachers for all types of music lessons.

Now, privately run regional "music schools" exist in many parts of the country. Most hire part-time private instructors and provide a place, the students, and take care of all the administrative details of the business. The teacher receives a percentage of the tuition fee. This may involve travel time for you but it could be just the start you need.

If you are hired to conduct a choir in a church or a synagogue, it may be possible to negotiate renting a room in the building for lessons. (In some cases, you might get this approval as part of your benefits.) Even without directing a choir, you may be able to rent a space during the week. You may need to keep the piano tuned as part of your contribution towards rent.

Other teaching options could be the use of community rooms in such places as historical societies, civic clubs, libraries or local theaters. These possibilities, however, may limit the time blocks available for your teaching.

In many communities there are private schools, some church affiliated, that may welcome a private teacher to come to their locations and serve their students several days a week. This arrangement may even be possible in public schools in some areas. As I mentioned in my last letter, if you are willing and able to provide a combination of keyboard, instrumental and voice teaching for a while, this may be an attractive opportunity for you.

THE NEXT STEP: TEACHING IN YOUR HOME

If apartment teaching is not a long-term option for you, you may decide to rent or buy a house. There are many things to consider. If you want to attract teenagers, you would have an advantage if you select a place close to the secondary schools of your community to draw a core group of students who can come to lessons immediately after school. In some school systems there is a relaxed policy for older students to come to lessons on "school time" if they have study periods at the end of the school day or if the study hall-lunch hour combination provides enough time. If you are located within ten minutes walking or driving distance from the school, this can be ideal. In addition, selecting a house within a reasonable distance of major highways can be an advantage in attracting students from outside the area.

One should be very careful to have adequate parking for the students who drive and for parents to wait. A very congested street with limited available space can create major problems when you schedule back-to-back lessons. If you live where it snows frequently, this is a serious consideration.

A major concern is finding a house where the zoning laws will permit the operation of a private home business. In some locales you will need to pay a yearly business permit fee. It is wise to check the zoning laws at the municipal office for all the areas in which you may rent or buy a house.

Recent newspaper and magazine articles report situations where private piano teachers have been forced to quit teaching due to zoning laws and neighborhood complaints. For example, a piano teacher in the business for over eight years in the suburbs of a Midwestern city was forced to quit because neighbors complained about traffic congestion when parents dropped off and picked up their children for lessons. Close to my home, a voice teacher and former student of mine was forced to sell his home and move to another neighborhood because of the zoning code.

You should check the zoning laws before buying a house in any district or township, if you intend to develop a voice studio. Some areas forbid this; some areas require a variance appeal and major fee; and others accept this with no problem. Each municipality has distinct zoning laws. For example, in my county, there are seventeen municipalities with different codes for each. Failure to abide by the regulations can result in huge fines as high as $1,000 per day.

The number of articles I have assembled regarding this situation seem to indicate that one is most vulnerable if there are neighborhood complaints. Thus, it is better to prevent this problem by checking the codes and to develop and sustain excellent rapport with your neighbors.

LETTER OF INTRODUCTION

As a new teacher or a new resident in your town, a letter of introduction sent to all area school music teachers and church choir directors is an excellent way to present yourself. The telephone directory has a list of most area churches and schools that you can call to get the appropriate names and titles of the people you wish to reach, or you may find such information on the Internet. This letter of introduction should include your name, address, e-mail, telephone numbers, academic background, and some of your performing experience. For experienced teachers who move, past teaching, performance highlights and professional involvement in NATS and other organizations could be included. You should address your interest in teaching private voice lessons as well as any other instruments if you are so inclined. Include the levels and ages you wish to teach. You may offer to meet with the person you are addressing to answer questions, share your philosophy or become better acquainted.

Several years ago one of my adult voice students received a degree in music with a horn specialty. She was interested in developing a horn studio, but with my encouragement agreed also to include beginning piano. As a result of her introductory letter and having lived in the neighborhood for several years, she had a studio of thirty students in her first year. Each year since, the number of horn students has increased, and very shortly she will no longer have piano students. Now that she has earned a master's degree, she has sent a second letter to school instrumental instructors specifying her new qualifications and experience and indicating that she only wants horn students.

Some teachers have placed a simple block advertisement in the newspaper. One of my former students put a notice in the classified section of the newspaper, but she received a number of undesirable calls and would not recommend this approach. Many readers of this volume may already be using media options now available; for example, a website can show performance samples, one's résumé, picture, and information about location, hours of operation, fees, etc. One also might make professional use of a Facebook page. After a number of years, one builds a referral system from the satisfied students and parents, as well as musical colleagues. But for now you need to develop a marketing strategy that is tailored to your circumstances.

CHAPTER 3
WHAT DO I NEED
IN MY STUDIO?

Equipment, Reference Books, Other Concerns,
Business Area, Personal Touches

Dear Mrs. B.,

I finally have found a place of my own where I intend to teach for the next several years. Even though I have several essentials such as a piano, a CD player, and my personal music and books from college, I would like to know what items you consider necessary to make a private voice studio complete.

Sincerely,
Nancy

Dear Nancy,

It will probably take you many years to get your studio set up to the point where you have everything you desire, but now is the time to consider all your options as you work towards that goal. Since my studio has been in the same home over the past 40 years, I will tell you about the things that I now consider important for my vocal studio business.

Sincerely,
Mrs. B.

EQUIPMENT

When you can teach in your own home or apartment, you have access to so many things that are unavailable while teaching in a rented studio or public facility. Your needs will be the same if you teach in a separate music room, a living room, or a family room. In addition, you should have a private "business" area.

Your most important piece of equipment is a piano. While it would be luxurious for all of us to teach with a nine-foot Steinway grand in our home studio, this isn't a practical option for many of us. Any good quality piano will do. It can be a grand, an upright, a console or spinet model. It must have a good tone quality and be able to hold a tuning. After these factors, it is also important that the piano is a good match for your teaching area. Can you situate it in such a way that if seated on the piano bench, you will be in an optimal teaching position? If the piano is too large for the teaching space, a student will feel claustrophobic. Make certain that you have room for all other desired items in the teaching area, including the bodies of the students and the teacher!

Maybe you're lucky enough to have inherited a piano from someone in your family. If not, you may need to consider a major purchase. If money is an issue, shop for a used piano using the classified ads and networking through music contacts. If you're very lucky, you may find someone willing to lend you a piano. There are many people who do not play and have pianos in their homes. It's conceivable that such a person might lend their unused instrument to a teacher in need, at least for a time. Rental is another option. Some piano stores have rent-to-own programs you might also consider. Plan to have your piano tuned at least twice a year. For those in winter climates, a good time for tuning is in the fall, a couple of weeks after the heating system has been running regularly in your home, and in the spring, a couple of weeks after the heating system has stopped running regularly.

Many teachers today have digital pianos. They are more portable, and use less space. Even though the overall acoustic quality will probably never be as musically satisfying as a standard piano, the advanced technology has greatly improved digital pianos. The price varies greatly, depending on the model and extras desired. You might even find a digital piano on sale, or find a quality used instrument to purchase. Visit a showroom to get a feel for the instruments. Some teachers find these instruments useful for ease of recording and using MIDI accompaniments, and for transposing songs into different keys.

Next to the piano you should have a quality device to record the student for college applications and auditions, etc., and lessons if the student forgets to bring his or her pocket size personal digital recorder, which is necessary for my studio. Some teachers also use video equipment in the studio.

Given the rapid advances in technology, a detailed guide to current devices that may be useful in the studio would soon be out-of-date. There are currently many articles being written and sources available to guide you in the selection process. Those teachers fortunate enough to have a complete studio room can have the space and set-up to include the most complete up to date teaching devices. Many beginning teachers work in situations where the piano is part of a room like the living room, den or family room. Since 1956, other than the first nine years teaching in my public school classroom, I have taught successfully in the same corner of my living room.

A mirror of some type should be available in your teaching area. You need to have a metronome to check tempos of unfamiliar repertoire even though the final tempo choice will vary with each student. A stopwatch is important to time recital pieces and selections for auditions and contests. A bathroom must be available stocked with tissues and cups for water if the kitchen is not close to the teaching area.

A telephone answering system, texting and e-mail capability is very important when you are operating a business and trying to build up a studio since some messages may be inquiries that lead to new students. Many teachers like to teach without telephone interruptions and therefore will check messages later. In my case, when a parent calls to give an important message to a student taking the lesson, I can process the message immediately. In other calls that take more than a few seconds, I will have the person call back at a later time when I am not teaching. If a longer call is a necessity, I will credit the student with that amount of time for a future lesson.

REFERENCE BOOKS

During your college days you used the many wonderful books in the music library. Now in your studio you should start to acquire some of these for your students to use as references as well as new materials for your own continuing research. With the advantage of the Internet in today's society, your students have access to additional information available. Using your books for reference can provide "unique teaching moments." I allow students to borrow some of my books, but I keep careful records so that I always get everything returned. Advanced students should be expected to do their own research on their own time using the Internet.

I feel it is important to have language dictionaries for Italian, German, Spanish, French, and any other languages you expect to teach. I also have several diction books for these languages available for my students and me to check for accuracy of pronunciation. In addition, *Word by Word Translations of Songs and Arias - Part I* (Italian) by Arthur Schoep and Daniel Harris, and *Part II* (German and French) by Coffin, Singer, and Delattre (Scarecrow Press), are the most used books by my students. All of my students who sing in languages purchase the paperback, *Pronouncing Guide to French, German, Italian, and Spanish*, by Jones, Smith, and Walls (Carl Fischer) which features a brief vocabulary of words in all four languages, taken directly from songs. My students are first required to translate their texts from this book and a dictionary, finally filling in the blanks with the *Word by Word* volumes. Once in a while, you may have a student who is fluent in a language other than English. The benefits to song preparation are obvious in these cases.

There is also a 1990 paperback book called *Arie Antiche* by Richardson and Rute (Paraclete Press), which translates all three volumes of *Arie Antiche* (Ricordi). Very valuable additions to your library are *Italian Song Texts from the 17th Century* Vol. I and *Italian Song Texts from the 18th Century* Vol. II, both by Martha Gerhart (Leyerle Publications). Many song volumes today come with word by word translations, but I still like my students to be challenged by the above process FIRST when they begin language songs. Later in their development, students find that these new volumes save time when they write the meaning of each word in their songs, but by then the student has a greater understanding of the language structure and familiarity with many words.

There are important song literature books such as *The Interpretation of French Song* by Pierre Bernac (Praeger Publishers), *Nineteenth Century French Song* by Barbara Meister (Indiana Press), *Eighteen Song Cycles* by Lehmann (Praeger Publishers), *Song: A Guide to Style and Literature* by Carol Kimball (Hal Leonard), *Art Song – Linking Poetry and Music* by Carol Kimball (Hal Leonard) and single composer books with explanations of songs by Schubert, Schumann, Poulenc, Fauré, Ravel, etc. These will help your students understand the background of many of the most well-known foreign language songs.

You should have several opera synopsis books at your disposal for your own research and so that a student singing an aria can read the story of the entire opera and understand how this fits into the story. Several I like are *The New Milton Cross Complete Stories of the Great Operas* and *Milton Cross: More Stories of Great Operas* (Doubleday), *The Kobbè's Complete Opera Book* (Putnam), and *The New Encyclopedia of the Opera* by Ewen (Hill and Wang). Two useful books for understanding individual arias are *An Interpretive Guide to Operatic Arias* by Martial Singher (Penn State), and *Bringing Soprano Arias to Life* by Boris Goldovsky and Arthur Schoep (Schirmer Books).

Many years ago I bought the paperback edition of the *Grove's Dictionary of Music and Musicians*. This is updated occasionally and is now only available on the Internet.

This tremendous source of musical information can be so valuable for you and your students. Additionally, several vocal technique and other song literature books should also be part of your library.

OTHER CONCERNS

There should be a place in or near your studio to put notices of future concerts, recitals and current programs such as school musicals and district and regional chorus programs that feature your students. I always underline the names of current students and use a dotted line for former students. Since my studio is a portion of our living room, I also place on the coffee table several music magazines including *Opera News, Music Educators Journal, Classical Singer, Journal of Singing*, and *American Music Teacher*. We also share *Time, Sports Illustrated* (except the swimsuit issue), and a variety of business and women's magazines for parents and students to read while waiting.

The waiting place for students, whether in the room where you teach or another room, should have accommodations for coats, book bags and umbrellas. There should be adequate seating and lighting for students, parents, and friends to read, study, use books for translations or reference, or to make final preparations while waiting for the lesson.

BUSINESS AREA

In your business work area you need a table or a desk with good lighting. Filing cabinets and shelf space are needed for storing music and books. It is helpful to have files of updated publishers' catalogues and distributors' brochures, information about music careers, and sample college music school brochures. I also keep lists of music and books from NATS conferences, studio recital programs, recital programs of other singers, repertoire lists of all my graduating seniors, hard copies of all reference letters written for my students, and reference materials applicable to private teaching. Do not forget to have a special place for all of your NATS publications.

I find it very helpful to have a computer, although I know some private teachers who operate successfully without one. There are those who are very fluent with a computer or tablet, have personal access to the Internet, and have all the updated music software which, in some cases, they use with students. Primarily I use the computer for word-processing such as preparing "camera-ready" recital programs, preparing handouts for my studio, writing letters of reference, preparing lectures and music lists, keeping track of retirement investments, making student telephone lists, etc. On the Internet you can bookmark important websites (music stores, publishers, research sites, organizations), participate in chat rooms of voice teachers, and build social media networking. I still prefer writing personal letters and thank you notes by hand and find that with the telephone, I can still have a successful "low tech" business with more simplicity.

One of the most important parts of my studio is my music reference library. Over the years I have been teaching, I have developed a large music library by purchasing items that looked interesting from catalogues, NATS music review articles, and browsing in selected music stores and libraries. Many of the items in my beginning library came from a wonderful second-hand music store I visited frequently while I was studying in Munich, Germany. Before the demise of city-based music stores, I would travel with my husband when he attended psychology and counseling conventions in large cities. I would spend most of the time in the music stores in the area. The books I have compiled have benefitted greatly from all the music I sent home from shelves and dusty basement bins. You will need to add bookcases and additional filing cabinet space as your library grows. If you live in a town or city without a comprehensive music store, you will need to purchase music to sell to your students. Music can be bought using toll-free number, online, or by conventional mail, and you will need storage room for those items you use on a regular basis. Other teachers may choose to have students make their own purchases of assigned items through recommended sources.

PERSONAL TOUCHES

The room where you teach should include the personal touches that make the studio area pleasant and say something about who you are. I was always so impressed during my teens to walk into my voice teacher's living room (part of a duplex house) and find that every two months she had a different oil painting on the wall. She subscribed to a local painting lending library and could have a great variety of original art. Some teachers' studios have photos of professional personal appearances, signed photos of artists they know, and programs from all over the world on the walls. Other teachers display music posters and memorabilia or collections of music figurines, bells, music boxes, etc. Still other teachers have a wide variety of green plants. I feature some of the oil and watercolor pictures I have painted and I change them seasonally. I also have four areas, including the piano, to have set-ups of fresh, dried, or silk flowers in different vases from my large collection. (Over the years we have planted specific varieties of flowers in our yard so that I have fresh flowers continually from the forcing of forsythia in late February through the last fading chrysanthemums in early November. Holiday decorations, poinsettias, candles, and favorite small three-dimensional art pieces take care of the remaining months.)

You need to be sensitive to the fact that some students have allergies. Pets in the teaching area can be a big issue. People who are severely allergic to the dander in animals will react, even if the animal is not in the room but has spent a good amount of time there in the last few days. It could be frustrating to try to sing when your eyes are watering and your nose is congested. Flowers and perfumes can also cause an allergic reaction in some people. I recommend asking a student in the audition appointment about allergies. If a student tells you that he or she is allergic to cats, and you love your cat and want to have it next to you all day as you teach, then, in the worst case scenario, you will have to decide between income from students or your pet's company. Beyond allergies, you need to be aware of the comfort level of students as they react to your dog or cat. A dog in the room can make some people very tense, and not all among us are cat lovers. If you are getting the impression that I think it's a bad idea to have pets in the teaching area, with the exception of service dogs, you're right.

By now you are probably overwhelmed and wonder how you can finance all of this. Remember that I am describing an "ideal" situation which is gradually attained over many, many years. When I first began teaching in our home after moving from a furnished apartment, I had only a piano, a stereo player, a floor light, four wicker porch chairs, a bench and a small cabinet in the living room for the first year. As my husband and I slowly furnished our seven room house, I still took a percentage of the payment of every lesson I taught and invested that into the growth of my music and reference library. As is addressed in another chapter, all business items are tax deductible, except for music purchased for students, when you file your Schedule C for your income tax. If you use my approach, as your income increases, so will the amount you can re-invest in studio growth. The important thing is to have a plan and then develop this on a gradual basis. A good teacher continually tries to learn more about vocal technique, repertoire, and music in general, and this is reflected in the continued purchase of books, music, recordings, videos, plus accessing performances on the Internet.

CHAPTER 4
JUST A FEW THINGS BEFORE WE START...

The Policy Statement, Musical Expectations, Benefits of Vocal Study, Visitors and Make-Up Lessons, Music Purchases, Payments and Other Topics

---

Dear Mrs. B.,

During the last several weeks, I have started quite a number of new students. I find that I spend a great deal of time explaining procedures and answering questions. Sometimes I forget to stress important topics and yet I feel there is so much repetition on my part. Do you have a solution to this problem?

Sincerely,
Nancy

Dear Nancy,

Your problem is one that I faced many years ago but eventually solved by formulating a policy statement which I had printed to hand out to each new student at the first lesson. There have been many revisions over the years because of serving my particular needs and the changing character of the students I accept in my studio. Let me share some ideas for a studio policy letter and also references to some sections from my present statement. Maybe this will help you to formulate guidelines that directly relate to your situation.

Sincerely,
Mrs. B.

THE POLICY STATEMENT

One can approach a policy statement in several different ways. A common method is to produce an annual document dated for the current studio year and distribute it to all students at the beginning of the first semester of lessons. Another procedure is to develop an overall policy outline that is given when an individual begins lessons in a studio. You may need to have more than one version of your studio policy statement for different types of students. For instance, you may use one version for children, one for teenagers, and one for adult students. Most of the comments in this chapter address teaching teenagers.

After reviewing sample letters from other private studios, I find that the updated yearly letter is very desirable if one is working with the defined contract system of payment. Such teachers need to specify which dates comprise the semester or term length for their payment schedules. They will usually note the exact number of weeks in a term and the beginning and ending dates. They will also list the holidays and vacation schedule for the entire year. The instructors also state the tuition costs for the term length or the teaching year and include payment due dates and the manner in which they wish to be paid.

Since I do not operate on a contract system, my letter, "Information for Parents and Students," tends to be of a more general nature. My first paragraph is really a disclaimer to take care of the parents who, for instance, cannot understand why after several months of lessons their son or daughter does not get the lead in the school musical. It also helps the students to realize that having tonal, pitch, rhythmical and other problems can be a very natural thing. Thus, I say in part,

> In analyzing beginning voice students, I find that some students are gifted with a well-placed natural voice, possessing a lovely, full, open quality, while others have too many problems to list. As a result, some students will make swift progress, while others will take many months of careful study before much progress is evident.

MUSICAL EXPECTATIONS

Since I am a strong believer in the discipline of warm-up exercises, the use of formal sight-reading and technique books, and an organized way of controlling practice time, I continue,

> In all cases, it is the exercises and vocalises which play such an important part in building the voice and developing good vocal technique. This technique is gradually transferred to songs. Some students prefer to work with these exercises in privacy. If your son or daughter feels this way, it is much better that he or she be left alone in the room while practicing. Several short periods of practice a day are recommended in the beginning weeks of study rather than one long period. Each student is required to bring a recording device such as a small digital recorder, a smart phone, or an iPad so that each lesson can be reviewed at least once before the next lesson. By doing so, the student will hear the results of constructive teacher comments and the student can work with portions of the song accompaniments. Continual practice is necessary for full benefit of lessons. Students with disciplined and organized regular practice sessions make the most progress. Occasionally, circumstances will arise where a student will not be able to practice as much as usual, and in this case the next lesson will be a supervised practice session, not a missed lesson.

In addition, I give students a practice procedures guide which I will review in a later chapter.

BENEFITS OF VOCAL STUDY

My next paragraph deals with the benefits of voice training for everyone and not only for the most naturally gifted singers. It begins,

Not all students who take voice lessons will develop into fine solo singers. However, many of them will find that as a result of this training they will be able to exhibit much more musical self-confidence. Many former students have found that this background has made them influential members in youth choirs, church choirs, community chamber ensembles, college vocal groups or musical theater organizations. In all cases, former students have gained a much deeper appreciation for all types of vocal music and music in general. They have also developed a much better speaking presence and self-confidence when performing in front of large audiences.

VISITORS AND MAKE-UP LESSONS

Occasionally parents ask to observe a voice lesson. Still other parents, especially those whose children cannot drive themselves to lessons, sit in for most if not all lessons. I give them the opportunity by writing,

> Parents are welcome to observe a lesson anytime they wish with the student's permission. However, you must understand that with some students this will be an unnatural situation and they will not be as relaxed and responsive as they usually are. You may feel free to call me to discuss the vocal progress of your son or daughter at any time.

With adult students, visitors are infrequent. Sometimes out of town guests, special friends, or others may be in attendance. In other cases, the student's individual comfort level naturally plays the deciding role.

Most teachers include a section on missed and make-up lessons. Policies on this vary greatly from teacher to teacher, impacted by a package pre-payment for lessons or a pay-as-you-go method. Some teachers make up only those lessons missed due to illness or extreme weather conditions. Others require a twenty-four hour advance notice of cancellation. Some studios have a "swap list" for those students wishing to arrange lesson changes among themselves. Other teachers never make up any lessons. My policy states,

> If a student is ill, I wish to be notified as soon as it is convenient so that a lesson change can be made. If there is a general conflict I need to know a week or two in advance because often a lesson switch can be arranged. Failure to notify me prior to the lesson missed after the first time may result in a charged lesson, except in the case of an emergency. All lessons missed due to scheduling conflicts for the student or me will be made up at an agreeable time.

For instance, since many of the teenage students are in spring school musicals, I know that "tech" week and the week of the show make it impossible for them to show up at regular lesson times. Also, I know which students are likely to miss lessons for district and regional chorus. I therefore add,

> I will sometimes begin to have make-up lessons in the early fall months (when schedules are not so hectic) for conflicts I know will arise later in the year. I will sometimes schedule a double (one hour) lesson to save additional trips for the student and parents or add fifteen minutes for two weeks to make up for a half hour lesson. At most, I see each student for lessons a total of seventeen or eighteen hours during an entire school year and this is why I consider every lesson to be important for maximum progress.

Since I have an open studio primarily of teenagers, all of the students quickly learn to adjust to the presence of students and others being present for part of a lesson at times. Clearly, this environment would not apply to all studios.

MUSIC PURCHASES

Students and parents need to understand that the cost of music is above and beyond the fee for lessons. Some teachers who sell music directly to students require a "music deposit" sum of money at the beginning of each term with a new deposit when it is depleted. Any remaining money is carried over to the next term or if the student discontinues lessons or the money is not entirely used, the remainder is refunded. Other teachers direct students to make purchases from music stores, toll-free numbers or websites. I include a paragraph with the actual range of music costs for a calendar year. This figure is adjusted periodically due to increasing music costs. I write,

> From past experience, I have found that many parents inquire about extra costs involved in the purchase of music. Because of the rapidly increasing costs of music, I try to use books whenever possible, as opposed to single song sheets. Three pieces of sheet music often equal the cost of an entire book, yet from time to time sheets will be used because many songs do not come included in book collections. Until I am sure of the vocal range of a new student, I may use individual songs and unison octavos before deciding on definite books. An estimate of music costs for the first year of lessons would range from $50 to $150 depending upon the progress, age and ambition of the student.

PAYMENTS AND OTHER TOPICS

I conclude my letter, "Many parents find it convenient to pay by check each week, or at the beginning or end of the month. If this is your case, please make out the checks to JOAN BOYTIM." I include my telephone number and address for any questions that may arise, since in some cases a parent is not present when I distribute this letter to a new student.

The teachers who hand out yearly policy statements usually include the actual recital dates for the year. I post this information in my studio at the beginning of the lesson year for the student to add to the family calendar.

There may be other issues you will need to consider, such as parking instructions, payment of fees for an accompanist if one is used for lessons or recitals, arranging recordings for college applications, scholarships or contest entry, and requests for extra coaching sessions for adults preparing public performances.

Discussion of studio policies for the private studio is a frequent topic during breaks at chapter meetings and NATS workshops. I encourage you to seek ideas from those who might offer other suggestions for efficient operation of your business.

CHAPTER 5
GETTING ORGANIZED

Lesson Cards, Revenue Records, Schedules and Telephone Lists, Repertoire Cards, Repertoire Lists, Clothing Chart, Other Lists and Computer Files

---

Dear Mrs. B.,

I have been experimenting with ways of keeping track of business concerns in my studio, and I seem to lack consistency with keeping records. Everything seems to be haphazard, and I might have a confusing time at tax season. As a result of your years of experience, what records do you keep, and how do you do it?

Sincerely,
Nancy

Dear Nancy,

As I have previously indicated, you need to treat your voice studio as a business and keep records that are easy to trace at a moment's notice. There are many ways to do this, but I would be happy to share the lists and records I have kept over the years to organize my studio so that valuable time is not lost.

Sincerely,
Mrs. B.

LESSON CARDS

Many teachers keep track of student lesson times and payment by using an account book or computerized equivalent. After trial and error, I developed a "lesson card," which is very easy to use in many ways. I have several hundred of these cards printed at a time to save on costs. They are 8" by 5" in size. Here is a sample for you to see. I have included the various symbols and comments I use. (See next page.) The same aim could be accomplished with computer files.

VI

NAME __MARY MELODY__ GRADE __11th__

ADDRESS __440 MICAELA LANE, CARMEN, PA__ CHURCH __FIRST METHODIST__

TELEPHONE __H-555-5555 C-666-6666__ LESSON TIME __WED. 2:00__

email: sopranomelody56@email.com

Music - Voice

MUSIC   COMMENTS

(AI-SII) Piano, Horn, Violin   German, Spanish

Credit - $.34

Italian 6.36
Purcell 3.30
& 11.66

Ger. 6.31
Mozart 3.71
God bo 1.33
& 11.35

Virginia Slumber 2.65
S. Black Fest 2.65
5.30

Get Contemporary operetta

Date		Date		Date		Date		Date	
SEPT. 1		NOV. 2		JAN. 4		APR. 1		SUM. 1	
2		3		5		2		2	
3		4		FEB. 1		3		3	
4		DEC. 1		2		4		4	
OCT. 1		2		3		5		5	
2		3		4		MAY 1		6	
3		JAN. 1		MAR. 1		2			
4		2		2		3			
5		3		3					
NOV. 1		—		4					

Prior to the start of a new academic year, I fill in the date blanks with the month and week number of that month, starting on a Monday. For example, if November 30 is a Monday, then for my accounting purposes, that is a November week. When I first started using these cards, I would write the actual date; however, that proved to be too work-intensive and made things complicated when a month changed in the middle of the week.

You will notice that I place an "X" in a lesson block if the lesson has been taken, a dotted "X" in a block where the lesson is to be made up at another time, and "Pd" in any block if the lesson has been paid.

This card is also used to verify name spellings, addresses, all phone numbers, email addresses, grade level (for teenagers) or class level (for college students), church or synagogue affiliation (if applicable), and lesson time (in pencil). Below this area of the card, I note the musical instruments played, the languages studied in school, and any other pertinent information (for example, the potential college major of the high school student, or times when makeup lessons will never work).

If I have ordered music for students, rather than asking them to make their own purchases, the cost of any music that needs to be paid is recorded on the card at the time when the music is handed to them. Upon payment this is crossed off. If books or music are loaned to a student, the titles are also listed here so that I have a record and can be sure to have all items returned. So many teachers have indicated they have lost a good portion of their library because of not keeping records of loaned music.

I keep these cards arranged in lesson order at the piano where I teach. If a lesson time is changed, the card gets shifted to the appropriate position in the stack. At the end of every week, it is easy to total up the lessons taught and the revenue collected by using the cards. If I need to get a message to a student, I take the card to the telephone. Several teachers I know have switched to this system and find it very convenient. The concept could easily be adapted for storage on your home computer.

REVENUE RECORDS

It is very important to keep accurate records of studio earnings throughout the year for tax purposes as well as to help you determine trends in your music business. My system includes keeping a yearly income record. It shows my lesson payment totals for each week, monthly studio earnings totals, as well as the extra income from any other music pursuits such as accompanying, performing, giving workshops, serving as substitute choir director, or whatever else is part of my professional income.

I also keep a record of business expenses for each month. It is a good idea to keep a running account of all donations and dues throughout the year. If you pay these by check, you can make a notation in your checkbook to facilitate your record gathering at tax time. If you use credit cards or electronic payment plans for studio expenses, mark those items that are business related for end of the year tax calculations.

Don't forget to keep track of mileage for concerts, shows, and professional meetings and conferences, etc. I keep a list of frequently used round trip mileage numbers to the major airports I use, area high schools, and theaters. I note the date and event along with the mileage and the cost of parking and the ticket. At tax time you will be ready to total these expenses and mileage costs.

A former student who is now a voice teacher and NATS member keeps a daily record book where she staples receipts to the applicable pages. There are many ways to keep your financial records, with computer options abounding these days, but the important thing is to be consistent and accurate.

SCHEDULES AND TELEPHONE LISTS

I like to keep a copy of my schedule at the piano and also one clipped to my telephone studio list of the current roster of students. Often I have to refer to it when a student requests a switch with another student for a future lesson. Many teachers today probably store schedules electronically. Some teachers have what they call "switch lists" which are given at the beginning of the studio year to those students who are willing to make lesson changes among themselves. With years of experience, you will become aware which days involve less conflict for individual students. In the case of teenagers, I make sure that all students from the same school are aware of each other's lesson times so they can make any necessary changes.

My telephone list is developed on the computer and kept near my telephone. With fewer people using land lines and, therefore, not being listed in telephone directories, many readers will keep a file of frequently used numbers on their smart phone or favorite electronic communications device. I do advise, however, keeping a hard copy of your studio numbers for convenience, for ease of updating, and just in case your file is compromised or your phone is lost. One of my musical friends lost over 500 telephone numbers in his file when he changed to a new smart phone; it required several days with the help of his computer specialist son to reestablish his list.

REPERTOIRE CARDS

I keep a repertoire card for each student I teach or have taught. This includes the student's name and grade or class for school or college students. Exercise books and all song collections are listed on this side whenever a student is assigned any music. On the opposite side, a column on the left is devoted to Christmas music, which is given every year to those interested students who may have the opportunity to sing in church or at holiday programs. The rest of the space is devoted to a list of single copies assigned to this student. When I am selecting new music for a student, these cards are very helpful in reviewing what they have already learned, particularly when it comes to Christmas and sacred sheets. Again, a comparable filing system for student repertoire could be developed on your computer or other electronic devices.

REPERTOIRE LISTS

In preparation for graduation, I give high school seniors a sample repertoire sheet so that they can format their complete repertoire history in a logical manner and make copies for college voice teachers and choir directors auditions. The title is "Vocal Repertoire" and includes the student's name underneath. This page shows all the student's repertoire under each category in a format that has each alphabetized composer's last name, followed by the song title. If the selection has been performed in public, it is noted with an asterisk. The categories I use are Italian, German and Austrian, French, Miscellaneous, British, American, Sacred, Christmas, Opera, Oratorio, Broadway, and Exercise Books. Some students will need to eliminate some categories if they have studied for a rather short time, or several groups may be combined if the repertoire is limited. Sometimes we will add Broadway roles, opera roles, or duets, depending on the student's experience. (See Mary Melody's sample list in Chapter 16.)

CLOTHING CHART

Some may find this idea absolutely ridiculous, but I have used a clothing chart each year since I began public school teaching in 1956. Every September, I divide a 9" by 12" piece of heavy card stock into grids for each teaching day. I divide the card in the middle so that I can get a full year on one side. What I wear on a given day is noted by color and type in each block so that I do not, for instance, wear the same outfit two Mondays in a row. When one is accepting professional fees, I feel that one should dress in a professional manner. For me, this means a dress, skirt or suit. I understand that many will find a suit of jacket and slacks or a coordinated pants suit combination perfectly appropriate. Whatever the specifics, I hope the spirit of "professional dress" is understood. Men may have an easier time determining "professional dress" for themselves.

In a letter to the editor of *Teaching Music*, June 1996, Joseph Romano, in speaking about professional images, writes,

> In this age of first impressions, our physical appearance is not something we can ignore. Consider how unlikely it would be to see a priest, senator, doctor, or civic leader report to work wearing jeans and sneakers. Members of certain professions, for example, lawyers, realize that their physical appearance shows how seriously they regard their work. By trying to have a professional appearance when we teach—men wearing suits and women wearing dresses—we will increase our chances of getting the respect we deserve.

I believe your students will have a greater respect for you based on your demeanor, your use of time, and your dress during the lesson.

OTHER LISTS AND COMPUTER FILES

Each year I keep a file with my teenage students listed by schools and grade level, so that I can monitor school referral trends and potential overloads in any one grade level.

Included with my current telephone information is my waiting list. I note the school of a teenage student, his or her address and telephone number, the musical background, the referral source, and the date of the initial inquiry. In the spring, after new students are auditioned and selected, I completely revise the file.

During the year, I keep a list of any gifts I receive from students so that I am sure to send a personal handwritten thank-you note for everything that was given to me. I have found that if it is not written down immediately, it is possible to miss someone. This also give me an opportunity to comment on the student's progress for the current year. In this day's rushed society, I still find a place for personalized correspondence.

You may think of other records that would help you to manage your studio, such as email addresses and telephone numbers of church choir directors, school music teachers, local college and university music faculty, accompanists, music store addresses and telephone numbers and websites. Some teachers have catalogued recordings, videos, books and music on the computer. It does not matter whether you keep records on the computer or by hand, or both, or what size cards you use. What does matter is that you strive to develop a system of record keeping and lists that will help you to be more organized, to use your time efficiently, and to make your business as manageable as possible.

CHAPTER 6

NEW STUDENTS

The Initial Contact, The Audition, Decision Time, After Acceptance, Transfer Students

---

Dear Mrs. B.,

My neighbors have accepted my studio and I am becoming known in this area as a voice teacher. As a result, my studio numbers are growing and I have taken everyone who has called for lessons. Should I be auditioning my students? What procedures do you follow in an audition? Thanks for your help.

Sincerely,
Nancy

Dear Nancy,

You certainly have made great progress with your studio since your last letter. In response to your question, I will share with you my ideas about auditioning prospective students.

Until you reach the maximum number of students you are willing to teach, I suggest that you audition your students as part of the first lesson. When your studio is near capacity, or if you wish to limit the number or type of students, and you can afford to choose which singers to accept as students, then I suggest that you schedule a separate audition for everyone who calls. I never charge a fee for the scheduled audition.

Sincerely,
Mrs. B.

THE INITIAL CONTACT

When a prospective student or parent calls about voice lessons, you should accurately record the full name, the address, email, the phone number, age and grade in school if this is a teenager, and the work schedule hours if this is a working adult. After getting more background information and learning the purpose for the lessons over the phone, if you decide you might be interested in this prospective student, then you should set up a mutually agreeable audition time. For the audition, you need to have the prospective student bring any type of prepared solo, church hymn, or a portion of a choral piece to sing. The audition should provide you with all the information you need to know about a prospective student in a very short period of time for you to make an intelligent decision to accept or reject this person for your studio.

If you decide, based on your phone conversation, that for whatever reason, this is not a person you wish to teach, do not set up an audition but immediately refer the individual to another teacher more suited to the immediate needs, or suggest an alternative route for the person to pursue such as piano lessons, a music continuing education class, or a non-audition community choral group.

THE AUDITION

My audition consists of several segments. First, I try to make the prospective student and parent (if with a teenager) feel at ease with some light conversation. Then I will hear a portion of the prepared selection, which is enough to assess the quality and strength of the voice, some basic musicianship skills, the musical sophistication reflected by the choice of audition selection, and the level of singing confidence. If the person does not bring a solo, I will have a Christmas Carol or a show tune to use.

At this point I hand the candidate a standard version of "America, the Beautiful" and ask to hear the melody while I accompany on the piano. Recently, I auditioned two teenagers who had never heard this song. After hearing a portion of the song, I ask a female to sing the alto line and a male to sing the tenor or bass line. This gives me an immediate evaluation as to the music reading ability of the student and the attitude regarding the challenge of trying to read another part.

Next, I vocalize the prospective student with a four-note arpeggio starting around middle C going to the top of the range and then a descending arpeggio to the bottom of the range. This tells me more about the natural vocal sound, the basic vocal problems and the present range limitations.

The most challenging segment of my audition is a tone matching exercise. I play a series of four totally unrelated note patterns in various up and down directions and wide and close intervals, and ask the student to immediately sing on "ah" the four notes played. When an individual matches all four pitches accurately, one has found a very good musical ear. When one or two notes are not accurate, this generally denotes a very trainable ear. When the pattern is sung back in opposite directions, or when there are no correct pitches sung, one has found a person with serious musical ear problems.

Finally, I may explore why he or she wishes to take lessons. If the adolescent student turns to the parent and says, "My mother wants me to take voice," this raises a red flag and I, in turn, suggest that the candidate re-evaluate and re-audition at a later time when he or she really desires lessons.

I ask about previous voice lessons, vocal solo experiences, school, community, and church choir participation as well as instrumental experience and language study. It is important to check the number of after-school activities and seasonal sports participation because of the possible lesson conflicts. I casually inquire about the work world of the parents and explore the transportation arrangements for getting the student to lessons.

In the case of an adult, I explore the musical background, review former vocal instruction, and discuss participation in high school and college musical groups or other choral, solo, opera or musical theater experience. Since I schedule my teenagers for after school hours, I will only accept adult students who can come during the day before 3:00 P.M. Working adults can usually schedule flexible lunch hours to come for a lesson. You may be in a situation where you want to teach evenings and weekends, which allows more options. I used to do this, but now I teach only one evening a week to accommodate my teenagers who are involved in scholastic sports, and I use Saturday mornings on occasion for make-up lessons.

DECISION TIME

After a final evaluation of all that has taken place and the knowledge of spaces in my present studio schedule, I will (1) accept, (2) reject, (3) refer the student to another teacher, (4) put the student on my waiting list, or (5) suggest a year of piano lessons after which I require another audition. Because of many more requests than spaces in my studio, I usually only accept female teenagers who have had at least a year of piano or instrumental lessons, or I request that the student take at least six months of keyboard lessons. For the interested male teenager I forego this requirement because peer pressure at this age assures that almost every male willing to audition is very serious and dedicated about potential lessons. In any event, I will only accept a male student after the voice change has taken place. Because of my personal preference and style of teaching, I generally will not accept a female student before seventh grade. There are exceptions! I have previously taught twin sixth grade girls whose maturity levels matched some older students. Teaching children is another specialty and there are many successful teachers working with this age group who share their ideas through workshops, conventions, and articles in the NATS *Journal of Singing*. (See Chapter 20 on teaching children for further recommendations.)

When I was first building my studio, I took all students who requested lessons, whether or not they could carry a tune. As a teacher you will learn from every student you teach. You will develop great teaching skills by working with the less talented students as you learn to teach them to match pitches and teach them to learn to read music. In the case of the student with severe musical ear problems, if the voice is excellent or has some potential, and the student is burning with desire, I may accept the student on a three or four month trial basis. A student with desire and a great work ethic can learn to overcome these deficiencies. Several of my students who began lessons barely matching pitches went on to achieve leads in school musicals, made district and regional chorus, or became active as church soloists.

AFTER ACCEPTANCE

Normally, I make a decision about accepting or declining the student by the end of the audition appointment. After agreeing to accept the individual, I will discuss my fee schedule and method of payment. In addition I will explain my style of teaching and what I expect from my students. I am a very demanding and strict teacher, and if the student wants leniency and fun, this is the time for the student to decline and to seek a teacher with a different teaching style. Each teacher develops his or her own manner of teaching and not every student will fit into each style.

Before the accepted student leaves the audition I will explain the rules of the house, for I want my students to be comfortable in the teaching area of my home. In my case, I want the student to walk in without knocking or ringing the bell. I point out the location of the restroom and the telephone, and encourage students to arrive a few minutes early so that we can begin each lesson on time. Because I record every lesson for my students, I request that the student decide what recording device to purchase such as a pocket digital recorder, a smart phone or and iPad. For certain students, I still have the capacity to use cassettes.

These audition procedures work for me but all teachers have their own unique methods. Some teachers provide an intake form for the prospective student to complete instead of the more casual approach I use. You may want to ask your former voice teachers about their ideas regarding auditions. This is also a popular informal discussion topic at NATS chapter meetings, regional conferences, and national meetings. Above all, remember the phrase from *The King and I*, "By your pupils you'll be taught." The great singer and coach, Lotte Lehman once said in one of her famous master classes, "It is very strange how much one learns when teaching. I learned things that when I was a singer, I didn't know myself." You learn more about teaching from each and every unique person you accept as a student in your studio.

TRANSFER STUDENTS

Carlisle, the town where I live, has the unique distinction of having the home of the U.S. Army War College. Over 300 students attend a ten months program at this institution each year, and many of the faculty come for a three-year term. Each year I usually get several teenage students as transfers for a one or three year term. In fact, the original Nancy who wrote major portions of the letters which head each chapter, was the daughter of a three year faculty member. Occasionally I teach some military students or their spouses who have had previous vocal training or who decide that this is the year to try voice lessons. These students who have lived all over the world bring an unusual rich background to the studio. I use the same audition routine with all transfers. In addition, if they have studied before, for the first lesson I request a list of their prior solo books and sheets to be shared. In some cases the student will bring a bag with all the music they have from previous lessons. This helps to provide a quick idea of the background of the student.

Another unique characteristic of Carlisle is that it is the home of the Central Pennsylvania Youth Ballet. With the success of many of their graduates being selected as soloists and corps members of major ballet companies in the United States, some families choose to relocate to Carlisle so that high school students can participate in this nationally recognized school. Several students wish to pick up voice training in addition to dance if they want to pursue musical theater training.

Depending upon the type and size of your community, many of your inquiries for lessons will come from people who have recently moved into the area as a result of job transfers, the decision to attend a college or university in the area or other circumstances. I have taught students from Shippensburg University, Dickinson College, Penn State Dickinson School of Law, Harrisburg Area Community College, Messiah College, and Central Pennsylvania College.

Many of these "short term" students make your teaching exciting and also help to keep your studio a thriving business.

If a student wants to transfer from another local teacher to me, I expect that he or she has terminated lessons for several months or has the consent of the present teacher to make the change. You do not want to be accused of stealing another teacher's student. On occasion, I have been part of a collaborative teaching situation which has worked very well. A local teacher who specializes in musical theater and I have shared students. She worked only music theater style and I worked only classical style with each student. The students felt very comfortable because they respected us both.

CHAPTER 7
LET'S START AT THE VERY BEGINNING

Starting the First Lesson, And Now We Sing, Important Discoveries

Dear Mrs. B.,

The ideas you shared for creating a policy statement have really helped me to set a business-like tone with beginning students. This fall, I started many new students, teenagers and adults. I find that the first lesson is so difficult for me since I am never quite sure how to proceed. What do you try to accomplish?

Sincerely,
Nancy

Dear Nancy,

Since beginning to teach in 1956, I still find the first lesson with every student to be challenging and exhausting. What I can accomplish depends upon what each individual brings to the lesson in the way of background, personality style, and motivation. Let me share what I do in the first half-hour session and the next several lessons that follow.

Sincerely,
Mrs. B.

STARTING THE FIRST LESSON

The minute a previously auditioned new student walks through my door I want to set the tone for all future lessons. In my mind there is a "lesson plan" for every lesson I teach, and especially for this most important beginning session.

After a warm greeting to put the student at ease and a review of the "no knock, walk right in" policy, I explain the house rules (where to put outerwear and back packs, the location of the restroom, etc.). The student is told to walk in at least five minutes before the scheduled lesson, so that valuable minutes of lesson time will not be lost as one student concludes a lesson and the next one begins a lesson. Students are made aware that I treat every lesson as a serious commitment on my part, and that I expect the same from them.

Since I have previously filled out my lesson card for this student, I will verify the information. I check the correct spelling of the name. (One year I had three students with the last name of Bair, Bear, and Baer; at other times, I have taught in the same year a Garrett and a Garett, a Karen and a Karin, and a Jenny and a Jennie.) I make sure I have the correct address, email, phone numbers and, if this is a teenager, the correct grade and school. Other information for the lesson card includes any languages studied, instruments played, any church or synagogue affiliation to determine if the student is interested in including sacred music as part of the repertoire, and the voice part sung in choral groups. I ask college-bound teenagers what major they wish to pursue after graduation even though this may change from year to year. I am very interested to hear adults explain more about their musical background and describe job responsibilities if they are working.

All students are then presented with a shortened copy of my résumé (see Appendix I). I believe students and parents need to be informed about our own professional and academic backgrounds if we are accepting money from them. Students also receive a copy of my policy letter and practice procedures sheet (both extensively explained in Chapters 4 and 8), a card stock copy of my sixteen basic warm-up exercises, and five sheets of fifty-five one line melodies in graded steps of difficulty that I developed many years ago to be sung with the printed solfeggio syllables (see Appendix II and III). I explain that this is basically a "cram" course in music reading and that songs will not be sung until the student has completed all of this material. In my experience, I find that the students who concentrate on discovering free quality vocal sound, good breathing concepts, and basic fundamentals of musicianship without the use of songs initially are on the road to teaching themselves by the time we do begin easy song literature. Students are prepared for this beginning phase of lessons to take from four to twelve weeks or more depending upon the experience and diligence of each person. In general the rare student with excellent vocal quality and musicianship skills will complete all five sheets in four weeks or less. The average student will take around eight weeks and those who struggle to read notes will take twelve or more weeks. After eight weeks I will pick out three to four easy songs for the students to try so that they feel they are making progress and can choose two to sing in the next recital four months later. Through experience, I have found that these preliminary materials have been extremely helpful even to some master's degree voice graduates I have taught.

AND NOW WE SING

If the student has remembered to bring a recording device, we begin recording. If not, I emphasize that a recording device is a requirement for the next lesson. After answering any questions from the new student, we begin with the student humming several descending notes on any pitch, progressing to a simple *sol, fa, mi, re, do* passage moving up or down by half steps. Some students hum correctly; however, most students need to learn to produce a vocally healthy hum. Next the hum is carried down the descending scale. We then go back to the five note passage and open the hum sound into vowels on *mi, re, do* and open the hummed scale to vowels on *fa, mi, re* and *do*. We concentrate on tension free open vowel production.

The next drill is a *sol, mi, do, mi, sol* pattern on connecting vowels preceded by the "y" sound. I follow this with vowels on a *do, mi, sol, mi, do* passage which often proves to be problematic for many students. The student needs to learn to approach ascending arpeggio passages from above and not by reaching upward which many beginning singers do.

In the case of students with breathy voices, severe tensions, or less than desirable tone quality, working with these simple exercises in striving to develop a vocal sound with freedom, yawn, and inner space may take the <u>entire lesson time</u>.

For those students who naturally sing with freedom, good resonance and an innate sense of quality vocal sound, I will move on to an explanation of breathing and have the student work on several breathing exercises. This student likely will also be assigned several more of the warm-up exercises. In the case of the very vocally gifted and highly motivated student, I may already assign the entire first sheet of syllable melodies for the next lesson. Each week I add more of the warm-up exercises until they are all learned.

By the end of the first lesson, most students, regardless of the level of advancement, have become aware that there is much to think about and practice even without the use of songs. Many comment that they understand why we do not begin with songs. I personally feel that the first two lessons are the most important lessons I teach because they set the tone for all the following vocal work that takes place.

IMPORTANT DISCOVERIES

Through the use of these syllable drills in the first several lessons I learn about many attributes of each student. I discover the student's:

1. MUSICIANSHIP. By this, I mean the ability or inability to sing a vocal line independently against a chordal accompaniment and the ability to read simple melodic patterns. Reading difficulties can also be detected at this stage.

2. VOCAL RANGE. By constantly shifting keys of the syllable drills, the student experiences the results of vocal development with good breathing and free sound, and I can discover the comfortable range and tessitura for the individual before songs are introduced. After a few lessons the range and tessitura will often be very different from that displayed at the time of the audition and the first several lessons.

3. PERSONALITY TYPE. I am able to discern if the student is an extrovert or introvert, lazy or industrious, sensitive or able to accept constructive criticism. Additionally, I can judge to what degree the student has developed a sense of self-worth.

4. PRACTICE HABITS. The weekly preparation of the syllable drills shows if the student is a fast or a slow learner, or if the person is self-disciplined or must be constantly prodded. In addition, I am able to assess the person's capacity for concentration.

5. MATURITY LEVEL. The work ethic and attitude assumed by the student during these weeks of learning breathing and vocal technique and developing fundamental musicianship skills are good predictors of success once we begin to apply these fundamentals to the study of songs.

All that I learn about each student in these first weeks will guide me in choosing beginning repertoire. If I were to select songs based upon an audition or the first lesson, I would possibly choose inappropriate literature in terms of range, sophistication, emotional maturity and level of difficulty. Further, I am able to have the student experience firsthand that learning basic technique and reading skills are tremendous challenges by themselves. By the time my students are ready to consider vocal literature, they are more comfortable with their voices and their singing skills are able to develop more naturally and quickly because a basic foundation of terminology, technique, musicianship and discipline has been established for them. One might compare this process to introductory art classes where many weeks are spent on drawing exercises and specific drills designed to experiment with and learn the idiosyncrasies of the medium, be it watercolor, pastels, acrylics, or oil paint, before a real painting is begun.

Recently a teenager came with four years of voice lessons and auditioned with a Tchaikovsky piece sung in Russian. She could not read music very well and she had learned by listening to her teacher sing the songs for her. She had one book of music (*Twenty-Four Italian Songs and Arias*) and several photocopies to show for four years. This student had no idea where middle C was on the piano. I had her begin piano lessons immediately with a patient teacher and with my approach and her piano work, she was making much progress in music reading and performance of easy song literature.

If your style of teaching lends itself to this approach, I hope you will consider some of my ideas in planning for beginning lessons with a new or transfer student.

CHAPTER 8
PRACTICE, PRACTICE, PRACTICE

How Often Should I Practice?, Warm-Up Exercises,
Learning a Song, Other Thoughts on Practice

Dear Mrs. B.,

It was interesting to try some of your ideas for a first lesson with new students. After the first half-hour, most of them were able to comprehend the reasons for not starting with songs in the beginning weeks of study. Previously, you indicated having a practice procedures guide for your students. Since many of my students would be more productive if they prepared for their lessons in a more organized manner, could you please share your ideas on this topic?

Sincerely,
Nancy

Dear Nancy,

The practice habits of voice students, teenagers in particular, vary greatly from person to person. There are those who expect you to do everything for them and they expect instant success without any work, and there are those who work in a meticulous, thorough fashion. In order that all of my teenage and adult students have a basis to understand my expectations for lesson preparation, I have written a general statement about practice that I will share.

Sincerely,
Mrs. B.

HOW OFTEN SHOULD I PRACTICE?

Quite often when I accept a new student, a parent will ask, "How much practice time each day do you expect?" This question probably is generated because many piano teachers have set policies and even have students fill out practice charts noting the exact length of time they have practiced each day. I answer that a student needs to practice the amount of time it takes to satisfy my expectations for each lesson. The student will be able to determine this as the lessons progress. This changes from lesson to lesson and from student to student. I explain that one student may accomplish in fifteen minutes what it takes another student thirty minutes to do. I also indicate that practice for voice lessons takes many forms. One needs to spend quality time at a piano, keyboard or other instrument, or listen to the recording of the previous lesson, or work with warm-up exercises while in the shower, or concentrate on proper breathing skills in a school choir rehearsal, or work with more resonance while singing hymns in church, or mentally memorize songs on the school bus or in study halls or even before falling asleep at night. In my mind, all of these things add up to voice practice. In order to be more specific, I hand all new students a one-page sheet titled "Practice Procedures—Keep for Reference."

My first paragraph stresses that,

> Daily practice is necessary for the full benefit of lessons. The amount of time spent in practice varies from individual to individual. The important thing is that each minute of practice be used carefully with complete concentration of thought. Fifteen minutes of careful practice is worth more than one hour of 'just singing.' Problem areas within exercises and songs need to be thoroughly analyzed and corrected at home.

Even though I consistently circle and mark incorrect rhythms, notes and complete musical sections, some students need to be constantly reminded to isolate and concentrate on these places until they are thoroughly learned before practicing in the context of the entire vocalise or song.

WARM-UP EXERCISES

Every lesson I teach begins with vocal warm-up exercises. My guide continues,

> One should always first warm up the voice carefully with exercises and vocalises. (Before a lesson it is beneficial, at the very least, for each student to do some humming exercises.) For the first several months, the exercises and the melodic sight-singing drills are the most important phase of the voice lessons and should be the point of concentration in home practice. One builds a good singing technique this way that is then transferred into the singing of songs. Later, when songs become more important, the exercises and vocalises must still be continually practiced for improved technique, reading skills and extension of range.

My philosophy is that one's technique must be so secure that when one performs, the technique takes care of itself, enabling the singer to concentrate on expressing the music and interpreting the text. I continue,

> Practice should be done in a standing position to achieve good body posture and support. When a song is mastered, those students proficient enough at the piano to accompany themselves should play with an extremely careful sitting position. Most of the time the piano should serve as a pitch check or guide or as an occasional accompaniment. Too often a student will learn serious mistakes when trying to play the accompaniment before the song is thoroughly learned.

LEARNING A SONG

Next I address an organized way of learning a new song.

> When songs are introduced, the text should be read out loud as a poem. Then the melody line should be vocalized on vowels or vowels preceded with consonants such as mah, nah, lah or bah. When the pitches and rhythms are correct, the words should be added. It is also very helpful to read the words in rhythm before

combining them with the notes. In problem passages where poor tone quality is evident, one should revert back to the vowels and then try to match the words into the same open vowel positions.

I realize that it is difficult for many teenagers to approach their songs in this manner; however, those who do generally have few problems and make rapid progress in the studio.

Since I ask each student to purchase a pocket musical dictionary (unless he or she already owns one), I write,

> It is the student's responsibility to know the meanings of all musical terms and symbols encountered in each new song. After consulting a music dictionary, many students write the meanings above the terms in the music until they become familiar with them.

I also expect the student to use a regular dictionary or the Internet to look up any words in the text with which they are unfamiliar when they first encounter the new song. In order to convey to the student that when we sing we express emotions, I add,

> In learning a new song, it is most important that the words of the song are carefully read to discover exactly what the writer is saying. What mood is being expressed? Is this a song about happiness, sadness, or another emotion? If you were asked what this song is about, could you explain it? Songs convey a feeling to the listener and you as a singer must relay this feeling to the best of your ability.

As a help for those students who eventually will be dealing with more advanced repertoire, I state,

> Foreign language songs for more advanced students require translating the text into English from dictionaries and from special books I have that you may use before and after lessons. The English written under the notes is merely a singing version and not the translation. Occasionally, some phrases may be close to the real meaning. You should not sing a foreign language song unless you know what you are singing about. When singing operatic arias, you need to read the story of the opera so that you know your character and where this aria falls within the context of the entire opera. I also have books to help you with this procedure. The Internet can be a major resource for you.

One of the most beneficial paragraphs in the procedures statement is the section on song memory preparation. It begins,

> All songs studied will be memorized. After a song is completely learned with the music, the memorization procedure which I expect is for you to write the words in poem form on 3" x 5" or 4" x 6" file cards. Include the title, the composer's name, the song category (sacred, French, Broadway, etc.), and any little helpful hints you need to sing the song accurately from the card. Practice for a week with the card, checking the music occasionally to be sure you are not learning anything wrong. Then the week after you have sung the song with the card for me, I expect you to sing it entirely by memory. These cards then become a permanent file of all the songs you have learned.

This is one procedure that I absolutely require. I find that as a result of this organized approach, my students eventually learn to memorize very quickly and it becomes a natural process. Some students will even start the process on their own if they feel they are ready. This also is a security factor in performance since a student has both memorized by looking at the entire song and also by looking at the poem.

OTHER THOUGHTS ON PRACTICE

Finally, I add a few comments on vocal health. I suggest,

When your voice feels tired, stop practicing for a period of time. Never push your voice beyond what seems to be physically comfortable. A head cold or a minor sore throat should not prevent one from singing; however, when the speaking voice has become affected and there is evidence of laryngitis, singing can be harmful.

It would be a teacher's dream come true if all students were disciplined to abide by each of these guidelines; however, it would be foolish to think that all students will follow everything on the sheet. Since this is given at the first lesson, it does make a statement that this is serious business and not "fun and games." It is interesting to note that many younger students who have learned this organized approach to voice lessons find that it carries over into their general schoolwork. Many parents have commented about the definite improvement in study skills and time management as a result of voice lessons.

Again, let me emphasize that your teaching style may indicate a less formal approach and not lend itself to these ideas. However, there may be a number of items that you can incorporate into your own statement of practice procedures.

CHAPTER 9
MUSICAL AND VOCAL FITNESS

Music Reading Techniques, Exercise Books and Vocalises,
The Importance of Vocalises

Dear Mrs. B.,

I have developed a practice procedures guide for students. In addition, I have created my own sheets of melodic syllable drills for my students but I wonder if you can suggest some things to help those who struggle with reading them. When your students finish your 55 melodic patterns and you start songs, do you use any other formal exercises?

Sincerely,
Nancy

Dear Nancy,

You will notice a tremendous difference in your students when you finally begin song literature as a result of the beginning lessons dealing primarily with fundamental concepts of sound production and reading skills. Let me offer you some ideas that work for me in helping those students who struggle with reading. Since I am a great believer in using formal exercises and vocalises for building vocal technique, I will describe the various books my students use in addition to working with song literature.

Sincerely,
Mrs. B.

MUSIC READING TECHNIQUES

When I start my students with music reading, we spend time with a one octave scale and various short syllable patterns and progress into one-line melodies (described in chapter 7). I play only chords and accompaniment backgrounds so that the student learns independence from the beginning. With some non-readers, it is necessary for them to clap and speak each syllable in the correct rhythmic notation before attempting to sing the vocal line. If a note is held more than one beat, I have the students clap and pulse the other beats. If there is a rest, I have them separate the hands and speak the word "rest." Some students have difficulty with this at first, but the students must be able to feel the rhythm in order to sing it accurately.

For those pupils who have problems with the intervals, I have them imagine that the piano keyboard is in a vertical position. The student is taught to "step" the scale with the hand held horizontally for each note up and down. We then "step" the syllable patterns and progress to the melodic patterns. You may find that the student who struggles will "step" with the hand sometimes moving in the opposite direction of the note patterns. This indicates a lack of eye to brain coordination. By constant work the student can eventually learn to recognize and reproduce the direction accurately. I have some four and five year students who will resort to modified hand positions when learning new repertoire because they know that the physical movement helps them with their reading skills.

In deciding where to breath, we make little sentences out of the note patterns and the student is already experiencing the concept of phrasing. I do not tell the student where to breath – we figure it out together.

While using these methods, I continually change the keys of the melodic drills as a means of improving technique. In addition, this helps me determine the most comfortable tessitura for the students as I choose beginning repertoire.

EXERCISE BOOKS AND VOCALISES

In my opinion, formal exercises that deal with all aspects of musicianship in singing and that improve agility and technical skill in a student help the teacher develop the complete musician-singer. The student learns the discipline of hard work, logical sequences of notes and rhythms, musical phrasing and vocal development in a way that merely singing songs will not accomplish at this stage of study. As a result of my weekly assignments, I am assured that my students are really spending at least some time on technique and music fundamentals.

If students are prepared for this type of rigorous study from the very first lesson, they will accept it without question. Many will find it difficult at first, but they recognize the value when they realize the strides they are making as musicians.

In an October, 1997 *Forbes* article, "What Do Teenagers Want?," Diane Ravitch notes that teenagers want order and discipline. They are tired of just doing the minimum to get by. She quoted Deborah Wadsworth, Public Agenda's executive director, "American teenagers hunger for structure, discipline and more rigorous standards. They complain bitterly about lax instruction and unenforced rules. Many feel insulted at the minimal demands placed upon them. They state unequivocally that they would work harder if more were expected of them." This observation still applies to today's adolescents.

Do not be afraid of losing students because of rigorous training. I find that young singers will respect you for making such demands. John Stuart Mill, a philosopher, wrote, "The pupil who is never required to do what he cannot do, never does what he can do."

What skilled pianist has not struggled with the scales and exercises of Hanon and Czerny? What good trumpet player has not worked through the Arban book? What serious horn player has not studied the etudes of Gallay, Kopprasch and Maxime-Alphonse?

There are many exercise and vocalize books available, but over the years I have settled into a sequence of books that really "work" for these students:

Concone: *The School of Sight-Singing* (G. Schirmer). Most beginning teenage students in my studio start with this book. They learn key and time signatures and the moveable *do* syllables. I personally do not like to use the fixed "do" system because the student never gets the feel of each of the intervals. With movable "do," most common in North America, there is more of a relationship of sound among the intervals as one moves from key to key. For most of the exercises I have the students write the first letter of the solfeggio syllables above the notes and for the chromatics they write the entire syllable. Some of the exercises lend themselves more to be sung on a neutral syllable. I usually lower the keys for alto and bass voices. Very musical students finish this book in six months to a year. The average teenager takes close to one and a half years, and some students will take two years or more.

This book introduces most of the basic musicianship skills the average student will encounter with a very gradual sequence of difficulty.

Marchesi: *Complete Vocal Method*, Op. 31, Vol. 1664 (G. Schirmer). This book follows the Concone for most female students. The first section involves a series of agility exercises and the second section (which I add after the student has finished exercise #36) consists of vocalises. Again I lower keys for altos. Many young students are still in this book when they graduate from high school. Occasionally, very talented students will complete this in eleventh or twelfth grade.

Marchesi: *Elementary Progressive Exercises for the Voice*, Op. 1, Vol. 384 (G. Schirmer). If I teach a good sight-reader, who will be with me for only one or possibly two years, I will substitute this volume. It is primarily the first section of the complete *Marchesi* and deals with scale and agility exercises. It eliminates the vocalises section.

Panofka: *24 Progressive Vocalises*, Op. 85, Book 1 & 2 (Kalmus). I use these books for male students after the Concone. The vocalises are not as complicated as Marchesi, yet are still challenging. For the lower voices I usually lower the key a step or more.

Vaccai: *Practical Method of Italian Singing* (G. Schirmer). After Concone I add this along with the Marchesi or Panofka books to introduce Italian as well as to teach the rudiments of ornamentation. I prefer to use the G. Schirmer edition which comes in three keys. A fourth book written in a very low key is available from Kalmus. When a student concludes this book, I always require a second time through for review. My students love to do this because it seems so easy the second time around.

Lütgen: *Vocalises* (G. Schirmer). This book was introduced to me by Elizabeth Mannion and comes in High, Medium and Low. This is a valuable book which I use frequently. When I have a student who reads well, but who I know will only be with me for a year or two, this is an excellent choice. It works very well with the male student. If a female finishes Marchesi, I will have her also use this even though she may find it rather easy after Marchesi. If time permits, I require the student to review this book.

Bordogni: *Thirty Six Vocalises*, Kalmus, Vol. 9148 for Sopranos and Vol. 9149 for Mezzo-Sopranos. This is an extremely advanced 150-page book of lengthy operatic agility vocalises which are excellent for the serious adult student and teacher who welcomes a musical challenge.

You might want to check with other teachers for names of their favorite exercise and vocalise books. This way you can make better decisions as to what will work for you.

THE IMPORTANCE OF VOCALISES

The role that such vocalises can play in developing young singers was addressed in an interview in *Etude* magazine in 1953, when the famous soprano, Bidu Sayão, said, "But my voice was too small for professional aspirations, and my friends discouraged me. However, I persisted in studying, and had the great luck to find a teacher who gave me the principles of bel canto, and kept me for several years on nothing but scales, vocalises and the Marchesi exercises. At the end of that time, my voice had developed, without the least forcing, into professional proportions."

A wonderful book called *Mastery*, with interviews of thirty remarkable people by Joan Evelyn Ames (Rudro Press, 1997), includes comments by the great singer-teacher, Margaret Harshaw, who stressed the importance of discipline in studying singing. She wrote about her teacher, "Anna Schoen-René was a real disciplinarian. Her students called her a Prussian General. When she instructed you, you did it, and you did it right away. She made a stipulation that she would not accept me as her student unless I agreed not to sing literature for two semesters…nothing but scales to build technique." I am sure this also included vocalises and flexibility exercises.

Today's lifestyles do not allow time for such rigorous training as experienced by these two singers. Nevertheless, we are in a position to incorporate some of the techniques into each of the lessons we teach so that we are providing each student the opportunity to become the best possible musician-singer he or she is capable of becoming.

Many teachers have told me that they can see a great difference in the progress of their students if they incorporate some of the ideas that have been discussed in this chapter. It is also satisfying when after several months, even middle and high school students tell me how great it is to be able to understand and have some reading ability for their school choral literature.

An adult singer with two years of lessons in Germany began lessons with me in the spring of 2013. She had a fine voice but she admitted she could not read very well. She was so excited that I would spend a great deal of time with my preliminary work with her on learning to read. In the fall of 2013, she decided to audition for the alto solo quartet work in a Haydn Mass with a quality community choral ensemble. In the meanwhile her voice had really blossomed and she was elated that she could actually read some of the easier alto solo sections without my help. She worked very hard to be completely prepared for the audition. Much to her surprise she was accepted as the soloist. She claims that there was *absolutely* no way she could have done this without the time we devoted to music reading fundamentals.

CHAPTER 10
THE SONGS WE SING

Choosing Repertoire for Beginners, Repertoire Readiness,
Appropriateness of Repertoire, Beginning Song Literature,
Sacred Songs, The Teacher's Continuing Search

Dear Mrs. B.,

Even though I have now taught for several years, I really struggle with finding new repertoire that is appropriate for beginning teenagers and novice adult students. I find that the things I sang in college are way too difficult and most of them were in a foreign language. Can you guide me through the process of how to choose repertoire, and will you share what you use in your studio?

Sincerely,
Nancy

Dear Nancy,

Your question is directed to the subject that is of primary importance to all teachers of voice. I will discuss guidelines in choosing repertoire, and later I will talk about anthologies, octavos, and single sheets that I find to be most accessible and useful.

Sincerely,
Mrs. B.

CHOOSING REPERTOIRE FOR BEGINNERS

In the book, *Profiles in Vocal Pedagogy*, Weldon Whitlock wrote, "In knowing what to teach, the teacher's knowledge and experience are constantly strained to the breaking point. No matter how wide and extensive the teacher's repertoire, it is never comprehensive enough. The demands for repertoire are different for each individual pupil. The good teacher continually carries on his study in repertoire and adds to it."

Making song literature choices for your students takes a great deal of time if you are serious about treating each student as a unique person. If you have taken my suggestions about teaching music reading for six to twelve weeks before introducing songs, you will better know each student's personality, practice habits, musical abilities, and vocal strengths and weaknesses. One result is that you will be in a better position to evaluate literature for these individual students.

The songs chosen must be appropriate for each person, musically worthwhile, and yet technically not difficult. We must keep in mind that these young people and beginning adults must be able to relate to the repertoire in some way in order to succeed. Some students will progress rapidly into "standard serious repertoire" while others will require several years before they are emotionally and musically ready for this. Most of our students require songs of a simple nature in the beginning years of study.

Sometimes students express a desire to sing current pop music, country music, or contemporary Christian songs. This music is not specifically addressed in this book. This type of literature might be appropriate with an adult student working on a specialized project, or the occasional instance where a teen student has an upcoming special event. In general, I find that guiding a student into classical literature, in addition to musical theater, provides much more rewarding vocal study. If someone only wants to sing popular music, and as a teacher, this is not what you wish to always teach, then you might reach an impasse, and the student will need to seek another teacher. My students are most often quite willing to work on popular music on their own, rather than in the studio, or perhaps with only occasional attention to it in lesson time. I do recommend that a teacher certainly can encourage students to sing solos, and to apply the technique they have learned in the studio to any music they sing.

REPERTOIRE READINESS

One must choose songs close to the level of a student's present maturity and then gradually lead and challenge the pupil through all types of music and musical styles. Musical tastes are only developed through exposure to all kinds of song literature. There is a definite time for introducing unfamiliar types of music which I call "Repertoire Readiness." Is it not better to have a student ask, "When will I get to sing songs in Italian?" than to hear, "Why do I have to sing this yucky Italian stuff?" It is our job to start with easy songs and have the student progress gradually to more complicated ones in a timeline that suits each individual. In mathematics, a pupil learns arithmetic before being exposed to algebra and calculus. The study of music requires a similar developmental approach.

APPROPRIATENESS OF REPERTOIRE

Beginning literature needs to be limited in range and have a comfortable tessitura. There should be no excess breath demands or extremes in tempo or dynamics. Songs should be at an easy level of musical difficulty with moderation in all areas. Short songs are desirable with slower learners as well as for other students as they learn the discipline of practicing and memorizing. Songs with movement and melodic skips are much easier for beginning students than slow, sustained pieces. The music can be challenging but not frustrating to the student.

Students need to relate to the text and melodic line of their songs. Political correctness has affected us in recent years, and as a result, we sometimes have to modify a dated text of a song. The songs must appeal to the student's present maturity level and still have lasting value, if only for the student's personal enjoyment. Values change, and as teachers we all have a different and unique sense of musical value. As an example, many years ago I found the music of Mrs. H. H. A. Beach (now known as Amy Beach) to be very unappealing. Several years ago I was asked to sing many of her songs for a special program. After digging deeply into the repertoire, I discovered that Amy Beach had indeed written some lovely songs including ones I had previously rejected. We are surrounded by change in our lives, and as a result our values and judgments are bound to change.

Musical literature also tends to follow a general, larger ebb and flow in tastes. A composer once thought passé may become relevant again, or music once highly regarded may later seem anachronistic. In classical literature for beginning students, one must seek beyond only the most major composers to quality songs by minor composers that match the vocal pedagogical purpose. One could define this valuable body of music as "pre-standard literature" or "teaching literature." Many of the songs in the four books I have compiled, *36 Solos for Young Singers* and *36 More Solos for Young Singers* and the *Easy Songs for Beginning Singers*, Part I and *Easy Songs for Beginning Singers*, Part II are teaching literature by this definition.

The use of common sense in repertoire selection can make the difference between the enthusiastic student and the one who discontinues lessons. One should never put a student in a position of feeling ridiculous. No "tripping o'er the violets" for male students. In my studio, with rare exceptions, the male teaching repertoire is completely different from that of my female students. One also needs to realize that there is often a lack of emotional maturity in junior high school females. Many of these girls just love singing songs like "The Lilac Tree," "Two Marionettes" and "The False Prophet." One of my most advanced high school seniors was *musically* very mature in ninth grade, already singing Italian and florid literature when her absolute favorite song to sing as one of her choices for the spring recital that year was "Animal Crackers," I knew that *emotionally* she was not ready to perform many of the more musically advanced pieces she had learned so well. By tenth grade I could see a tremendous difference in her recital preferences as her emotional maturity level had caught up with her intellectual level. She went on to get a doctorate degree in voice. As teachers, we must be insightful about a student's aesthetic capacities. We should not project a highly experienced adult's tastes onto young students not ready to communicate subtle and sophisticated emotions.

Standard Broadway show tunes and easy sacred and folksong style octavo pieces can provide the necessary bridge between the student's beginning tastes and the teacher's goals. This can also add lots of fun to the studio. All of my first and some second year students work on Broadway songs. For many years I had been using SA and SSA octavos for my sopranos because the keys were more suited. Since then, Hal Leonard published my compilations, *The First Book of Broadway Solos for Soprano, Mezzo-Soprano/Alto, Tenor* and *Baritone/Bass* Part I and II. The songs were chosen and the keys altered in many cases to make this a viable choice for the non-belting classically oriented studio singer. Several songs can be sung by both male and female voices.

Through my extensive work with teenagers, I find that my students prefer very melodious songs, of which many seem to stir their inner emotions. It seems as if, in the case of shy students, the things they are feeling can only be expressed through the medium of song. These pupils also like character songs, which allow them to portray a person different from themselves.

BEGINNING SONG LITERATURE

When beginning middle school or junior high school students are finally ready for song literature, I will often begin with unison and SA octavo pieces, both sacred and secular, Broadway solos and sometimes single song sheets. I want to be very sure about the student's comfortable tessitura before I have him or her purchase books. In most cases, when beginning senior high school students are ready for songs, their voice classification is usually pretty well set and I can decide on specific art song anthologies. Even with this age I will use some single sheets and sacred octavo literature to keep music purchases efficient.

My students are usually working on more songs than we can cover in a lesson. These songs are all at different stages of development. There may be a "memorized" song, a "carded" song (a week away from being memorized), a song learned to the point where it can be "carded" for the next week, and several songs in the beginning stages of learning. The student is expected to work on the songs in this same logical order for the lesson. Songs memorized are dropped unless they are later chosen to be sung for a recital, competition, or church service. At that point, these songs are then perfected to the point of being "performance-ready." The student learns the difference between songs memorized for vocal and musical growth and those memorized for audiences, but all songs are memorized.

SACRED SONGS

Quality sacred music is very important for many of my students because there are opportunities to sing in churches or synagogues. For instance, in our church I provided a soloist for a period of 31 years for each Sunday at our 8:15 A.M. service. In addition to using our own church soloists, I am able to provide many solo opportunities for those students in my studio who were interested. This often resulted in opportunities in their own religious services. Every year I make sure that these students have learned several new Christmas and Lenten pieces for their future use. In the case of Jewish students, it will take more research to find appropriate literature, although many Old Testament based solos are appropriate. You may find useful songs in some books by two music publishers that specialize in Jewish music: Tara Publications, and Transcontinental (both distributed currently by Hal Leonard). You may need to get resourceful in dealing with students of other religions. You will need to check the interests of all new students, however, because you will sometimes have students who do not wish to study any sacred music in the studio. These wishes should be respected.

THE TEACHER'S CONTINUING SEARCH

One of my missions in song literature development is to provide a smorgasbord of all types of music from all periods of music. In this way the students gain an appreciation for musical styles which form a basis for their musical preferences in later life.

The students purchase all the music that they study and learn. Since music costs are dealt with in my policy statement, there is never a question from parents regarding this cost.

Wherever I go, I am constantly searching for new books and songs for use with students. It takes time and energy to search for suitable repertoire, but for me it is like the thrill of finding the prize in the scavenger hunt! Happy hunting!

CHAPTER 11
WHAT'S AN OCTAVO?

The Octavo Format, Sacred and Secular Octavos, Obtaining Octavos

---

Dear Mrs. B.,

Your last letter challenged me to think carefully when choosing repertoire for young singers. Previously I had never considered that the emotional, musical and intellectual maturity in a teenager may not always be at the same level. Recently I accepted several junior high school students with limited musical backgrounds, and now I understand why I have been frustrated in finding suitable song literature. I would not have thought about using selected octavos as solo repertoire for my students. Please tell me more about octavos.

Sincerely,
Nancy

Dear Nancy,

Even though I had used a few octavos for my private students as a result of my experience as a choral director and public school music teacher, it was not until the 1972 NATS workshop in Winston-Salem, North Carolina that I became so excited about seriously using this type of music in my private teaching. Harvey Woodruff, now deceased, gave a wonderful session on octavos, and this led to my ongoing search for new pieces to this day.

Sincerely,
Mrs. B.

THE OCTAVO FORMAT

Usually at my workshops on repertoire, I find one or two voice teachers asking, "What's an octavo?" An octavo is used in choral singing. In the printing industry it represents one-eighth of a large sheet giving you eight leaves and sixteen sides, thus the origin of the term. In most cases the octavos I recommend are unison or two-part—usually soprano/alto arrangements—and are adaptable for young voices.

There are many appealing aspects about octavos. Because most educational and sacred choral music is designed for average school and church voices, the ranges are moderate, often just an octave, and as a result, many are perfect for beginning voices. Most of the pieces work best for medium and high voices, although there are some I like specifically for low voices.

Simplicity seems to describe many octavos. The melodic lines are generally predictable, yet sometimes present occasional surprises. The rhythmic patterns are either straightforward or, in some cases, tend to have a jazzy flavor. One often finds a variety of time signatures in one piece, and they are easily learned with the simple texts and easy range demands. There are, however, some secular and sacred octavos that are moderately difficult and demand musical maturity.

The texts are often of a folk song style or easily understood pictorial moods. There are lullabies and sea songs as well as solos that are also available in the more expensive vocal/piano sheet format. In the case of sacred octavos, the texts speak to teenagers since many of these were written for junior and youth choirs. One needs to evaluate carefully what you use because there are pieces one could use with seventh or eighth grade students where the texts would not be mature enough to give to some ninth grade students and older.

The length of these octavos is generally on the short side. The accompaniments are usually not complicated and often support the voice line. One finds a great deal of repetition and key modulation.

The SA octavos usually are written in such a way that the second part, whether alto or a descant, is not needed because it is represented in the accompaniment, or can be totally eliminated or easily added by the piano. One often has options to create different note combinations for final phrases depending on the student's range. Some women's chorus octavos (SSA) will also be very useful as solo pieces.

A key advantage is the minimum cost per octavo versus a standard piece of vocal/piano sheet music. The main disadvantage is that *these pieces can go out of print very quickly*. For this reason, a voice teacher's search must be continual. I have found that there are many more choices appropriate for female voices than for males. If you find a song you *really* like and multiple copies are available, I advise you to buy some for future use for students because many of my favorite pieces of which I purchased over the years are no longer in print.

Through the years I have searched choral catalogues, displays at workshops and conventions, unison and two-part bins of octavo music and files of choral music in many music stores. In addition, I have received boxes of single copies of youth and children's church choir octavos from retired choir directors which provide free occasional suitable solo literature for students. It is not unusual to find only two or three possibilities out of every thirty to fifty pieces you see. Each teacher's taste will determine a different selection of music.

SACRED AND SECULAR OCTAVOS

The voice teacher, in many cases, can help to create singing opportunities for students in churches or synagogues. For 31 years, I volunteered to provide special music for our early worship service at church for every Sunday in the year. There was no choir at this service, and I felt that, in addition to using our own church soloists, I could provide a service to the church and for my students. Eventually, several other church choir directors asked me to supply talented singers for their regular summer services. One choir director calls me every spring and asks for the names of my new teenage talents so that he may invite them to sing in his church throughout the summer. There are several choir directors who want to know when I start students from their congregations and when these students will be ready to sing their first church solos. In many cases, opportunities arise when parents question why their son or daughter gets a chance to sing in my church and not in his or her own house of worship. This has led to many more solo offerings in the churches of our community and nearby areas.

Professionally speaking, I feel that even the voice teacher who does not have a personal religious affiliation needs to be able to encourage and direct this musical opportunity and need in students. To neglect such an important avenue would be a disservice to the interests and growth of some students.

When an interested student who attends our church is ready to sing, I will feature this person as a soloist as many as five times in a calendar year—in the fall, during Advent, at one of the Christmas Eve services, during or immediately following Lent, and late spring. If I have two compatible students, they will also sing duets at least three times during the year.

A high school senior formerly studying in my studio began lessons in eighth grade. Her junior choir director had her singing little solo bits with the choir, and a Christmas solo at a nursing home. When she was ready, she sang in her Lutheran church as a soloist. As an adult she cantors twice a month and sings a solo at least once every three weeks. She has numerous sacred octavos, in addition to many sacred vocal albums and sheets. This young woman will be a church soloist the rest of her life, even though she did not major in music in college.

When students begin song literature, I usually include sacred octavos unless the student expresses disinterest in sacred music. The texts, ranges, and relative simplicity of the pieces are appealing to teenagers. These songs are learned very quickly and the student experiences immediate vocal accomplishment. Many of the selections I regularly use may be sung by either male or female students. It is important to teach different solos to students from the same congregation so that duplication is avoided.

Many interesting unison and SA secular octavos are published by English companies such as Boosey & Hawkes, Novello, Roberton, Elkin, and Oxford. In addition, many American and Canadian publishers such as Choristers Guild specialize in choir music for children and youth. I particularly like the secular unison animal songs written by Peter Jenkyns – "The Owls," "The Tiger," "Snakes," "The Crocodile," and his "Little Spanish Town," and "The Wizard." "The Bouquet of Rosemary" by Robert Elkin (Elkin & Co.), "Arcady" by E. Markham Lee (Leonard, Gould and Bottler), "My Sweetheart's a Sailor" by Geoffrey Winters (Oxford), and "The Path to the Moon" by Eric Thiman (Boosey & Hawkes), are several favorites of my beginning young females. This is merely a sampling of what is available.

OBTAINING OCTAVOS

It is most likely that you will find these items by ordering from a music store or music company that also stocks a large selection of choral literature. If a piece is out of print and you have a copy, write to the publisher and request permission to make an exact number of copies. Some firms will grant this free of charge; others will require a flat fee per copy. Still others will charge a fee per page. Several publishers will sell you authorized photocopies, and others have a special service built into their production structure. In the case when a publisher decides to delete a piece because of poor sales, the copyright may be returned to the composer, or to the arranger if the material was in Public Domain (even though the arrangement itself is copyrighted). When this happens, one needs to contact this person directly. Most publishers will supply an address. If the publisher has retained the copyright, the firm will most likely grant you the permission you seek. "Print on demand" is becoming more likely with today's publishers, but actually obtaining copies of permanently out of print material requires a great deal of effort from the private teacher. This can be frustrating, but from the publisher's point of view, if the piece was at all profitable, it probably would have remained in print. Publishers accommodate the occasional request for a permanently out of print title as best they can. You will have to determine if the pursuit is worth the effort in some cases. At times, it may be best to make an alternate selection that is readily available.

Whatever the case, be diligent as you explore octavo literature, and you will find it to be a fascinating opportunity for expanding song repertoire for beginning students.

CHAPTER 12
ANTHOLOGIES FOR
ADOLESCENT AND NOVICE SINGERS

Elementary, Middle School and Junior High Students, Freshman and
Sophomore High School Students, High School Juniors and Seniors,
Christmas and Sacred Collections, Thoughts About Contest Solos,
Songs for Novice Adult Singers, The Quest Goes On

Dear Mrs. B.,

You certainly added to my repertoire awareness with your ideas for secular and sacred octavo music for young students. I wonder if you would review some of the all-purpose anthologies available for my use. In particular, I'd like suggestions of appropriate collections for teen students. Even though I use several of your compilations, I would like you to explain how and when you use them.

Sincerely,
Nancy

Dear Nancy,

I'd be happy to tell you about the collections that I find useful in my studio. You might also want to ask some of your other teacher friends to share their favorite anthologies for additional ideas.

Sincerely,
Mrs. B.

ELEMENTARY, MIDDLE SCHOOL AND JUNIOR HIGH STUDENTS

You will note that we have included all collections for which I am compiler in the Appendix VII with the complete Table of Contents listed for each volume. As you read this chapter, you may want to refer to the Appendix for the books with which you are not familiar. Included in these volumes are many songs that had been out of print for years or previously available only in single sheet form, very familiar songs that should be part of a singer's repertoire, and many songs that are worthy of bringing into the repertoire of young singers. There are so many wonderful volumes available these days by many publishers that I also use in my studio, but space does not permit me to mention everything here.

As noted in Chapter 20 dealing with children, I developed two books specifically for singers ages 9-12 and slightly older with limited experience, *36 Solos for Young Singers* and *36 More Solos for Young Singers*. These books include lullabies, folksongs from several nationalities, camp songs in solo arrangements, spirituals, humorous selections and a few standards that remain popular with each new generation of singers. The majority of these solos have a range of an octave from D to D with a few extended notes below and above. Most of the melodic lines are supported in the accompaniment.

In the past, one of the reasons I used octavos so heavily is because I had not been satisfied with many books for this age student. I was a great fan of the old *Art Songs for School and Studio* – Vol. 1 (High and Low) by Glenn and Spouse (Presser) for the seventh and eighth-grade girls. They really liked these songs, which are so appropriate to the temperament and musical sensitivity common to young women of this age. For girls with very limited background, the *Pathways of Song* Vol. 1 (High and Low) by LaForge and Earhart (Warner Brothers) provides easy and short songs for a first book. On occasion, I will still use these books.

The books I rely on heavily now are my Part I and Part II of the *Easy Songs for Beginning Singers* (G. Schirmer) for all four voices. They were developed for 12-15 year-old singers, or even high school and adult singers with very limited backgrounds. There are between 22 and 24 songs in each book with a companion CD of recorded piano accompaniments. The songs are all in English and most of the ranges are an octave to a tenth. Semi-popular songs, folk songs, easy art songs, humorous, spiritual, and short traditional songs round out the collections. As in all of the male volumes I have compiled, every song included has a text that is specifically suited for a male student. One of my previous complaints was only finding volumes with one or more songs suited for a young male student. The songs in these sets are also on the short side, which helps the student to experience vocal progress more quickly.

For a very musical male student I often add the *Arnold Book of Old Songs* by Quilter (Boosey & Hawkes). The songs in this book make it ideal for the "bari-tenor" student whose range sits between baritone and tenor. Many of the songs can easily be transposed up or down a step to accommodate those voices that are changing. I find that working with this book guides me more definitely into the direction the voice is moving. This is also published in a high key.

A supplemental book elementary, junior high, and middle school girls like is my *Daffodils, Violets, and Snowflakes* (High and Low) with 24 songs. It is a book of short, cute vignettes about nature and love, and includes encore style songs ideal for those who enjoy story-telling texts. Some minimal florid singing is introduced. This volume appeals to the innocent young girl who lacks some of the maturity of her peers. Two other supplemental books I sometimes use at this age are *15 Easy Folksong Arrangements* and *15 Easy Spiritual Arrangements* (both Hal Leonard). These are very easy, familiar songs with new settings. These books come in High and Low with recorded accompaniments and performances.

All of my students use a Broadway or Disney volume because many of these songs are so familiar to them. I have the student bring what they have at home first, but usually the big books they have contain such low keys that there are only a few usable songs for the purpose of voice lessons. The wonderful *The Singer's Musical Theatre Anthology* series edited by Richard Walters is entirely too intense for this age student, but I recommend it for the older teen or college student interested in Musical Theater. I developed an eight-volume set of Broadway solos for Soprano, Mezzo, Tenor, and Baritone. Each book includes 22-24 songs for use in the studio. These feature some of the most used classic theater songs in keys that are suited for beginning study. The first volume is available both with and without a companion recording. The second volume comes as a combined Book/Audio package. Theater songs can be particularly helpful in encouraging dramatic involvement and expression in a student. In my studio, when using Broadway songs, the same issues of breathing and freedom of tone are stressed as in classical literature. On the other hand, students learn that diction is somewhat more relaxed in this style of song. These songs were chosen to be sung in legitimate style, yet, in the type of character featured in the show. Belting style is taught when a student has a role in the show which demands this type of sound.

FRESHMAN AND SOPHOMORE HIGH SCHOOL STUDENTS

When a student comes to you at age 14, 15, or later, there are many more choices for anthologies. In some cases, you may have to use books designed for younger students. Depending on the student, you may be able to start with more musically substantial material. As you might expect, since *The First Book of Solos*, Part I, II, and III for Soprano, Mezzo-Soprano/ Alto, Tenor, and Baritone/Bass (G. Schirmer) were compiled with my students in mind, I use these books extensively with my students. Since these books are all usable for this level student, I usually choose two of the three books and work the easier songs out of both books. Now the books are available with the three "Part I" volumes spiral-bound together for each voice part at a great savings. This is being made possible for the teachers to use at the piano, but students love having all three volumes together, and it gives greater song choosing flexibility.

Depending upon the students' personality and maturity, I will sometimes use *Pathways of Song* Volume III. (I do not use Volumes II and IV because there are not enough songs I use in teaching to justify purchase.) Occasionally, I will use Volume II of the *Art Songs for School and Studio* that was mentioned earlier.

There is an interesting, inexpensive set of three books called *Selected Solos for Contest*, Part I, II, and III (High and Low), edited by Grier (Heritage Music Press). Most of the songs have a contemporary flavor that is appealing to certain female students. The keys are well suited in both the high and low versions.

HIGH SCHOOL JUNIORS AND SENIORS

For beginning senior high school students, all the books I have mentioned so far may be appropriate, including a small inexpensive book called *Basic Repertoire for Singers* (Southern Music Company), which is a collection of 12 Handel, Purcell, Haydn, and Old English standard literature suitable for a soprano or a tenor.

Occasionally I will have a powerful and dramatic high school female voice. With this student I may use *Singable Songs* (High and Low) by Mason (Ditson), since several songs are suited for this rich quality.

Infrequently you may teach a student with an extremely low bass voice who is unable to handle the usual baritone and bass books. Van Camp edited the book *Songs for Bass* (Carl Fischer), which includes thirteen selections. The songs range from very easy to quite difficult within one volume, but the ranges are extremely low.

Hal Leonard has published a series for the four voice parts called *Classical Contest Solos*. The ten songs in each volume have been taken from several of the official state contest lists, and information is provided for students on how to learn a song, as well as translations, composer biographies and interpretive suggestions. Performances, pronunciation lessons, and accompaniments are included on the companion recordings. The original intent was to provide the student without a voice teacher the means to participate in state festivals, although the books may be useful in the studio.

Classic Songs (high and low), edited by Taylor (Alfred Publishing), can serve as a first book when the teacher seeks a volume that includes very easy Italian and French songs with updated English versions, in addition to Old English songs. Prior to the publication of The *First Book of Solos* I used this for some beginning male and female students. It still is used occasionally in my studio, particularly for a student who struggles with beginning Italian, because the songs are very short and the Italian is not difficult.

For the older adolescent student with a medium to low voice who is not academically-oriented or is not going to sing in foreign languages, I enjoy using the Spaeth book, *55 Art Songs* (Summy-Birchard). This volume is entirely in English, and it also contains many songs we traditionally teach in other languages, such as some early Italian arias and German Lieder.

Several other supplemental anthologies can be used by many high school students from Freshman through Senior grades. *Lovers, Lasses and Spring* for sopranos is a popular book, which I call the "baby coloratura" book. It contains 14 florid, melismatic-style, flashy soprano showstopper solos. This is a book for students with excellent musicianship and artistry developing at this age. Young sopranos love this book. *Roses, Laughter and Lullabies*, with 18 songs, was developed for mezzos, and includes several songs that have lengthy melismatic passages, and challenge the musicianship and interpretive strengths of this darker sounding vocal quality. For the male student, I compiled *Young Ladies, Shipmates and Journeys* in Tenor and Baritone/Bass volumes. These 21-song volumes feature many sea chanteys and robust male songs.

In addition to my Broadway volumes, *The Singer's Musical Theatre Anthology – Teen's Edition* by Richard Walters is an excellent book with songs taken directly from the shows for all four voices at the high school level.

When students have learned at least five or six of the Vaccai book vocalises, they are often ready for an Italian anthology. I personally prefer the *28 Italian Songs and Arias of the 17th and 18th Centuries*, published now in five different keys by G. Schirmer. These volumes have study translations, pronunciation guides and added information. The John Paton Edition *26 Italian Songs and Arias* (Alfred) is filled with wonderful historical information and pronunciation guides and translations and suggestions for ornamentation. (My students prefer the G. Schirmer editions because of the richer sounding, more supportive accompaniments.) I use the Paton as an auxiliary reference for many of the songs. A favorite Italian book I often use for light, lyrical, and very musical sopranos is *Twelve Ariettas* by Righini, a contemporary of Mozart. These songs were researched by Edwin Penhorwood and they are simply delightful.

Many talented high school juniors and seniors move very easily into *The Second Book of Solos* Part I and II for Soprano, Mezzo-Soprano/Alto, Tenor, and Baritone/Bass (G. Schirmer), after singing songs from the first series for a few years. If your student has a well-trained technique, these books are very accessible, and young singers really relate well to the repertoire. Another more advanced series available is *The Imperial Edition of Songs*, by Northcote (Boosey & Hawkes). I find quite a few of these songs to be too heavy for the teenage voice, but there are still possibilities for certain students.

There are many books available from various publishers dealing with specific vocal styles, such as spirituals, contemporary American songs, French bergerettes, more Italian anthologies, German Lieder, and Spanish books. There are also collections which have good literature, but the high and low ranges are mixed together and for this reason I do not use them. There are also many books of folk songs available.

If the student is ready for it, a full move beyond teaching literature into standard classical literature is possible at this point, depending, of course, on the student's ability. As classically trained singers, our college education in voice prepared us in at least a basic education in standard song, opera and oratorio. A discussion of how the music can be applied to private studio teaching is beyond the scope of this book. I refer you to the many books available about these topics.

CHRISTMAS ANTHOLOGIES

For years I have had interested students add at least three Christmas solos each season to their repertoire because I encourage seasonal solos for church, Sunday School, banquets, private parties, and club celebrations. Hal Leonard released several volumes with original arrangements by Richard Walters called *Classical Carols*, and also *The Classical Singer's Christmas Album*. These two volumes include occasional duets and several instrumental obbligatos.

Christmas Song Album Volume I and II (Boosey & Hawkes) are sets of eight and nine songs but with the high and low keys mixed together, which make them less practical for a teaching anthology. *The Christmas Soloist* (Alfred Publications) comes in Medium High and Medium Low; however, the Medium High version may be too low for many sopranos. Two books called *Cradle Carols, Set I* and *Set II*, arranged by Powell (Concordia Publishing), include four very familiar and easy carols for medium voice, with instrumental parts (in B-flat and C) for each carol, usable for oboe, cello, flute, clarinet or violin.

In wanting a book that I could use with beginning students as well as with older students, and have them revisit it each year for more advanced repertoire, I compiled *Christmas Solos for All Ages* (Hal Leonard). This very comprehensive collection in High, Medium and Low Voice versions has 45 solos, with carol arrangements (eight by Boytim), art songs, traditional standards, some more unfamiliar solos, and several secular seasonal songs, all of which should work for most holiday occasions and at a very affordable price.

Another anthology called *The Christmas Collection* (Hal Leonard, edited Walters) contains fifty solos of all types, including art songs and more involved carol settings than those found in my collection. Both of these provide a singer with a rich library of the genre.

SACRED ANTHOLOGIES

Most of the sacred music I use for first and second year students comes from the octavo libraries (see Chapter 11). I include some modern SATB pieces that can be readily adapted for solo voice. After that, I have had to rely on single sheets or several collections which have worked well for teenage students.

Sacred Song Masterpieces Volumes 1 and *II* for High and Low Voice (edited by Fredrickson, R.D. Row Music) tend to be the first volumes I've used. Many of the pieces are adapted from melodies of the great composers but the popularity with my teens justifies this practice for this age group. Both volumes are used with the same frequency.

The Soloist's Practical Library of Sacred Songs Volume 1 (High and Low Voice, R.D. Row Music) is another book I consider. I do not like to use Volume 2 for teens because too many of the selections are unappealing to them.

The Church Soloist (edited by Pfautsch, Lawson-Gould Music, in High and Low) is a book I sometimes give to a student with a great deal of natural musicianship. It is primarily a group of fifteen Baroque and Classical selections.

There are quite a number of spiritual collections available for students. You will need to evaluate these books individually in matching them with a singer's needs.

My search for a more comprehensive sacred collection for student singers resulted in my compilation of *Sacred Solos for All Ages*, for High, Medium and Low Voice, published by Hal Leonard. This volume has 43 selections, including the most beloved "old chestnuts," many solos previously only available in single sheet form, traditional church solos with Biblical texts, selections for Thanksgiving, Lent and Easter, three Ave Marias, and a number of unfamiliar songs that I consider worthwhile to add to the church repertoire. This collection should be useful for many years of church solo singing.

Adults using this collection will find the High Voice suits the trained soprano and tenor. The Medium Voice is good for many typical soprano and tenor soloists. The Low Voice is quite low to accommodate the baritones and basses singing in early church services.

The Sacred Collection (edited by Walters, Hal Leonard, in High and Low) is a totally different source of sacred material. There are 70 selections, combining sacred art songs, traditional songs, 28 spirituals set by Harry T. Burleigh, and 14 solo and duet concert arrangements of hymns and sacred folksongs set by Walters. This is designed for the more mature singer, but could be used by some teens.

THOUGHTS ABOUT CONTEST SOLOS

Many states in the United States have official repertoire lists for the middle and high school "contest solo" events. Some of these have literature categorized by the size of enrollment of the high school, which obviously can be quite at odds with the level of the student. Most voice teachers who have encountered the contest solo phenomenon would agree that in many cases the literature on the state lists is poorly recommended and can be much too difficult for high school singers. Stories abound of advanced opera arias or heavy vocally sophisticated art songs appearing on state high school contest lists!

If you are in a state where you must prepare contest solos with students, I recommend that you find out as much information about the repertoire lists and official rules as possible, perhaps consulting a school choral teacher for advice. After studying the requirements, guide your student in making the best possible choice within the rules considering what is an appropriate challenge within the student's ability.

Those of us in the voice teaching profession need to do what we can to seek appropriate changes in the compilation of contest solo repertoire. Perhaps we can cultivate tactful and constructive relationships with our choral colleagues, some of whom are the compilers of these lists in most states. We can make a difference!

SONGS FOR NOVICE ADULT SINGERS

Most adults who have had no previous voice lessons can use the anthologies discussed in this chapter, as long as one avoids texts that are too childish. An exception might be if one is building a program for young audiences. For those expressing an interest in musical theater, *The First Book of Broadway Solos* series is very useful. For beginning classical singing the *Easy Songs for Beginning Singers* series should be considered. Adults with some high school and college vocal experience will naturally find my *The First Book of Solos* and Part I, II, III to be starting points. Many will move quickly into *The Second Book of Solos* and beyond that to standard vocal repertoire.

In all cases, the repertoire interests of adult students should be respected. Since each comes to the studio with a unique agenda, I allow the adults to set the tone for their lessons, as is explained more thoroughly in Chapter 19.

If you have students with an interest in singing duets, I compiled *Easy Classical Duets* for High and Low Voice combinations. There are 18 duets with a wide variety of pieces. For those who are looking for church duets, *18 Traditional Sacred Duets* for High and Low Voice combination should provide interesting possibilities. Teenage students as well as adults have performed many of these selections.

THE QUEST GOES ON

As teachers, we assume that our students know most of the pieces we knew while growing up. Experience tells me this is not the case. Recently, I had a forty year old man who had never heard the spiritual "Deep River." I have had young people report that they had never heard of the musical *South Pacific*. Just because it is tried and true material for us does not mean that it is not brand new for our students.

With the continued shrinkage of the publication of the single sheets suitable for the studio, there is an expansion of published compilations, which offer many song choices within each volume, and at a more affordable price per song for students of all ages. Every teacher will have favorites they will be willing to recommend when you chat with them at chapter meetings, workshops, and conventions. I encourage you to continue the search to find appropriate songs that are developmentally sound, intellectually rewarding, and enriching for the musical and vocal growth of each of your students.

CHAPTER 13
GOING PUBLIC

Scheduling Student Recitals, Where to Perform?, Publicity and Programs, Choosing Recital Songs, Recital Preparation, The Big Day Arrives, Lasting Benefits of Recitals

Dear Mrs. B.,

During the past several years I have held short informal studio recitals because I have not had enough students for a public recital. I know some teachers who never hold recitals and other teachers who present annual programs. I now have 20 students and I believe I am ready to try a more formal presentation. Do you have any guidelines to offer to help me in planning this?

Sincerely,
Nancy

Dear Nancy,

A public recital is the most visible marketing strategy you have available. The parents and others in attendance have a firsthand view of your teaching skills as evidenced by the performance of your students. For the students, *when properly prepared,* **performing in a public recital can add confidence and a surge of musical growth equal to at least four lessons in the studio. Let me elaborate on the procedures I use in planning a recital.**

Sincerely,
Mrs. B.

SCHEDULING STUDENT RECITALS

Students are informed of the dates of my yearly recitals during the first few lessons in the fall. From many years of experience, I have found that students progress much faster with two recitals rather than only the traditional one at the end of the school year. They have a midpoint time in the year to measure their progress and to compare themselves with their peers. Singing with more frequency also makes them more comfortable with the performing challenge. In order to provide new students adequate time to prepare two selections and to avoid the holidays, I usually schedule my first recital the first Sunday afternoon in February. Even if the Super Bowl game is scheduled for that same day, people in attendance can get to their parties in plenty of time. I schedule my spring recitals for Mother's Day afternoon. Since I draw students from many area school districts, I can generally avoid conflicting school concerts with this date. In addition, extended family members have expressed joy at being able to attend on this special day.

In my studio, recital participation for teenagers is mandatory. All ages can be combined at first if your student population does not merit separate programs for children, youth, and adults. Since you are trying to increase your teaching numbers, I would advise you to have adult programs if your students have the interest.

After many years of featuring my adults in separate recitals, I dropped these, since almost all of my adult students get many performance opportunities in church, music clubs, community theater, chamber ensembles, and choral groups of all sizes. There are many occasions for me to encourage and help adult students prepare programs on their own, or in combination with two or three other singers or instrumentalists. In such cases, my role becomes more that of advisor or consultant rather than organizer of the recital and, in many cases, the invited accompanist for such presentations. You may wish to do the same for your other singers as well.

WHERE TO PERFORM?

Your biggest concern is finding a convenient place with adequate parking for the program. Most teachers who belong to a church or synagogue can usually rent or be granted permission to use a large space with an adequate piano in the facility. (For many years, I used the fellowship hall of my church that could seat 150 people and provide an informal, non-threatening setting.) In lieu of rent, sometimes one can negotiate to pay to have the piano tuned several days before the program. You can check the use of public halls such as a civic clubhouse, an historical society home, a community building or the local library. In my case, with the unification of my church with two others, and the sale of our building, I have moved my recitals to the community room of the newly renovated public library, for which I donated a piano so they can feature musical concerts of all types.

PUBLICITY AND PROGRAMS

Publicity of the event occurs on several levels. I send a press release to the local papers at least two weeks prior to the event. I include the names of each student participating and, in the case of teens, the school districts represented. Those of you who use social media regularly can consider this as an outlet for publicity. In addition, I make sure that I have the completed programs from the printer at least two weeks before the recital so that each student can take a copy home to share with family and friends, and a copy for each of the represented choral directors in the schools. I choose to make simple one or two-sided programs on various colored paper for each recital. Other teachers prefer elaborate style programs. Since some of my graduates enjoy seeing the programs, the one page sheet is much easier to send with personal notes.

The actual "camera ready" programs are prepared on the computer after spending much time in deciding the performance order of the students for the recital. Those teachers who do not have a computer available will need to write the program in long hand or type it and take it to someone for final preparation. As long as I teach twenty or more teenagers, I will schedule two recitals with an approximate break of fifteen minutes between them. I keep younger and inexperienced students in the first program and the older and more advanced students in the second one. The younger students are encouraged to remain for the second recital, unless they have a legitimate conflict.

I try to make the program as interesting as possible by varying the voice types and by alternating male and female singers. I try not to have any selection performed more than once a year in the winter and spring programs. Because for some, this performance experience is difficult at first, I always try to position each student where he or she can come across to the audience most successfully. Being very careful not to place a soft voice immediately following a strong voice, I have my programs progress in terms of advancement as well as vocal strength. A male student can help to solve this problem because when he is placed between two females, the females immediately before and after him will not be compared. It is important to vary the position in consecutive recitals among friends with the same general ability. As a rule, I like to end each program with a strong selection. One needs to use a great deal of psychology in student placement to assure a successful program for all concerned.

CHOOSING RECITAL SONGS

About six or seven lessons prior to the recital I ask students to give me a list of the five or six of their favorite pieces they have learned or are presently finishing in lessons. Together we try to reduce this to four songs. During the next lesson I listen to and time each song with a stopwatch. Together we decide which two pieces will be their best choices in terms of sound, preferences, technical ease, and variety. Sometimes it will take yet another lesson to solidify the choices. Since my students memorize all their songs, by this time the choices need only to be *carefully polished* for public performance. By using this method, the students are always in charge of what they wish to sing and still I have the opportunity to guide them to the best choices. In most cases, young students will not perform pieces well that they did not choose to sing. My students always sing two selections so that if something goes wrong in the first piece, they have the chance to redeem themselves.

Some teachers like to have theme recitals. This is fine if they are supplemental programs but I believe at early stages of development there needs to be more freedom of choice. In the past, at some of my spring recitals I have also featured seniors in duets, trios, and even an ensemble piece or two. In the last number of years, difficulty of scheduling adequate rehearsals have prevented this because of the complicated schedules of my students, the number of schools I serve, the dominance of show choir engagements, and increased school trips for all types of reasons.

Once I have all the choices and respective timings, I can build a program. The timings guide me as to when to split the recitals, the time to schedule the second recital, and the time needed to record the complete program. In order to keep the recital length within one and a half hours, I shorten piano introductions, lengthy interludes and postludes. I always explain to my students the reasons for these changes.

RECITAL PREPARATION

A portion of each of the next several lessons is devoted to final preparation of the recital pieces. Students need to be so prepared that nervousness will not destroy the ability to perform well. I continually stress that this performance is a chance to *share* some of the student's favorite songs with family and friends. I do not mention the term *nervousness*. As a result of having the solos completely ready and thoroughly memorized, I rarely have a student who does not do his or her best in this situation. Only after the fact do we discuss "nerves." At that point, the student usually says that he or she would probably not be nervous for the next recital. This is a positive approach to the subject of nerves. Some students experience severe anxiety but their extreme preparation and mind set usually overcome the severity of the fear. At the next to the last lesson before the program I record each student on my audio equipment. To sing into a microphone creates a stressful situation for most students and if there are memory slips, there is still another lesson to make the corrections. (If teenage students remain with me through high school graduation, this composite record of all their recital pieces through the years become my graduation gifts. They are presented at the conclusion of the last recital as I announce to the audience each student's plans for attending college or beginning employment following graduation.)

In the case of students singing in foreign languages, the students are required to condense the essence of the song into their own words using a few written sentences to be spoken as introductions. Together we correct and make necessary changes. Each summary is memorized and practiced several times. In front of an audience, young students tend to speak too fast and are not deliberate enough without careful practice. At this stage of development "off the cuff" remarks cannot be trusted because of stammering and timing restrictions.

If you do not play piano well enough to accompany your students, and some voice teachers do not, you will need to hire a pianist, or perhaps pianists. In this case, you need to provide the music in plenty of time, and carefully plan for or supervise practice time with the pianist for each singer. If the accompanist cannot make the scheduled lesson time, you need to make arrangements for special rehearsals. Accompanists should follow NATS guidelines and play from the original scores, not from photocopies!

Time is spent discussing recital dress and etiquette. Female students are required to wear a skirt or a dress. (Several years ago I had a major problem on the definition of appropriate slacks so that I have had to become more precise in explaining my dress code.) Male students are required to wear a traditional two or three button jacket (a borrowed one if necessary), a conventional dress shirt and a tie. One year one of my older male students pleasantly surprised me by wearing a rented tuxedo he wore the day before while singing for his sister's wedding. I believe that when students are professionally dressed they are likely to sing like professionals. (Given that I accompany all my students in recitals, my husband insists that I wear a brand new outfit on recital day, since I sometimes have teenage students for six consecutive years.) Several years ago at a graduation party I was shown a scrapbook including pictures of me with the student at twelve different recital programs. If you don't like this method of building your dressy wardrobe, you can always wear black.

THE BIG DAY ARRIVES

The performing students sit in the front row. I expect them to arrive about ten minutes before the recital after properly warming up at home. They are instructed not to get up to sing until the applause has ended for the previous student in order not to "steal" another singer's applause. The students are encouraged to bow after the second selection. If a student so much as whispers while another person is singing, he or she is subjected to a very unpleasant glare from me while I am accompanying.

It is important to make quality recordings of recitals. One of my adult students who always attends the recitals is responsible for recording the programs. In turn, I provide a free lesson to her knowing that I do not have to concern myself with this part of the procedure. My husband is the usher who hands out programs, greets people, sets up additional chairs, handles emergency phone calls, provides cough drops, seats latecomers, etc. If you aren't as lucky as I am to have a gracious family member help out, you may need to recruit the assistance of someone to play this role. Because of logistics, back-to-back programs, and the number of people involved, I decided when I began to hold recitals that I would not get into the process of holding receptions. (However, it is a time-honored tradition for my husband and me to eat at a quality restaurant after the recitals as part of the debriefing and celebration!) Other teachers feel otherwise, and host informal to elaborate post-recital receptions.

It is important to welcome the audience and remind them to silence all electronic devices. At the end of the program I acknowledge the tremendous support they afford these young students by their enthusiastic response. They get a real music appreciation lesson because for many parents this is an opportunity to hear music that is not in the realm of their everyday life. They are generally very pleased to hear and see the students' artistry. This comes from having carefully planned the programs and leaving nothing to chance. Parents even become very supportive of other students over the years through these twice-yearly performances. We have some regular attendees who are not parents who simply enjoy hearing these young people perform.

LASTING BENEFITS OF RECITALS

In addition to the wealth of repertoire to which the students are exposed through the recital format, the students gain a great deal of self-confidence from program to program. They observe those students who are able to freely express the texts of songs and feel very comfortable in front of an audience. Processing the student's performance at the post recital lesson is important. I try to be very encouraging and praising of the student's efforts, yet we still deal with areas that need improvement. We discuss the performances of other students that an individual particularly enjoyed and why they were impressive. It is amazing how years later students will remember which students sang given selections in former programs. Students experience musical growth in the performance of their peers as well as themselves. This recital participation makes them comfortable in auditions, competitions, and even when competing with adults for solos in community performances. When they go to college, high school students who have enjoyed success in recitals have absolutely no fears of performing. They are also confident singing for juries and any other solo opportunities that come their way.

Based on the feedback I get from many former students, the preparation and performance in recitals has given them transferable skills in other challenges as well.

CHAPTER 14

VOCAL TECHNIQUES:
A FEW TRICKS OF MY TRADE

Learning Technique, Breathing, Resonance, Diction,
Artistry, Belting, Conclusions

Dear Mrs. B.,

I am wondering how you approach some technical aspects of voice teaching. Do you stress and teach the same vocal concepts to beginning students and more advanced students? How do you remedy a breathy tone, particularly in younger singers? I am interested in how you address high notes in your teaching. Is clear diction an impossible goal? How do you accomplish these things?

Sincerely,
Nancy

Dear Nancy,

The answer to your questions is to have patience, perseverance, and work toward the establishment of good vocal technique from the very first lesson. A former student of mine, while working on a master's degree in opera at the New England Conservatory of Music, was at a recent master class with a Metropolitan Opera coach. This woman commented that singing was really very simple. She mentioned that all one needs is to "breathe low" and "place high." Others have said this and it makes so much sense. Here are some techniques I use that my students seem to grasp rather quickly to make a difference in their vocal production as they learn to "breathe low" and "place high."

Sincerely,
Mrs. B.

LEARNING TECHNIQUE

Crucial to teaching voice is the ability to listen with an extremely critical ear. This skill develops through experience, and one becomes more sensitive through teaching each new student. Everyone hears sound differently, so this is a very subjective matter. Two teachers would evaluate the same sound in a different way. Daniel Ferro in *Opera News*, November, 1978, described the requirements for a voice teacher: "The teacher must be a technician, a linguist, a musician, and an artist in his own right."

Even singers with naturally beautiful voices must learn technique to survive. This is a combination of knowing what to do and how to accomplish it, which assures excellent singing even when one is not feeling well. Since a singer cannot hear himself or herself accurately, he or she must experience something else to stimulate the sensations needed to control the overall sound. The student learns through feeling the formation of the sound.

There are many techniques and different approaches, but the end result of beautiful singing is all that matters. The teacher essentially guides the student to find his or her most secure, comfortable, and lovely sound through sensation.

In *Opera News*, January 22, 1994, Richard Bonynge wrote, "I think too much is talked about technique, too much is made of it. Singers should have a technique that's as simple as ABC." He went on to say that when his wife, Joan Sutherland, had retired, she became fascinated with the shelf full of vocal manuals he owns from the eighteenth, nineteenth and twentieth centuries. He continued, "Before, she just did it. Now she is reading all about it, and she says much of what is written is *absolute rubbish*!" However, she reacted favorably to the simple exercises for controlling the breath, which trains the muscles long before a student sings big arias.

Bonynge observed, "Part of singing has to do with memory. Singing is sensation. You have to remember what it feels like when you do it correctly, so you can reproduce that feeling at will." Later, he summarized, "A good technique allows you to do what you want when you want to do it."

Some students come to my studio with everything in place, and it takes only suggestions here and there to keep their voices growing along with their maturing understanding of the vocal process. If they do use a correct approach at first (for instance, a free, open hum sound), I will explain what they are doing to make this happen. In this way they have a technical understanding as to why it works. Many other students need every bit of help to guide them to a singing technique that will carry them through their lifetime.

Recently, I questioned students about what I have said to them over the years regarding technique that they could really understand and that made a significant difference in their sensation "bank." The following is a summary of the main themes that emerged in their responses.

BREATHING

At the first or second lesson, after we have experimented and achieved a nice resonant hum on the first four exercises of my warm-up sheet (see Appendix II), I discuss breathing. Here are some recommendations on the topic, some of which already may be in your own repertoire of ideas:

1. Explain in very simple terms how the diaphragm is positioned in the body. Tell the students that it has no nerve endings and even though it is horizontally attached to the lower ribs, one cannot feel it as it moves up and down. The students learn that what they commonly refer to as their diaphragm is really the epigastrium.

2. Place your hands on the sides of your ribs and then on the back to show the outward movement, suggesting the similiarity to filling a bicycle tire with air. Then ask the student to do the same to themselves.

3. Next, ask the student to sit on a bench, putting the elbows on the knees and the head in the hands. When breathing this way, most students can feel the outward movement in the lower back area, and you should be able to see it.

4. Ask the student to raise his or her hands high over the head with hands clasped. Then ask the student to slowly lower the elbows close to the body with the palms open and away from the side of the body, with the chest remaining high. In this position, most students can feel the natural low breath.

5. On occasion, when nothing else works, I ask the student to lie on the floor and breathe as if going to sleep. They usually can do it correctly in this position, but often must work with this concept a great deal before they can do it while standing up.

6. It is particularly difficult to work with ballet students because they are taught to contract the mid-section of their bodies. Those athletes who are so used to high clavicular breathing may also have problems grasping this concept.

7. An exercise which works for me is having the student pretend one is filling a balloon with air. With the student placing his or her open hands on the lower ribs, give the instruction to take a breath and then over a long exhale, to make a strong "hiss" sound, then stop, and "hiss" again, then stop, until finally he or she slowly hisses out all the air. The singer feels the "kickback" and learns how to control the "hiss" stream of air.

8. In addition, I teach the low abdominal tuck prior to high notes, without disturbing the diaphragm action. I ask the student to cough or blow his or her nose while feeling the lower abdomen. In this way he or she can feel the action of support. I refer to it as putting the car in overdrive prior to passing another car. I stress that everything must be flexible with no rigidity.

9. When going back to the warm-up exercises, ask the student to put his or her hands on the lower ribs until obtaining a natural feeling for the breath support action. Some will grasp this immediately, and others take several months of reinforcement and working with the concepts before it is a natural process.

RESONANCE

After beginning with humming and singing vowel sounds, it is time to talk about the feeling of an open throat with a pre-yawn sensation. I draw an open mouth picture with the uvula and its upward movement in yawning. In addition, I find it helpful to ask the student to feel space in the roof of the mouth by having him or her put the thumb at the very top of the hard palate (a tip learned from Ellen Faull in a master class). Some students may experience the sensation if I suggest they think about having peanut butter stuck in the roof of the mouth. I constantly talk a great deal about inner space for richer sound quality.

When using Warm-Up Exercise 9 (see Appendix II), I draw mouth shapes for the five vowels listed there. I draw a tiny circle for the "oo" vowel, a long and narrow vertical oval for the "oh" vowel, a wider oval for the "ah" vowel, a sideways egg for the "ee" vowel, and a square for the "ay" vowel. I ask students to think of these mouth shapes as we go back to the beginning exercises. Since each student opens the mouth in a different way, it is important to explain that these are not rigid shapes, but merely models to help achieve purity of the vowel sounds.

After working with these ideas, by the second or third lesson, already there is a tremendous difference in the tone quality of the student who comes with a harsh or breathy sound, or even a tiny little sound. Students admit by the end of the second lesson that there is already too much to think about to be working in song literature at the same time.

If the student has grasped the breathing, space and resonance concepts by the second or third lesson, I will add the first solfeggio syllable sheet (see Appendix III) while gradually completing the remaining warm-up sheet exercises.

By this time, the students will have experienced the following concepts and vocal imagery:

• Standing with an imaginary chain attached to the sternum and hooked to the ceiling, tilting the head slightly forward like the hood of a cobra snake.

• Feeling the sensation of a hollowed out pumpkin head or the space of a cathedral dome inside their head.

• Feeling an "inner smile," or actually biting a huge apple, or feeling the sensation of trying to spread the back upper teeth.

• Imagining that all of the sound resonates in the area of the upper teeth and mouth, or imagining the feeling of throwing away the lower jaw, or imagining that the face is made of wax and someone holds a candle under it for the wax to melt to relieve facial tension. (Don't go too far with the heat metaphor here!) Some students relate to the concept of a wide open expanded throat feeling.

If the student's sound is too dark or too bright, I might draw a mushroom and demonstrate that if we only sing with the vertical stem space, the sound will be dark and hooty. If we sing with only the horizontal cap space, the sound will be too bright and spread. I tell my students that we are continually searching for the correct balance of spaces.

I often ask the students to actually physically recreate a "dive" as one approaches higher notes, particularly for the octave jump in Warm-Up Exercise 8 (see Appendix II) on the warm-up sheet. Start with a light bounce in the entire body, as if on a diving board, bending over at the waist with arms outstretched to the floor and the head vertically pointed down "in the water." The head and hands should go "into the water" just as the student sings the highest note. While singing the exercise, the student continues with the body in this position, keeping the head totally vertical "in the water" until the exercise is finished. Arpeggios are also good to use in this manner. I will not accept "belly flops," meaning that the head is not vertically fully extended. Those who have not experienced head sound will find this to be most enlightening since there is no tension whatsoever, and the resonance is easily felt. Then I will have the student stand up in a straight position and try to reproduce the same feeling in singing the same sound.

Often I talk to students about imagining throwing the sound up and over, like a horse jumps over the hurdles, or an Olympian pole vaulter gets over a bar, or a player shoots a basketball into the basket. I try anything that works in the student's imagination to understand the feeling of vocal lift without a push to the sound. As teachers, we need a number of ways to communicate the same concept. With some students, we practice the fire engine's siren sound, starting at a high pitch in head resonance and taking the sound as low as possible.

I speak about energy in the sound much of the time, whether or not it is fortissimo or pianissimo. I also stress the difference between *making* the sound and *letting* the sound happen, regardless of dynamic level. I often even write "LET" on the student's solfeggio syllable sheets or warm-ups. We always strive for a natural, supported sound. To reduce body tension, I sometimes ask the student to move around or make arm movements while singing.

To emphasize sound focus, I compare the point end of a pencil with the eraser end and ask the students to try to project with the pencil point focus. I sometimes illustrate projection and focus with imagining the dropping of a rock into a lake (thud), which causes no movement of the water surrounding it. Conversely, when you throw a pebble into the water, circular ripples surround the place of entry, and go on and on like the sound projection of the voice.

To illustrate a buoyant, dance-like sound, I compare the goblets on the dining room table, which are weighted down, to the ornaments on the Christmas tree. When one walks into the dining room, there is no movement of the goblets, but the ornaments dangle and vibrate when one walks near the tree. (I use dangling hands to illustrate the lightness; students need tangible visual imagery.)

I do not talk about register changes unless the student has a problem. Most female students have learned to bring the top voice down naturally as a result of the beginning weeks of exercises. These approaches, including the siren and the warm-up exercises (see Appendix II), usually fix the problem in a student with a severe break. Teaching the "lift" usually has taken care of everything else.

When the students encounter higher pitches, I teach them that the high note is usually not the problem – it is the approach and the preparation which need to be corrected. I start the "inner space" concept much lower when starting ascending vocal lines to help with tonal balance problems. As a result, most of my students develop the natural concept and very rarely have issues with high notes even as the range increases. This is not as easy with male students as they deal with passaggio problems until the voice settles in later years.

I do not teach boys with unchanged or changing voices, and since this is a specialized topic, I refer you to those experienced with it. In the young changed voice, the male students need special care in learning how to negotiate the passaggio area. This requires much patience, because one week it may work and the next week it will not work. Then one day, months or even a year or two later, it all fits together and they know they've "got it."

Occasionally I use colors to illustrate the quality of the sound. For instance, deep blue could represent dark sound, and lemon yellow could represent bright sound. Further color imagery of this type is certainly possible. Some students respond well to this sort of visualization.

Above all, we strive to keep intact the integrity and uniqueness of the sound of each student. No two voices sound alike, even though they sing with the same basic principles. During my teen years I sang with a manufactured voice like a mature woman. It was a detriment for years. If only I had understood then about finding my own natural voice.

DICTION

From the first words that are sung in my studio, I stop for every final consonant that is not articulated. Sometimes this can happen several times in one sentence, but I stop until the student automatically does it without thinking. This can take anywhere from a month to two years for some students. Once the singer has learned good diction, I never have to stop for this again. With some students it really takes the patience of Job, but I never give up.

Most students have never learned the rules for pronouncing "the." Though they may unconsciously do it correctly most of the time in everyday speech, in the elongated words of singing they may become confused. I illustrate by asking them to name various fruits, putting "the" before each: "thee" apple, "the" banana, "the" grapefruit, "thee" orange. This helps them understand the correct sound in common usage: "the" before a consonant and "thee" before a vowel.

By the time songs are introduced into lessons, the vowel sounds are usually quite good and consonants gradually match them so that the text is usually intelligible. Some particularly troubling words are "hosts," which comes out as "hose" or something like it, and "acts," which comes out as "ax." These need a great deal of attention.

I sometimes use vowel modification for upper register notes and for notes a singer must hold for a period of time. What works for one student does not work for another; therefore, it is a constant trial and error process. Also, what works this year may not work next year for the same singer. I find that, in general, flexibility is the key in establishing techniques.

I constantly talk about recognizing note patterns, tonal groupings and phrases when singing. We sometimes read the text to identify the logical breaks when speaking. I also talk about using the final consonants and the diving board approach when springing over problematic pitches and jumps.

Those students who have learned these simple concepts of basic technique find that their warm-up time has shortened considerably since they begin with relatively trouble-free freedom of singing. In other words, I try to teach my students to teach themselves.

Students need to learn that diction differs according to the style of song that is being sung. One does not sing a folk song or a show tune as one would sing an art song. The folk song demands a much more laid back kind of diction and the show tune needs less emphasis on consonants, particularly in the middle of words, whereas the art song needs very clear diction.

ARTISTRY

For linear smoothness, I often ask students to sing only the vowels of the words of the text. Then they sing it again and add the consonants without cutting the vowel line. This they find very difficult to do. I may invite them to pretend that they are pulling taffy out of their mouth to get the sensation of a long, drawn out line. I also sometimes speak of the conveyer belt traveling over big rollers. The belt (the vocal line) is very smooth, yet it has touched each roller (the notes). There are no bumps along the way where the belt has touched the rollers.

For ending sustained high notes, I draw an illustration (below) and ask the student to visualize two stairsteps from the side. I show that the sound (the top step) quits before the support (the bottom step). I compare this to a golfer who follows through with the swing of the club after striking the ball.

| SOUND |
| SUPPORT |

If a phrase ends with the same note that begins the next phrase leading to a higher note, these identical notes cannot be sung in the same way. A phrase should begin with the same inner space that is needed for the highest note within that phrase. For instance, in the song "Into the Night" by Edwards, there is a phrase, "As from the east he comes thro' the dark and the dew," which ends on C. The next phrase begins on the same C and moves immediately to the higher four note pattern of E's with the words, "The flowers lift their heads, the night is gone." If this second C is not sung with a lift, the next notes will invariably be sung flat. Another concern is the singing of a continuous line on the same pitch. If care is not taken to think about lifting each note higher, the entire phrase will sink lower.

Styles of singing for different languages and various periods of music need to be discussed. When singing a Baroque song such as Purcell's "I Attempt from Love's Sickness to Fly," there is no rubato and the beat is very steady and straight-forward, moving ahead with relatively little dynamic change. In Tchaikovsky's "None But the Lonely Heart," one must sing with a great deal of rubato and employ a number of crescendos and decrescendos.

Some students can immediately create the essence of the song into a very expressive experience. Most young singers need to learn to express their understanding of the text in a sincere, professional manner, and this takes much work to develop. Again, if the student feels a freedom of technique while singing, this is easier to achieve as the student learns to perform in an artistic manner.

A performing idea I learned from voice teacher Caroline Dorff, who was a student of mine for several years, has helped my student's presentations tremendously. In order to address the entire audience, if the student places three imaginary teddy bears in the right and left corner and the middle point of the back of the audience and continually sings to each of them you almost have to be expressive and it eases the nerves tremendously. Of course, like all things, this must be practiced because the student needs to change positions by appropriately reacting to the phrases and various sections of the text.

BELTING

I do teach "belting" if a student gets a role that requires it in a musical. Many singers have a "belt" sound, but sometimes it is not a healthy sound. I help them find the safe "belting" quality so that they know what they are doing without causing damage to the voice. It can be difficult to find, but most teens can make several possible sounds in this mode. Vocal projections one would use to get another person's attention outdoors can help students find this voice. For example, I might ask a student to call out "Hey, Joe!" to someone at a distance in various voice ranges. Another technique, which I learned from Mary Saunders of Pennsylvania State University, is loudly speaking the phrase "mayo mayo my" by quickly descending like an arpeggio. The trick is finding the sound that works for each individual student.

A recent student, an excellent soprano, performed the lead role of Winnifred in the musical *Once Upon a Mattress*. Her "belt" sound was so intense that it almost hurt my ears. We were able to modify it by slightly changing her focal point. To her director, it sounded the same, yet she felt completely comfortable for the duration of the show and her voice was not adversely affected.

CONCLUSION

By the time students get to the first song in lessons with me, many of these technique issues have been resolved through the use of the warm-up drills and the syllable sheets. By then they have an understanding of a solid, reliable singing process. They are ready to learn repertoire at a rapid pace. Many are able to almost teach the songs to themselves. They become very aware that a voice student works on technical issues all the time, but when they perform, they can totally forget about technique, because by now it is part of their being. As a result, they can concentrate on communicating the song.

In the January 2014 issue of *Classical Singer*, Marilyn Horne stated, "You have to get the technical stuff first. You cannot get the cart before the horse, and I am always saying if you get your technique down, you really will go so much faster."

One of the most significant things to have changed the studio in recent years is the opportunity for students to see and hear all types of singers, good and not so good, performing the same repertoire on YouTube. A seventh grade beginner of mine sang the unison octavo "The Path to the Moon" by Thiman. She located a children's chorus singing this on YouTube. What wonderful resources our students have today to reinforce what we are teaching in the studio.

CHAPTER 15

EXPRESS YOURSELF: TEACHING STYLES AND PROCEDURES

Song Teachers vs. Voice Teachers, The Delicate Balance,
Fairness and Honesty, The Incompatible Teacher/Student Agenda,
Choosing to Teach, The Independent Student,
23 (Plus) Questions About Voice Teaching,
Personal Thoughts and Observations, More on Individual Teaching Style,
50 Ways to Say "Very Good."

Dear Mrs. B.,

I have taken on several new students who recently moved here. It is evident that all of them were exposed to different styles of teaching. As a result, I find myself questioning my teaching methods. Can you discuss the various styles of teaching, and some of your teaching procedures?

Sincerely,
Nancy

Dear Nancy,

There are as many styles of teaching as there are voice teachers. We all have entirely different personalities and backgrounds, varied musical and academic training, and have been exposed to different voice teachers in our lives. Family influences, personal triumphs and disappointments, role models we have had in music or other endeavors, motivational factors for being a voice teacher, and numerous other life experiences help define our approach to helping those who wish to improve their singing skills. I will tell you about some teaching procedures, both positive and negative, with which I have had direct experience through my own observation, or through the experiences reported to me by many of my former students. My own style of teaching, as you will be able to tell, is constantly evolving as each new student walks in the door.

Sincerely,
Mrs. B.

As voice teachers, we are all unique. We should come to the profession with musical experience and education that give each of us a thorough knowledge of basic music skills, including piano proficiency. (If one is not proficient, continuing piano lessons are in order.) We should have some background in Italian, French, German, Spanish, Latin, and English languages, at least by having sung in each of them. Of course, facility in other languages will add to a teacher's knowledge base, as well. One can continue the study of languages as you are teaching, as I did with French and Italian.

One should have a broad knowledge of repertoire other than what he or she personally sang in high school and college. Beyond that, a 1975 American Academy of Teachers of Singing statement on "Qualifications for Teachers" reads, "The legitimate teacher of singing is not just a musician, but one who throughly understands the functioning of the vocal instrument in singing and in speech, and knows how to develop the potential inherent in each voice. Otherwise he or she is not a bonafide teacher of singing—regardless of musical ability." Very few of us start out teaching fully confident, but along the way, with the help of other teachers as mentors, private study, or by attending graduate schools, workshops, seminars, National Association of Teachers of Singing chapter meetings and conventions, we keep adding to our knowledge and confidence.

SONG TEACHERS VS. VOICE TEACHERS

One method of looking at teaching style is to consider if one's focus is on product or on both process and product. The first group of teachers I call SONG teachers, and the other I call VOICE teachers. The SONG teacher has the student learn to sing songs with a melody recording made by the teacher, or often by singing along with the student. This teacher may do a few warm-ups, but adds nothing further technically. Over a period of time, the student has learned few vocal technique skills or music fundamentals. The SONG teacher is often someone who sings, but does not have the proper credentials or motivation to be a quality voice teacher.

I know a person who was the rehearsal accompanist for an opera company for several years. A studio teacher who advertised regularly sang in this group. The accompanist reported that this voice teacher absolutely could not learn the intricate rhythms, could not come in correctly on some of the entrances after constant drilling with the director, and had a terrible time with the Italian language. Yet this teacher had a studio full of voice students.

Several years ago, I had a high school sophomore student transfer to me who had a very difficult time until I learned that, in two years of lessons, her former teacher sang along on everything she sang, including warmups, except when working on a recital piece in the weeks before it was to be performed. She reported the obvious, "My teacher liked to sing!"

On the other hand, the VOICE teacher teaches vocal refinement, technique, and all the skills necessary to make students better musicians, with the ultimate goal of having individuals who are capable of teaching themselves. When Isaac Stern gave a recital in our area, he said in a radio interview, "To those students who are in search of a teacher—find a teacher who will teach you to teach yourself."

I had a student who told me, "I don't play piano very well, but I've learned more about piano from voice lessons than I ever learned in piano lessons." I also had a young baritone claim, after two months of voice lessons, that he learned more about music in this time than in four years of clarinet lessons. He had never understood time and key signatures, subdivision of rhythmic patterns (such as dotted notes), or musical phrasing. Obviously, such students had never been taught to be independent learners.

Your experience differs from every other teacher, and whether we realize it or not, each new student we teach adds to the wealth of background we all carry with us constantly. My teaching improves each year as a result of what I have experienced musically, professionally, and personally. My husband comments that, years ago, I approached the molding of each student's vocal accomplishments as a beginning ice sculptor would approach a block of ice with an "ice pick," but that now, at my age and with years of experience, I am able to use a "chain saw" approach to "Boytimize" each singer. He doesn't mean I force a result, but with a motivated singer and my background, we are able to accomplish more in less time than it would have taken years ago.

THE DELICATE BALANCE

Your personality is the key factor as you market your skills as a successful teacher, particularly to children, teenagers, and community adults. I suggest that you:

- Be yourself—stay relaxed and pleasant
- Be enthusiastic—about music and your students
- Be encouraging, but not gushy
- Be patient, yet constantly challenging
- Be empathetic and understanding
- Demand and expect excellence—not mediocrity!

In the column *Sotto Voce*, "To Admire or to Teach," in the *National Association of Teachers of Singing Journal*, March/April 1986, Richard Miller wrote, "By the nature of the teaching function, the teacher is placed in the role of critic, whatever the level of student. One of the delicate duties is to find the right balance between diagnosing what is in need of correction, and letting the singer know what is admirable."

Miller stressed that one must not make the student feel good all the time, but must analyze, correct, and show him or her how to improve. He stated, "When a plumber is called in, he is not expected to admire the bathroom fixtures, but to repair them."

He indicated that we need to teach in a way that makes real praise and admiration possible, and he cautioned that "the student is not paying for friendship." Miller believes that the teachers who really teach, instead of "flattering," are more successful in the profession.

FAIRNESS AND HONESTY

My style of teaching, particularly for teenagers, requires complete concentration from students. At the same time, I try very hard to be absolutely fair and honest regarding basic problems that exist. The singers know if they have a tendency to sing flat, if their voice is very tiny at present, if their reading skills are quite poor, or if they remain expressionless when they sing, etc. Even though I initially set the stage for a serious approach to all lessons, there are several students I find I have to lecture week after week until they give me the kind of work that I expect from them. In the case of those students to whom I have to "raise my voice," I make sure they understand that I care for them as people, but I am very upset with their inadequate preparation or sloppy musicianship. (So that the reader doesn't think otherwise, let me say that my lessons also include moments of mutual laughter, psychological "high fives," and celebration of significant technical breakthroughs!)

I believe we should be totally honest with our students. Early in my career, I knew an instructor whose style was to praise everything the students did, usually with additional words about how wonderful they were. Even though she taught some highly motivated students with great potential, they could never quite understand why, if they were so good, they never made district chorus, got important parts in a musical, or received incidental choral solos. The students liked her, and she was a delightful person and a good singer, but were the students getting the vocal training they required for success?

THE INCOMPATIBLE TEACHER/STUDENT AGENDA

As one increases the standards in a studio, the teacher can expect this to lead to the loss of some students, as several examples will show.

I once had an eighth grade student who was not with me for a very long time. She did not want to work on vocal technique exercises, and she fought me all of the way on fundamentals of reading music. Finally one day, she said, "I know I have a bad attitude. You see, I am used to manipulating all of the teachers I have had in school, and *I can't seem to manipulate you.* You *make* me work like I never have before, and I want you to know I appreciate it." While this may have been one of the greatest compliments I have ever received, she was not willing to change her ways. She quit shortly after sharing these thoughts.

Several years ago, I taught a really good tenor who was a tenth grader. I was very pleased with his work ethic, and he seemed happy with lessons. It was exciting to assume that I would have him for two more years. After his first recital of the year in February, he quit lessons. He told me that when he started, his primary aim was only to sing in one recital, and then pursue something else, such as dance. He landed leads in the next two yearly school musicals, and went on to college in musical theater.

Another student I had was a trombone player who could read so well that in a few weeks, he was already singing songs. About ten weeks into lessons, he quit. The parents were really upset, but his reason was that he had "already learned all he needed to know" about singing.

Students may bring demands that test your values as an instructor. This happened in my studio some years ago when three high school juniors (two males and one female) wanted to talk to me as a group at a time other than lesson time. These were three very sharp students. They wanted to persuade me to limit their studies exclusively to Broadway solos for the next year and a half. Since I have a definite plan for teaching each teenage student prior to college, I was not going to bend to their wishes. I explained that when they walk into my house for voice lessons, they are really entering my store. I have certain products that I sell in my store. If they did not like the variety of goods that I offer, they were free to go to somebody else's store where they could get the products they desire. The female student quit, and the two male students stayed through graduation. Both were successful with choral singing in college. In my opinion, if I had succumbed to their wishes, it would have been the beginning of "anything goes" with my teen students and the start of many compromises in my personal philosophy of teaching.

It is different if your philosophy embraces the idea of total freedom of literature and lesson structure at this age level. Such an approach might possibly work for some teachers, but even then, the teacher must make some choices about what to encourage. Whatever the studio approach is, I believe each teacher must be able to articulate a philosophy of teaching carefully, and plan his or her style accordingly. Otherwise, be prepared to have your services defined by students and stage-door parents with limited vision.

CHOOSING TO TEACH

To be really effective, you must actively *choose to teach*. Your attitudes and personality will be reflected in your style of teaching as well as your accomplishments. When teaching voice, we are working with human instruments whose owners have a wide range of emotions and feelings. This may be why, on some occasions, people have the need to express feelings because they are too upset to sing. Most of the time, they need someone they can trust to listen, even if the issue is unrelated to the vocal lesson. We are not trained therapists, but on such occasions, we can try to be effective listeners as we guide them back to the task at hand.

In the October 1984 issue of the *Music Educators Journal,* Helen Hoff wrote, "Good teachers see themselves as good people. Their views of self are, for the most part, positive and touched with optimism and healthy self-acceptance. When teachers have essentially favorable attitudes toward themselves, they are in a much better position to aid their students in building positive and realistic self-concepts."

My half-hour lesson, once the student has graduated to song literature, consists of five minutes of warm-ups with constant technical help, ten minutes of work from formal exercise books, and fifteen minutes on literature, starting with the memorized songs, then the songs that are carded (in process of memorization), and finally the newest pieces. The student always has more exercises and songs assigned (generally two or three art songs and folk songs, a show tune, and possibly a sacred piece) than what we can cover in a given lesson. (For this reason, many of my students love occasional make-up lessons that are one hour in length!)

I find that today's serious students respond favorably to a demanding and disciplined lesson structure, although they may not admit this until they have some distance from my teaching. To get the most out of a session, many students start a lesson with all their music open to the appropriate pages and in the order we follow. Most will have warmed up walking or riding to the lesson. All learn that even if there are only one or two minutes left in a lesson, we can set tempos of new songs, check the areas in a song from the previous week which presented problems, or I can hear a portion of a song about to be carded.

There is no wasted time in a lesson, since I do not play introductions, interludes, or endings until the student is at the memorized stage of the given repertoire. If a student is preparing to perform in public, of course, more time is devoted to those selections over the next several weeks.

THE INDEPENDENT STUDENT

It is sad to say, but one cannot expect new students to always know basic fundamentals of reading. For instance, I taught a beginning student with four years of piano who could not correctly identify whole, half, quarter, and eighth notes, or comparable rests. But once the students learn to read during the first several months of lessons, it is usually the case that the intervals and rhythms of songs assigned are learned independently by the student prior to the lesson. I sing only to demonstrate vocal qualities, phrasing, a nuance here and there, or an expressive feeling. I do not play melodic lines for students at any time unless they are written in the accompaniment.

Singers in my studio are so used to the fact that I am a competent pianist that they are bothered at first as they encounter new teachers when they move from the area, or start with college instructors who have limited piano skills. I have heard that some teachers almost ignore the student while trying to play along at the piano. We all recognize that the ability to teach voice and the ability to play piano do not always come in the same person. Today's technology can help these teachers to be more effective by the use of companion recordings. The quality of most of the commercially-produced accompaniments has improved greatly over the past several years. For teachers with or without great piano skills, these also provide the opportunity to watch the student as he or she perfects the song using the companion recording. The students in my studio hear the accompaniment on their lesson recordings as we work each week. For students not afforded this benefit, the recordings can be used as a great teaching aid, provided they understand that tempos, nuances, dynamics, and interpretive feeling will change greatly when they rehearse with a live accompanist for performance. The teacher must carefully guide the use of all recordings in the studio.

23 (PLUS) QUESTIONS ABOUT VOICE TEACHING

In exploring various styles of teaching, I would like to pose a series of twenty-three (plus) questions for you to ponder. These have been generated by personal experience, observations and past mistakes, as well as relayed student experiences. According to your responses, some answers will add to studio effectiveness, while others might suggest counterproductive outcomes that need to be examined. (You may want to pause after each question and write down your thoughts.) Be completely candid in your answers. This is a private tool for your own evaluation of your teaching. Later, you may want to discuss your responses with others interested in some of the topics.

1. Do you teach a new vocal concept each week to all the students in your studio? What are some examples? What are the advantages and disadvantages?

2. Do you apply this weekly concept to the songs the student is presently studying? How does this add to your effectiveness?

3. Do you assign repertoire that is really too advanced for some of your high school students? If so, when you realize this, what do you do? Can you give an example or two?

4. Do you assign arias that you could not correctly sing if they were in your range? If so, how do you lead a student to a polished performance?

5. Do you assign songs with texts that make teenagers cringe, or that, in today's world, would be considered politically incorrect? Can you give an example? What do you do when you discover this problem?

6. Do you thoroughly prepare your students to speak the correct pronunciation of the title of a selection sung in another language, and the name of the composer, so they can do so if required at a performance?

7. For a recital, do you have your students practice delivering a short prepared synopsis of the foreign text in English?

8. Do you keep the lesson moving forward without any lag time? For you, what is lag time? What have you learned to do to avoid wasted time?

9. What percentage of the lesson do you use in talking while the student is waiting to sing? If you could modify this, would you increase or decrease time in talking? Why? How?

10. How often do you talk about things from your past career in lessons? In your opinion, how does this help the student?

11. Do you enjoy singing your favorite songs and arias for your students? Again, how does this help the student?

12. Do you play recordings of your singing during a student's paid lesson time? Once again, how does this help the student?

13. How do you react to a student who is late? How do you break the habit if a student regularly shows up five to ten minutes late? Do you make up this time? Why or why not?

14. What do you do when you are late starting a lesson? Do you make up this time or not?

15. How do you check whether or not what you are communicating to the student is understood? When he or she honestly doesn't get the point you are making, or doesn't know how to fix the problem, do you use alternative examples or explanations, or simplify the vocabulary you are using? Can you give several examples?

16. Have you ever had a student sing in a high range for such a concentrated time that the voice becomes very tired? When you realize this is happening, what do you do to save the voice? How do you determine when to abandon a piece as being in the wrong tessitura for the student?

17. When a student is very hoarse, how do you determine if a scheduled lesson should be postponed? What advice do you offer the student if that decision is reached? If you don't delay the lesson, how can you use a non-singing period productively with the student?

18. How would you describe your relationship with your students? Do you tend to "mother" some students? Do you single out certain ones to take to concerts and shows, while denying this to others who would also benefit from the experience?

19. What do you think is appropriate interaction with students outside of the studio, especially children and teenage students?

20. What is your reaction when a student expresses interest in changing to another teacher? Do you become possessive, get angry, make threats, or do what you can to be supportive during the transition?

21. When you believe it is appropriate, do you recommend that a student change to another teacher whose style may be more beneficial for this individual? How do you assist in the process?

22. Do you make physical contact with a student when you are working with breathing and posture? Is this only a one-time situation when first teaching breathing? Is this something you do constantly? Do you first ask permission from the student? What are some alternative ways you could accomplish the same end result without touching?

23. Do you still maintain a professional and ethical approach when using e-mail, texting, Facebook, Twitter and other electronic communications?

PERSONAL THOUGHTS AND OBSERVATIONS

My goal in interaction with all students is to treat everyone with equal respect, regardless of talent. I make a great effort not to have favorites, even though there is a wide variety of talent and personalities among students. One of my former students observed me teaching while she was a music major in college. She was surprised to find that, even though she always thought she was "special" in my studio, she observed that I treat every student as if he or she were "special." For me it is only after students graduate or leave the studio that those who keep in touch over a period of years may become very close friends.

Several talented students who were used to working hard in high school found that, as college freshmen, they were expected to do very little in comparison. Others, however, were being continually challenged and were very happy with their college experience. One recent high school graduate made such a smooth transition that I got a beautiful letter from her new college teacher thanking me for her preparation. How wonderful that was to read! The student was not a music major, but had performed more as a semi-professional soloist than many of the music majors during her college career.

No matter how one tries to use good judgment with young singers, there will always be surprises in the studio. Once I had an excellent young junior high school student whose brother, in high school, was dying of cancer. I was extremely careful to be especially empathetic with her during this difficult time. Several months after he died, I decided it was time to bring her back to the disciplined work I generally expect from my students. Apparently, I may have misjudged, and it was too much too soon for her. Several weeks later she came to her lesson and said, "This is my last lesson. I've decided to go to an easier teacher." I was very nice to her (although very shocked and disappointed) and wished her well, saying there was always a place for her if she ever decided to come back. She spent the next two years trying several other teachers. Late in her junior year, she called me very timidly, and asked to come back for lessons. She indicated that she realized that she really needed the discipline that I demand in my teaching, and she was now willing to work. She went on to complete two degrees in vocal performance at a major east coast university.

A few years ago I lost a good student because of my honesty. A young singer with a high, sweet soprano voice had several show leads. She had developed a safe belting style for her character roles. She struggled very much with fundamentals of reading and basic musicianship, and she was not thrilled with art song repertoire. When she told me she planned to major in music in college, I was worried about her. I carefully explained why this may not be a wise choice in her case. I recommended that she select another major, but keep music and voice foremost as an avocation. She and her parents were very upset with my comments, and she immediately switched teachers. She spent two years in college as a music major before she switched to a major totally unrelated to music. I wish I had been more persuasive in my initial advice to her.

We can't always succeed in urging the changes we perceive are necessary for a student's progress. I taught a young music school graduate who had already established a studio of about twenty-five students. She really came for teaching advice as well as personal voice work. Her practical knowledge of teaching repertoire was very poor. I could tell that she was not too eager to make changes in her thinking. I discovered that she just had her students bring anything they wanted to sing to the lesson, and she claimed she had several folksong books she would let the students borrow. My influence was short-lived since she married shortly thereafter and moved away.

Contrary to the past student, I had a wonderful experience with a singer who had graduated in voice from an excellent institution. She was out of school for part of a year and already had more than twenty voice students. She was heading for a graduate degree in vocal pedagogy the next fall. She wanted a complete crash course in all the vocal flexibility and exercise books I use with students, since she had never experienced this in her previous voice work, and thought such a concentration would enhance her own capabilities. She also wanted help in choosing repertoire for various types of students. She was a marvelous singer and musician, and with such motivation, she wanted to become the best voice teacher she could be for her students.

Before concluding my remarks, I'd like to comment on several issues that you need to consider as you develop your style of teaching. The first has to do with performance anxiety. Some teachers may be unaware how they instill the fear of performing into their students by dwelling on the onset of nervousness while singing for an audience. I have learned never to mention the word "nervous," but instead emphasize being so adequately prepared that any kind of interruptions and minor slips will not affect the performance. I stress that nobody knows their selections as well as they do, and that it is their job to make the audience like the songs as much as they do. Even though I know some of them are quite nervous for the first several recitals, the students rarely have a problem.

One recital presented a challenge. A sophomore in high school, who loved lessons, liked me, and had already performed well in three previous recitals, apparently was very upset and crying outside of the recital room because she was afraid she would let me down with her performance. She did not want to come in. When the mother approached me as I was waiting for this final student, it was one minute before starting time. Given that she was more than ready at her last lesson before the recital, the mother asked, "What shall we do?" I told the mother to inform her daughter to get herself into the first row *immediately* or she would *never* sing another note for me anytime or anywhere. She came in, composed herself, and sang beautifully when it was her turn. The mother said afterwards, "You certainly had the right words to say at the right time. Thank you!" It may seem a tough tactic, but seemed to be the right solution for this particular student.

A second issue has to do with being called upon to support a former student who seems to "get lost" in college. I am not a teacher who believes I am the only one who can help my students. There are *many* excellent teachers in our profession. I want students to grow and move on to other valuable vocal and musical experiences. Sometimes, though, a student seems to have some bad luck with subsequent vocal study. My heart always goes out to those who have an experience similar to a former soprano student who went to college as a music education major. Due to sabbatical leaves and staff replacements, she had three different teachers in two years. They all had different teaching styles. She liked the third one the best; however, it was frustrating for her because this teacher seemed to like everything she did, and failed to critique her shortcomings. She told me that she knew there were areas that didn't feel good vocally, but the teacher always said, "That's fine." She transferred to a college in our area where I had been an adjunct teacher for several years. There she received special permission to finish her last two years of voice training with me. While I was happy to help her get back on track, it was a shame that she did not progress through another positive voice studio experience.

Your teacher intuition should let you know when it is prudent to "back off." Invariably there will be a day when a student will end up crying due to personal frustration, emotional overload, or my pushing a bit too hard. After the tears are wiped away and the student realizes I was not trying to make her (or sometimes him) cry, I relate how, even at age 37, I cried after some voice lessons in graduate school when I was not able to accomplish what my teacher wanted. I refer to these episodes as "growing pains." There is nothing wrong with instilling the principle that making mistakes or struggling with change is part of the growth process. As teachers and nurturers of people, we need to always be tactful and supportive at such times.

MORE ON INDIVIDUAL TEACHING STYLE

In closing, let me share a very valuable class assignment I completed over forty years ago. While attending Indiana University as a special non-degree graduate student, I took a doctorate level course called "Seminar in Teaching of Singing" from Dr. Ralph Appelman. Our charge was to observe five voice professors teaching five separate lessons. We had to categorize *every* statement each teacher made from start to finish about breathing, phonation, resonance, range, dynamics, diction, and interpretation into Psychological, Acoustical-Phonetic, Psycho-Physical, Physical, and Musicality systems. After observing these master teachers of voice and analyzing the systems used, I was convinced that there is no one "correct" style of teaching voice. All were striving for the same goal—beautiful, controlled singing. However, each teacher had a different preconceived idea of what is beautiful. Achievement of the perfect vocal technique to produce beautiful singing is reached by as many roads as there are teachers. No one professor used a single system exclusively. Each teacher used the Psycho-Physical system most frequently. The Psycho-Physical System is a combination of two basic opposing pedagogical concepts—the psychological approach and the scientific approach. In recent years, through graduate study and workshop sessions, the opportunities for teachers to become more knowledgeable about scientific vocal research has expanded rapidly. Those who have studied the literature that now exists are able to teach scientific and physiological truths with the use of psychological terminology or imagery, with which a student can more easily relate.

It is very prevalent in today's youth to focus on "me." Many of these young people have everything they could possibly desire in material goods and they have an inflated amount of self-esteem built on flattery. This comes about in part, because as children, these students are exposed to getting prizes and trophies and accolades for everything they do whether such recognition is deserved or not. In many cases, accurate, honest feedback is very challenging for today's youth and they have become "praise sponges," and find it difficult to have to really work hard to achieve success.

As mediocrity is becoming more accepted in the world, I become more determined to help young people build their character on the truth. Honest feedback based on day-by-day effort builds self-esteem. Students often will not try because of making mistakes. I stress that "I do not grade you here. You need to struggle at times and make mistakes in order to learn to have self-confidence." I never allow the word "sorry," and I try to be careful to praise "effort" and "change" as much as possible. As Joe Gibbs, a former professional football coach has indicated, "with some players you have to get on them to perform – others react to a little bit of sugar." Since all of my students are different, I try to personalize my approach with each one so that each student can maximize his or her productivity on a weekly basis. If I am particularly demanding in a lesson, I purposely back off in the subsequent session. There is always the "give and take" factor in play. My husband has come up with a statement which holds great meaning to me on this subject. He says, "Self-esteem needs to be matched with SELF-STEAM."

In a February 2008 issue of *Time*, Claudia Wallace wrote that great teachers are those who imbued us with a deeper understanding or enduring passion, and are the ones who opened doors and altered the course of our lives. She claims that a good teacher is the single most important factor in boosting achievement. In addition to having a deep knowledge of one's subject, with patience, care, intelligence, competence, respect, training, and encouragement, this teacher shows an unbelievable belief in a young person's capacity to learn.

Ultimately, one's style of teaching comes down to being a guide and a leader. We guide a student from the very first meeting into our world of expertise. We may start with his or her several "good" notes until they fill an entire range. We take what the beginning student offers us like we take a rough diamond from the earth. We polish each facet of the gem over and over. But it is very important to remember that it is the student's gem placed in our care; it is not ours. We commit ourselves to help each student to become the best possible singer by guiding him or her to establish the foundation blocks of technique, musicality, and communication skills. We lead each student to strive for excellence and the highest standards in singing, and then we need to let them go.

In encouraging our students, teachers tend to use the same few words or phrases over and over again. Here is a list of 50 alternatives gleaned from various sources that you may want to consider using from time to time. These are phrases which I try to review periodically to keep my vocabulary more fresh and stimulating.

50 WAYS TO SAY "VERY GOOD"

1. You sang that very well!
2. You are really improving.
3. You are on the right track now.
4. That's coming along nicely.
5. I am really pleased today.
6. You've got that down "pat."
7. You make it seem so easy.
8. You figured that out fast.
9. I'm proud of the way you worked today!
10. I knew you could do it.
11. That's the sound I am looking for.
12. See what happens when you set a goal.
13. That's the best you have ever done for me.
14. You have certainly been practicing.
15. This kind of work makes me very happy.
16. You are getting better each lesson.
17. One more time and you will have it.
18. You have just about mastered that.
19. Your wonderful sensitive nature is showing.
20. Your musicianship showed practice today.
21. You've got your brain in gear today.
22. Can you feel that difference?
23. Finally, your practicing paid off!
24. You have accomplished a lot today.
25. That's two good lessons in a row.
26. Good for you!
27. Terrific!
28. Way to go!
29. WOW!
30. Keep on trying.
31. Fantastic!
32. Right on.
33. You remembered!
34. Super job!
35. I believe in you.
36. You've solved that problem.
37. Well look at you go.
38. That's so musical.
39. Excellent interpretation.
40. You are full of potential.
41. What an improvement.
42. You are learning fast.
43. I knew you would improve.
44. That's great, now do this.
45. Yes, more of that!
46. Give it all you've got.
47. Keep up the good work.
48. Good lesson.
49. You have nailed it today.
50. See, I'm nice when you practice.

CHAPTER 16

SHOULD I MAJOR IN MUSIC?

Tracking Level of Interest in a College Bound High School Student, Narrowing the Choices, College Visits and Auditions, Preparing for Transition to College, Mary Melody's Vocal Repertoire

Dear Mrs. B.,

Several of my students who wish to major in music are now at the age when they are asking me where they should go to school. How do I answer them? What are some things I should consider in assisting my students to make college choices?

Sincerely,
Nancy

Dear Nancy,

When one teaches teenagers, he or she is expected to help with career guidance and college choices. We certainly do not take the place of school counselors or parents; however, we should provide some meaningful input since we know the student so well. Private voice instructors should provide as much pre-college experience and preparation as possible in the time we have with the student, including any assistance we can offer in the application process.

Sincerely,
Mrs. B.

TRACKING LEVEL OF INTEREST IN A COLLEGE BOUND HIGH SCHOOL STUDENT

I always ask a new teenage student what major he or she anticipates studying if planning on going to college. Each September I ask this question again, because the answer for a given student may change from year to year. When a student still expresses a serious interest in music at the beginning of the junior year of high school, we have a preliminary talk. There are students who would never consider another major, and there are those who are weighing music against other areas of concentration for their college experience.

If I am thoroughly convinced that the student wants no other major than music, I will support him or her fully if possible. But if he or she does not have adequate ability or preparation, I will try to explain why another choice for a major would be more beneficial, and advise the use of music as a minor or as a strong extra-curricular activity and life-long avocation.

NARROWING THE CHOICES

At times, the student who is completely set on music will ask, "Mrs. B., what college should I select?" or "What is the best music school?" I explain many of the variables that are involved in the final choice. First, the student must identify whether he or she is interested in teaching, performance, musical theater, conducting, composition, musicology, arts management, music business, music therapy, or some other career. School counseling departments have information on colleges offering majors in all these areas, and this should be explored by the student. Ultimately the question the individual may ask is, "What is the best music school for me where I can be accepted, compete, grow, be challenged, and succeed?"

I will ask the student about preference regarding institutional size—small, medium, or large. Does he or she want a school in a large city, a small city, or in a rural environment? Is the person interested in a music program found in a private university setting, a conservatory, a liberal arts school, a state comprehensive institution, or a junior college? What kind of school can the family really afford? In addition, the individual needs to decide if the institution should be close to home, or hundreds of miles away, which adds to the transportation costs associated with higher education. Scholarships and grant opportunities, study-abroad options, honest appraisal of academic preparation and institutional expectations, and school "culture," including extra-curricular opportunities, need to be assessed as well.

After the student has done the preliminary research, I have the individual bring me a list of the colleges under consideration. Then we explore other possibilities if there are additional schools that fit his or her preferences, but have been missed. I encourage the potential applicant to provide the current lists of voice faculties of institutions under review, in case there is some personal connection which can provide us with more insight into a given music department or division. Most music faculty information can be easily found on the Internet.

A student should always include a "safety" school or two in case his or her expectations are too high. Some students only apply to two or three schools, while others will broaden the reach to six or more. One high school senior applied to ten schools that offered a musical theater major. He had a résumé that included numerous equity and non-equity community theater roles, as well as school productions. He had additional experience as lighting technician, stage manager, choreographer, and in dance and voice. He had appeared on stage since the age of five. He was a top academic student as well. Even with this highly unusual set of credentials, and excellent auditions at each institution, he was accepted at five schools and rejected at five schools. The school he attended accepted a maximum of three male students in musical theater that year from applicants throughout the country. An area school, one which I had anticipated would be an easy acceptance for him, took only six freshman males—he was not included. One can see that acceptance into musical theater programs can be extremely difficult. I make a point of this because so many students have the "Broadway dream," and we must help them to face reality. It is so important to carefully and honestly discuss their potential with these young people, so that they have time to rethink their future if necessary. On occasion, I have lost a student simply because of my honesty in expressing my doubts as to the student's innate musical ability and prospects for completing a degree in the field.

COLLEGE VISITS AND AUDITIONS

It is wise for the student to visit all the schools being seriously considered, in order to experience the environment and have an opportunity to interact with some of the students, faculty, and staff on campus. For example, a few years ago, I had a voice student who planned to major in French horn performance. He arranged to have a trial horn lesson with the major horn professors at eight schools before he finally made applications at all eight institutions. Because of the very limited number of freshman horn spaces, he was elated to be accepted at five, and could choose according to his teacher preference.

For vocalists, the personal audition is the most important part of the final process. Each school has its own requirements. Encourage the student to research a school's audition recommendations and bring each set of instructions to you, so that you and the student can select the best repertoire. It is much better to have the student use pieces that have been sung previously in recitals and competitions, so that they are well-seasoned and well-matched to the student's ability. For majors in music education or voice performance, audition selections should be standard art songs or solos from oratorios, with at least one song in Italian or another language, and a contrasting song in English. Some schools will accept all songs in English. Show tunes may not be acceptable. It is wise not to use operatic arias unless the student is exceptional, with a very mature voice. Some schools require as many as four contrasting selections.

College auditions can be brutal these days, particularly for musical theater. A new policy that is being used at most schools is the requirement to send a pre-screening audition video before being selected to actually audition. Some students apply to upwards of 10 to 20 schools. The top colleges audition over 1,000 candidates each year for a selection of 10 to 24 per each freshman class. At most, an audition consists of two monologues, a dance audition, and usually only 16 bars of a ballad and 16 bars of an up tempo song from a musical show. On occasion, students of mine have been requested to sing part of an art song. Sometimes the monologues and the dancing auditions are more valued than the singing.

A very informative article is *Preparing Singers for College Audition – Musical Theater and Vocal Performance* by Matthew Edwards and Jonathan Flow from *American Music Teacher*, August/September 2013, Volume 63, No. 1, Pg. 32-36. The authors relate "the arts have been drastically affected by the economic hardships of the last ten years." This writing stresses some very important information regarding audition procedures.

Since the accompanist will be playing without a rehearsal with the candidate, the applicant must be confident enough to keep singing regardless of what happens at the piano. Any special spots or instructions in the music need to be clearly marked. Often this turns out to be a very good experience, but I have had some students singing almost a cappella. The student must be very gracious throughout the audition and be receptive to the wishes of the evaluating faculty. If you know any of the teachers involved, it is a nice gesture to send your greetings via the student. I always advise my students to dress conservatively for the auditions. This means wearing a dress or skirt below the knee with no platform shoes or sandals for females, and a traditional shirt and tie and jacket for the male students.

PREPARING FOR TRANSITION TO COLLEGE

The repertoire I assign students through the years provides a smorgasbord of styles and periods of music, which prepares the student for the literature that will likely be found in the college studio. One of the assignments which I require before my students graduate is the formulation of a complete repertoire list, with songs in categories, to hand to the college voice teacher and choral director. I even require this from students who will not major in music, or even go on to college. If they have kept all their memorization cards, this is not a difficult task, especially with the help of the computer. I give the student a sample sheet with guidelines for creating categories and format. (See the repertoire sample at the end of this chapter.)

Students majoring in music at college who have studied more than two years may have learned songs in each category. A student not majoring in music with only two years of lessons will eliminate several categories or even combine several under the title, Art Songs. Those students wanting to major in Musical Theater will still have a good number of art song repertoire in English and in several languages in addition to the extensive Broadway listing.

A one-year male senior, who planned to major in Art, initially could not match pitches. He had a total of 30 easy songs in five categories – Art Songs, Folk songs, Christmas, Sacred, and Broadway show tunes. In contrast, a superior female student I taught for seven years and who was planning on music as a major, assembled a list of 145 memorized songs and four completed exercise books representing all the categories and languages listed.

Another male, now a successful first grade teacher, studied for four years and listed 120 memorized songs and four completed exercise books at graduation. I am so excited to learn that under his leadership, his young class does some singing every day of the school year.

A very motivated female pre-music major studied for two years and still prepared her list, showing 40 memorized songs representing all the listed categories.

Probably the last helpful activity you can undertake with your student prior to college entrance is to discuss the successful transition to a new teacher in an academic environment. These young people are usually only exposed to one or maybe two teachers up to this time, and they expect each college professor to teach the same way. I try to explain that everyone has a different style of teaching, but that we are all striving for the same goals for our students. As teachers, we all have our strengths and weaknesses, and it is the student's job to take the best from each of us to eventually mold his or her own technique. One of my former students spent part of his career as a young opera tenor. He once told me that when he got to college, he finally understood some of the things I was trying to teach him, and when he came back to me in the summers, he finally understood what his college teacher was trying to teach him. In other words, a different way of expressing ideas may enhance your student's ability to understand and apply instruction. Once in a while there may be a conflict with a college teacher simply because of teaching styles, personality, or inability to teach sophisticated and advanced freshmen. In these cases, I advise the student to find the best match with other studio options at the institution, and make a switch at the end of the first year, or even at the end of the first semester.

At their final lesson with me, I ask my students to keep in touch and let me know how they are enjoying their college experience. I tell them I will always answer their notes, but I will not make the first inquiry. Many students do remain in touch, while others leave the studio to be gone forever. If your experience is similar to mine, some will call, some will write, some will email, some will visit when at home on vacation, some will arrange to take lessons during semester breaks and summers, some will send recordings and programs of recitals and concerts of their performance groups, some will let you know when their touring group will present a concert in your area, some will make you proud when you hear them sing in NATS college-level auditions, some will ask for recommendations for internships and even graduate school, some will invite you to their weddings, and once married, will send you pictures of their children. Meanwhile, I move on to that new group of exciting young talents who are most eager to absorb all the knowledge I can help them learn about singing, and this is what you should do, also!

(sample copy)
VOCAL REPERTOIRE
MARY MELODY

I.   Italian
         Ciampi – Quella Barbara catena
         * Handel – Bel piacere

II.   German and Austrian
         * Haydn – The Mermaid's Song
         Schubert – Lachen und Weinen
         Wolf – Verborgenheit

III.   French and Miscellaneous
         Fauré – Ici-bas
         * Grieg – I Love Thee
         * Rachmaninoff – Lilacs

IV.   British
         Carey – A Spring Morning
         * Quilter – Love's Philosophy

V.   American
         Barber – Sure on this shining night
         * Charles – Let My Song Fill Your Heart

VI.   Sacred
         MacFarlane – Open Your Eyes
         * Malotte – The Beatitudes

VII.   Christmas
         * Hamblen – Mary's Slumber Song
         Caldwell – In the Bleak Mid-Winter

VIII.   Opera and Operetta
         Lehár – Vilia (*The Merry Widow*)
         Mozart – Un moto di gioja (*The Marriage of Figaro*)

IX.   Oratorio
         Benedict – I Mourn as a Dove (*St. Peter*)
         Mozart – Alleluia (*Exultate Jubilate*)

X.   Broadway
         Kern – Make Believe (*Show Boat*)
         * Rodgers – My Favorite Things (*The Sound of Music*)

XI.   Exercise Books
         Concone – School of Sight-singing
         Lütgen – Vocalises
         Marchesi – Vocal Method (Complete)
         Vaccai – Practical Method

* performed in public

CHAPTER 17
WILL YOU RECOMMEND ME?

Student Background, Introductory Paragraph, Voice and
Musicianship, Musical Honors and Special Accomplishments,
Related Information, Some General Guidelines

Dear Mrs. B.,

You didn't mention letters of recommendation for college in your last letter. I am never sure what to say and, as a result, I find writing these letters to be very difficult, particularly for the student who is not as talented as others. I would like some guidelines and maybe some samples from letters you have written.

Sincerely,
Nancy

Dear Nancy,

Writing the letter of recommendation is very time-consuming for me, but it is very important if it is to have any real value for college applications, scholarship awards, or special camp or competitive ensemble consideration. When I first began to write these, I had no idea how to begin, so I'll be happy to share portions of letters I have prepared for my students (of course, using fictitious names and locations).

Sincerely,
Mrs. B.

STUDENT BACKGROUND

When a student asks me to write a letter of recommendation for college or for scholarship awards, I ask the individual for an updated résumé (most students have these prepared by this time for school counselor uses) and a stamped addressed envelope for each destination. If the letter is to be sent with the student materials, I still want the name and destination for the envelope I will use.

I will not write a "universal" unsealed letter to give directly to the student to be photocopied for inclusion with all applications. I have read some of these generic letters, and they could apply to each of my students and still not reveal anything specific about a given person's strengths and limitations. Because I am convinced it carries more weight, I will only write a "blind" recommendation. This is a personal evaluation of the student, and the letter is sealed in an envelope with my signature written over the flap. For example, I did this when I wrote letters for a former student who was a college senior applying for a summer internship at either Wolf Trap or the Kennedy Center. Neither place would accept letters unless they were prepared with the signature written over the flap. My husband, a former college professor, says that this is a common expectation when completing recommendations for graduate school applicants.

INTRODUCTORY PARAGRAPH

After carefully reviewing the individual's credentials, I begin my letter with a statement about our relationship, such as, "It is certainly a pleasure to write a letter of recommendation for Mary Melody, who is finishing her senior year at Largo Senior High School. I have been her voice teacher for the past four-and-a-half years, and I can speak with confidence about her abilities." Or I may begin, "Jane has asked me to write a supporting letter to include with her application to your college. I have taught Jane as a private voice student for the past three years, and it is with great pleasure that I honor this request." Another example is, "It is indeed an honor to recommend John for your scholarship award. He is a very motivated young man who has made amazing vocal progress in my studio these last two-and-a-half years."

VOICE AND MUSICIANSHIP

In this paragraph, I discuss the type and quality of voice, the musical abilities that particularly stand out, overall vocal strengths and weaknesses (if any), and performance skills. If a student is exceptionally gifted at ornamenting Baroque music, portrays character songs with a special kind of humor, sings with a deep sense of passion, has special language skills, or possesses a special talent, I will make note of these attributes. Here is an example:

> Donna is a very bright, vivacious young lady who is gifted with a velvet quality lyric soprano voice. Her learning skills are excellent, and as a result, she has progressed from a novice singer to an accomplished vocalist in these past few years. Her sense of pitch, vocal flexibility, and sight-reading skills rank her way beyond her peers. Donna is a joy to teach, for she absorbs what I have to say very quickly. She is a fine musician and has learned the art of teaching herself new literature on her own. She has a keen ear for language and sings well in Italian, German, French, and English. She has sung repertoire from Baroque through the Contemporary styles of music. She is particularly skilled at creating ornamentation for the Baroque arias she enjoys so much. Her outstanding, innate sense of song interpretation brings everything into focus as she becomes the 'complete singer' well beyond her chronological age when performing in public.

It is obvious that this is an outstanding student and it is not often that I am able to write such a glowing evaluation. She went on to receive advanced degrees in voice, performs as a soloist, and has begun her own voice teaching studio.

In another case I wrote:

> Sam is an enthusiastic young man with a special drive in whatever he tackles. As a singer, he arrived with many vocal and pitch problems. There is still a certain roughness in his vocal quality, and we are still not quite sure whether he will be a

tenor or baritone when his voice finally matures. His work ethic, which is so strong, has enabled him to conquer most of his problems so that he made the tenor section of district chorus ranking in the teens, and moved up to sixth position for regional chorus. Two years ago I never would have thought this to be possible, but his drive to achieve is unusual for a young man of his age. The charisma and presence he portrays when doing roles in musicals makes up for many of his present weaknesses.

This young man, after auditioning several times before being accepted as a musical theater major, graduated midyear from college in musical theater, and one week later was already at work for the season in a major touring musical. He was in the original cast of *Hairspray* for four years on Broadway after years of regional and Off-Broadway roles. He has now broken into the Hollywood scene.

Here is another example:

Sue is a bright young lady who has a very sweet, clear and flute-like soprano voice. She is musically gifted with an excellent sense of pitch, rhythm, and vocal flexibility. She works hard at everything she strives to accomplish. Sue is a real joy to teach because she always comes to each lesson prepared. She has fine sightreading skills, and a great deal of innate musical feeling and sensitivity. This is not a huge voice; however, she has learned to project to the back of the auditorium, and I am convinced that it will continually grow as she matures. This voice can provide a core to a section, yet not stick out. It is the type of voice that is especially excellent for Baroque and Classical music.

This young woman was not a music major, but she attained coveted positions in the small select choral groups of her college all four years.

Another support letter starts:

Alex is a very mature individual, and whenever there is a goal to achieve, he always seems to succeed. His young bass voice is continually growing in strength and quality. Alex has had to learn to read music with me, and his skills are constantly being refined. When singing in front of an audience, he is able to project much musical sensitivity and honest emotion, which produces a very satisfying presentation. This young man loves to sing, and he is open to exploring all facets of the bass repertoire. I find him exciting to teach. In this short amount of lesson time, he has been able to learn songs in Italian, Latin, German, and French, as well as English. He seems to have a special affinity for Handel and Vaughan Williams. Alex has an excellent sense of rhythm and pitch, but he is working very hard to overcome his struggle with certain intervals. He has a very wide range with a fine balance of sound throughout.

This student was not a music major either, but received one of five $10,000-per-year music awards just to sing in the choral groups and be a soloist at his university. The attributes you write about will certainly appear through auditions or during early semesters of study. It is important that what is written is totally honest without "fluff" or "put downs," in case the contents should be revealed to the applicant.

A letter for a student who has limited ability might read:

> Anna is a very pleasant young lady who loves to sing. At the present time her range shows room to grow and her voice quality is showing constant signs of improvement. Reading music has been a constant challenge for Anna, but she is gaining more confidence with each lesson. As a result, we have not done much work with foreign languages at the present time. Anna is so cooperative and works diligently.

MUSICAL HONORS AND SPECIAL ACCOMPLISHMENTS

This paragraph of your recommendation outlines the school and school-related musical achievements, as well as community involvement. Many of the students also play musical instruments, and success in related musical activities should be included. Rankings in district and regional choruses are significant items to note if you serve in a state where such activities occur. Specific leading roles in school and community productions should be addressed. Recently I wrote:

> Trish has sung the last several years with the Midland Youth Chorale, soloing last November. In addition, she sang with an adult women's ensemble of eight this past year. As a sophomore, Trish made district chorus, placing twenty-second out of 150 Soprano I singers. Last year she placed fifteenth; in competition with other combined districts, she placed fifth for regional chorus. Last month, as a senior, she captured first place out of 150 Soprano I singers for district chorus. She performs as a soloist in area churches, and has participated in the Valley College solo competition for high school juniors and seniors from four states. She recently won third place at the NATS auditions in the senior high female category. She was one of nine vocalists from the state of Pennsylvania to be selected for the Governor's School of the Arts for the summer. At the same time, she was selected as one of thirty from a field of ninety for the Eastminster Solo Voice High School Academy this summer. She auditioned for solos in our 140-voice community Messiah production, and was given a major solo. Also, she has had the lead in her school musicals the past two years.

Another example:

> Amy's school musical activities are somewhat limited because the Baptist High School does not participate in the county, district, and regional choral festivals. She did win second place in the Valley vocal competition, and third place in the NATS auditions. She has been active with the Central Opera Association, and has been a frequent church soloist. She has won first place in many Christian school arts competitions, in both piano and voice, since seventh grade.

For another applicant I wrote:

> From a field of approximately 100 Bass II singers auditioning for district chorus, Nick, as a junior, placed third chair, then seventh for regional chorus, and second chair for state chorus. Now, as a senior, he again placed second for District Chorus. In the Valley Vocal Competition, he won the $200 second place award. For the past two years, he has been a bass soloist in the 140-voice community *Messiah* production. Nick had roles in the last three school musicals, and was featured in the Central Commonwealth Youth Theater for several shows.

RELATED INFORMATION

Another paragraph of your recommendation letter may be added attesting to involvement in church, community and volunteer activities, scouts, and part-time work. Other school honors, such as National Honor Society, school government, grade point average, rank in class, athletic participation, science fair participation, scholastic art and writing awards, recognition in other school disciplines, and special interests can be included. I also like to add statements dealing with the character and general personality of the individual applicant.

Some awards are based partly on need, in which case I may write, "Amy is one of three children who are supported completely by a mother with no other financial help. Amy has kept a part-time job in a food store as well as a restaurant on weekends for the past two years. Even with the limited time available, she always comes prepared for lessons. The need is very great in this situation." On the other hand, I may write, "Lee comes from a family where there is no real financial problem. Even though he is very worthy of this award, there may be candidates of equal ability who would have much greater need."

In closing, I may write, "This fine young man has a genuine sense of loyalty and the highest standards. I feel that Mark is very worthy of your consideration for the vocal award." Or I may close, "This young lady is one of my really all-time beautiful performers. Her personality makes her even more charming as a singer. Always a top honor student, she should have a very successful career in the field of music." Yet another closing might be, "This young woman is very goal-oriented, and I sincerely believe that, as she continues to gain confidence in herself, she will be very successful in your music department. I give her a very high recommendation."

SOME GENERAL GUIDELINES

Above all, be completely honest with what you write, yet be gracious. If a student is limited in ability, you can state things in a way that suggests types of problems, such as, "She is struggling with the mechanics of music reading," or, "She has not yet found the true core of her performance vocal sound," or, "He is trying to learn to be completely focused when practicing." Or you may simply choose to omit specific reference to problem areas in your letter, which is acceptable as long as the letter is not misleading as a result. Obviously, these students will not exhibit the honors and awards comparable to the students who have been cited previously; therefore, these letters will be shorter. Sometimes if you have too many negative feelings, it is best to have the student find someone else who perhaps "knows you better than I do" to write the letter. But if I do write, I always find some positive things to say that are completely true.

You may be asked to write letters of college recommendations for non-majors as well, as noted in several of my samples. There are a number of institutions that award grants and scholarships to recruit quality leaders for their choral organizations. These letters are just as important as those for music majors. Some schools offer work study grants to sing, providing from $500 a year to $12,000 a year or more, as I previously noted. One of my former male students received $750 a semester to sing in a small group, and a former female student was given $1,000 a year to be a soloist and alto leader in all the choral groups. I find that writing recommendations for non-music majors competing for scholarship money is becoming more frequent.

You may be asked to write letters for music camps, local scholarship awards from small choral groups, music club awards, intensive summer study programs similar to the Governor's School, select college programs for high school students, summer-abroad touring groups, or the National Honor's Chorus at Carnegie Hall, New York City.

To make it easy to keep track of these letters, I keep them on the computer in a file devoted to this activity. In addition, I always keep a hard copy of each letter I have produced. Since I never write more than one page (although I may use different spacing and font sizes), it is easy to update on a moment's notice those "I need it tomorrow" requests you get late in the year.

CHAPTER 18
HOW DID I DO?
Winning and Losing in Competitions and Auditions

A Perspective on Competitions, Auditions for Musicals, Selective Competitions and Auditions, Dealing with Judging Results, Learning to Lose Gracefully

---

Dear Mrs. B.,

Do you enter your high school students in competitions? How do you determine when a student is ready to compete? How do you handle the disappointment when a student does not win? Is a competition worthwhile or not? I would like some advice as I begin to encounter this issue with increasing frequency in my studio.

Sincerely,
Nancy

Dear Nancy,

So much of what your students do is competition-based. There are auditions for county, district, regional, and state chorus, auditions for special school choirs, auditions for roles in school and community musicals, auditions for incidental solos in choral works, and auditions for college. In addition, some states have solo competitions, and if you belong to the National Association of Teachers of Singing or the Music Teachers National Association, there are auditions at the chapter and regional levels. Recently in our area, several of the small adult chamber choirs have held yearly scholarship/performance competitions for top high school soloists. Let me share some ideas that have helped me.

Sincerely,
Mrs. B.

A PERSPECTIVE ON COMPETITIONS

There is so much discussion these days regarding the self-esteem of teenagers. Much has been written about the need for the student to always feel good about everything. Honest hard work and real discipline very often are lacking even in some students who are high achievers. The student who expects easy praise and little suggestion for improvement is one who may be affected negatively by competition.

In a sense, a student taking lessons is in a competition between how he or she performs given tasks and the present expectations of the teacher. Voice lessons are a continual progression of steps, either forward or backward. If the weekly expectations are satisfied, the student builds self-esteem, the teacher's expectations are met, and accomplishment can be celebrated. If the student fails to work and satisfy the teacher's expectations, discouragement and disappointment may set in for the week, and the teacher needs to assess how to deal with the student's loss. The teacher must constantly set the stage for the student to be able to win (achieve), yet be prepared to deal with the student who loses (falters). Thus it is the competitive experience and progression of each student with which we are dealing, and not the finality of who wins or loses in a given public performance.

Naturally, one would assume that students taking private lessons would increase their chances to make auditioned choirs in middle and high schools. Then, in competition for groups such as county chorus and honors choirs, where there are limited people accepted on a part, one might expect that, in general, qualified upperclassmen will be chosen first. Failure to gain a position in such select groups is easily understood by inexperienced, younger students.

However, when we come to the competition to be an audition candidate for district chorus, or solo contests in those states that sponsor these events, there are even tighter restrictions on the number of entries allowed in each voice category from each school. Experienced private voice students may have the edge over other students, but it is likely that some faithful upperclassmen and naturally-talented singers will be chosen. This creates problems if the voice student believes that private lessons guarantee preferential treatment in the local tryout.

In our geographical area, district chorus tryouts are extremely competitive. The schools usually send a total of around 200 Soprano I and 180 Soprano II students to compete for 25 spots in each part. There are somewhat fewer entrants in the other voice categories, especially Tenor I. The music must be learned to perfection, and even then, a slip here and there could easily eliminate a student. My job as a teacher is to prepare the students for this occurrence. For example, if a student follows five terrific singers, the chances of a successful audition are less than if a student follows five poor candidates. I tell students that in the past I have taught excellent singers who never made district chorus who have gone on to become successful voice majors in college. I inform them that I have had students make district, regional, and state chorus as sophomores, and then not get beyond preliminary tryouts in their junior year. It is necessary that each student be well-prepared for such a loss in advance so that he or she doesn't treat it as an "end of the world" experience.

When one of my teen students fails to meet the cutoff for district chorus acceptance, together we discuss what possibly went wrong. In most cases, the student is aware of missing an entrance, singing a crucial rhythm incorrectly, or having a scratchy voice due to a cold. Yet there are some cases that are not explainable. For example, one of my best mezzos qualified in her senior year within the top five positions in district chorus. During her judging for regionals, four out of the six judges ranked her very close to the top, and two of the judges ranked her last, which prevented her acceptance when the averages were calculated. This was devastating for her, but as a teacher I had to assure her that she was still a valuable singer and a worthwhile person. She is now a successful music teacher in the midwest.

AUDITIONS FOR MUSICALS

The most problematic scenario is the final audition result for a musical. Very often the best singers are not chosen for the leading roles because they are subject to typecasting. Overall looks, role-reading ability, dancing skills, personal demeanor, and even height and weight are factors that may be used in the decision. The students trying for leading roles must understand all the variables that go into the final choices. They need to realize that, for example, if they are playing a lead as a sophomore, that the shows chosen in their junior and senior year may not have leading roles that suit them. Very often the private teacher must deal with the parents in such times of disappointment. Once I had an upset mother call me because the school musical had just been announced, and it contained an obvious soprano leading role. In a frantic voice, she said, "What can we do about this? My daughter is an alto!" Should this happen to you, I suggest you encourage her to audition for the chorus and hope that maybe the next year there will be another opportunity for a lead in her range.

Currently in our area, most of the schools send home photocopies of the possible tryout songs from the show produced. This is only a melody line without chord symbols or any kind of accompaniment. Unless you know the show well, it is very difficult to expose the student to the correct chords to help with learning the song in several days. I usually suggest finding the song on YouTube. Years ago, students were able to sing something in their best range and something that showed their best effort.

There are times when you may feel that your student has not been judged fairly for certain musical roles, but you need to remember that these choices are made by the staff directing the show. It is not in the place of the private teacher to interfere, but to support the decision of the staff and help the student in question to move on. As all teachers know, "life lessons" are often a part of voice lessons.

SELECTIVE COMPETITIONS AND AUDITIONS

I feel that all students who wish should try out for all the school choral, show, and solo competitions, or community musicals and choral ensembles. There is a difference in my feeling about private competitions, for which there are always entrance fees to be paid. I participate in the National Association of Teachers of Singing student auditions, and in the past entered students in another private four-state high-school-age competition. These are more advanced competitive experiences, and I do not feel that all students should enter.

I explain auditions and competitions such as these in a letter to my juniors and seniors indicating that these opportunities are designed for those students who have enjoyed successful solo-singing experiences to date or who are planning to enter the field of music in college. I explain that I must send students that possess excellent potential at the present time. I then ask those students who are interested to check whether I feel this would be a valuable experience for them at this time in their vocal development.

I very strongly encourage those students I believe would make a good showing. To those who would be out-of-place in the situation, I gently say that I don't feel they are vocally ready for this, but I wanted them to be aware of the opportunity and, with another year of experience, it might be appropriate. Sometimes these non-competing students may benefit from attending the event, if this is a practical alternative. If your students have been taught in an honest way, the ones not ready will likely realize this, and withdraw themselves, but will appreciate the opportunity to be informed and will support the others.

Regarding competitions and auditions for college there are excellent guidelines written by Kathy Kelton and listed in the *Classical Singer*, September 2009 – Vol. 22, No. 9, Pg. 64-66. Some of her suggestions are, "Sing something simple and sing it well," "Strive for perfection when you perform," "Select repertoire appropriate for your age as well as your level of musical and technical development," "Select pieces that will be familiar to the adjudicators yet are not overly performed," and "Sing music you are absolutely confident about."

DEALING WITH JUDGING RESULTS

For those students who enter more selective competitions, I prepare them for the comments they will receive. I emphasize that this is a learning experience, and that winning is not important. In many cases, the adjudication will reinforce what I am trying to teach. In some cases, the judges may have picked out areas we have been neglecting, and offer new ideas for us to consider. In still other cases, the comments are not valid and they must be explained to the student as poor judging. As an illustration, a girl who has studied with me for four years has struggled with a non-musical ear, and has overcome it to a great extent. Occasionally she will revert to being slightly under pitch. At a recent contest, two of the judges talked about her occasional flatness, and the third judge wrote that she was consistently sharp throughout. While other observations of the third judge may have had merit, this one had to be ignored. Finally, some comments from judges are confusing to both the student and the teacher, but most of them are clearly understood and helpful. Regardless of the outcome, I try to teach my students to learn to deal with the results with dignity, even if they feel the conclusion was not fair.

College audition results can be confusing to candidates as well. One of my students received rave comments about her singing from one school, while the next week, at another institution, with the same repertoire, she received devastating comments about her vibrato. The main point I am trying to make is for you to prepare your students for all possibilities, because some of these young people view all judgments as absolutes.

In my view, self-esteem comes from accomplishment, and not from false words of praise. A student with positive self-esteem can weather the traumas of competition with adequate preparation, even if there are tears to be dried and emotions to be put back together with the teacher's support. Formal competitions are very important for those students you teach who are planning to major in music. It allows them to observe and meet similar students from other geographical areas who have the same talents and goals. You must be aware that these competitions bring increased effort, added stress, and pressure for the teacher to abide by deadlines and prepare the proper required repertoire with the applicants. Sometimes, if the teacher plans well, the pieces chosen may be selected by the student for performance in the next studio recital. I believe that, overall, competition can be very worthwhile if approached honestly and with sensitivity within the studio walls.

LEARNING TO LOSE GRACEFULLY

I'd like to describe a singer who studied with me for five years. This girl had a great personality, wonderful showmanship, and a lovely alto voice, but was endowed with a poor musical ear. She struggled to learn intervals, to read music, and to be able to hear subtle pitch differences. Later on, she was very successful as a church soloist, and always did a beautiful job in my recitals because these were hand-picked songs for her. At every competition for district chorus and in other competitions, she met with disappointment. The most difficult one for her to accept was one where four other singers from my studio competed, and all four got honorable mention or were winners. The other four felt she had sung excellently (open auditions) and should have been cited. Although I put on my "psychologist's hat," many tears were shed, and she went home very upset. At her next lesson, she was her bubbly self and explained to me that over the weekend she had finally "learned to lose." After she shared her thoughts, I asked her to write them down for me. She has allowed me to share them with you, as well as my other students who are in need of reinforcement. Here is a condensed version!

> When a person comes to the realization that the world will not fall to his feet, that he will not always win, and that 'everyone' will one day lose, he is 'finally' able to realize and understand the true insignificance of winning. Winning creates a brief moment of happiness, but that flicker of time quickly fades amongst old memories, only to be forgotten and later considered unimportant. Winning is merely 'a drop in the bucket' when compared with the significant worth of the inner strength and state of mind gained when a person copes with losing, while learning to accept, overcome, and move on with life.

> It is important to continue to stand strong, to make progress, and to continually try. The attempt should not be made in order to earn a pointless trophy that will only later collect dust, but to make an attempt and work hard for the betterment of yourself. Greatness lies in the opportunity to become a better person, and the chance to learn more about yourself, in order to find contentment and inner peace. We cannot and do not achieve this glory through winning, but through failure.

> The strength gained through losing is enduring, and provides a person with something to stand on and lean against as protection for the next battle for 'greatness.' Losing is something that has happened before to many, many acclaimed 'winners,' and it will happen again in every person's life. Failure is the inevitable reality of living and taking great chances.

> Learning 'to lose' is what will change a person's outlook on life and on competition. It is important to learn to 'smile' and accept losing with honor and pride. Each person defines his or her own greatness and can conquer life's many challenges after the acceptance and growth gained from losing.

> The inner strength and self-empowerment gained from losing will enable a person to change and achieve her or his own greatness. What a person learns from losing is not something a person can point to, or touch and easily explain. A person can feel this strength deep within, growing each day through the misfortunes of reality.

Getting her thoughts on paper allowed this teenage student to continue to grow as a musician and to receive many forms of recognition as a student (top 5% of her class), leader (senior class president), and competitor who went on to "win" an appointment to one of the nation's military academies.

One of my long-term adult mezzos has had an amazing career in regional dramatic and musical theater on stage as well as producing and directing many shows. At a mature age she penned this poem after she was not selected for a part she really wanted to play. It helps to express those feelings we all experience throughout our lives.

WINNING
By Fran Horkowitz

No matter how often I succeed,
Accepting rejection isn't easy.
It's an aspect of life that, indeed,
Makes me humble
Makes me think
About what's truly important.

No matter how accustomed
I become to success, I must remember
That someone else must lose.
When *I* win, her heart cries,
As does mine
When *she* shines.

In every competition I give my best.
That's not to say
All the rest don't do the same.
And so... sometimes I lose.
But I'll be back
To win again
Another time.

CHAPTER 19

WHEN YOUR STUDENT IS YOUR AGE OR OLDER

Short-Term Adult Customers, Long-Term Adult Students

Dear Mrs. B.,

Recently I have been getting phone calls from adults for lessons. My clientele has been mainly teenagers, but now that I am becoming better known in the community, I have had requests from adults with relatively little background, some quite elderly, and some having unusual reasons for desiring lessons. Should I take adults as students? Is your approach to teaching adult students any different from that which you use with teenagers?

Sincerely,
Nancy

Dear Nancy,

Some of my most enjoyable teaching experiences have been with community adults over the past 55 years. Few have had aspirations to be full-time professional singers. It is my opinion that any adult, regardless of age, should have the opportunity to take voice lessons if this is his or her desire. What follows is a collection of vignettes of several of my adult students, to show you the endless possibilities of singers—amateur, semi-professional, or professional—that may appear at your doorstep.

Sincerely,
Mrs. B.

One of the major advantages of teaching adult students is that many can take lessons during the day when teenagers are in school. Professional people such as lawyers, doctors, clergy, college professors, salespersons, self-employed individuals, retirees, and full-time homemakers can usually adjust schedules to arrange weekly or bi-weekly lessons. With the increase of more flex-time options in the work environment, many working adults can also schedule lessons over the lunch break (11:00 to 1:30), or even before work begins (8:00 or 8:30). (Yes, people can and do sing at this hour of the morning!)

In a *Business Week* article, "Your Inner Musician Is Just Waiting to Be Found" (May 13, 2002), Robin Schatz wrote that the Music Teachers National Association reported that 25 through 55-year-olds are the fastest-growing group of new music students, and that these music lessons provide a creative outlet for most adults. A similar article written today would suggest that the upper range of potential students is 65 or older.

For a very small percentage of private voice teachers "adult students" may mean professional opera and oratorio singers. For all the rest of us, probably 99%, adult students can mean just about anyone who has a desire to sing.

Many adults are looking for the opportunity to learn something new or looking for ways to enrich their newly found spare time after retirement. Some of these people are searching for an aspect of life that was neglected in their younger years because of cost, time, or even because they were discouraged in the grade school years because a teacher misunderstood the changing voice. Most adults I have taught have a great attitude about learning to improve the skill of singing particularly when they understand that you are never too old to learn new skills.

The older students tend to question more and want to know the "how" and "why" of many aspects of singing. They want so much to experience the capacity to grow and develop their knowledge and they need constant reassurance as they progress.

You must enjoy working with adults or you will not be a good teacher for them. I personally treat my adult students quite differently than my teenage students in what I expect from them. The lessons are created to fit the individual whereas the college student and the teenager lessons are formulated with a specific academic-based plan. I do not require memorization for adults unless they do a great deal of solo singing. I do not require singing in other languages unless they wish to pursue this type of repertoire. I tailor make my sessions to suit the basic reasons they are taking lessons. In some cases the adult may develop into an "academic voice student" by choice.

Several years ago I chatted with Tony Bennett after he performed a concert in our town. He expressed to me that he believed the bel canto tradition is the only way to learn to sing even though he has always loved the popular standards. He told me that he continues to study with his voice teacher as much as time permits.

Even though it was written some years ago, I refer you to a very informative article by Marty Heresniak in the NATS *Journal of Singing*, Sept./Oct. 2004, Vol. 61 #1, Pg. 9-25 titled "The Care and Training of Adult Bluebirds" (Teaching the Singing Impaired). There is advice on teaching the non-singer that is very helpful. This is information that will never be dated and is always useful. There is little written on this topic.

SHORT-TERM ADULT CUSTOMERS

You may have short-term adult customers as well as long-term adult students. The short-term customer has a specific goal and "gets what he or she pays for." The long-term student often does not have an immediate goal, but gets much more over the time he or she studies. I'll tell you about several short-term customers first. These people have a well-defined purpose and may be with you for as little as two weeks, or as long as one year. A teacher must be especially nimble, flexible and willing to adapt to answer these specific needs and requests. For example…

• There was the hermit poet in a nearby rural county (the only county until 2012 in Pennsylvania without a traffic light) who wanted to be able to sing to the poetry she wrote, in addition to other folk songs, at her poetry reading sessions. She had never learned to project her very weak speaking and singing voice, so we worked primarily on breathing, vocal resonance, and projection, ending each lesson with several of her folk songs.

• There was the Mennonite farmer and feed mill operator who wanted to sing in his church choir (all a cappella), but he needed clarification as to which part he should sing. With several weeks of vocal fundamentals and experimenting with his music, he felt comfortable settling in on a definite part as his contribution to the choir of his church.

• I remember the performer who sang at various Sheraton Hotels, and had been sent home for six months to get her singing voice rehabilitated. It was in very bad shape, and we carefully and slowly rebuilt her basic singing technique to the point where she could go back to lounge singing without damaging her voice again. The majority of the time was spent on careful sound production, although we did work on songs near the end of her time with me.

• I had a referral from a laryngologist to give six lessons to a patient of his who was part of an acoustical duo. He wanted to be sure she was singing correctly before dismissing her as a patient.

• A number of young pageant entrants came strictly for one or two coaching sessions on their selected talent presentations. This involved helping to solve high note problems, and to improve overall showmanship—somewhat like applying a band-aid for the moment!

• There was a barbershop quartet in which two of the members were already long-term students. This involved working with the entire quartet as they prepared to enter quartet competition. We worked on blending, ringing chords, and stylized motions. (In retrospect, I probably learned more about the barbershop style of singing than they did!)

• A member of a recording Gospel quartet needed help with vocal resonance. This was my first experience with modern shaped-note music—I always thought it applied only to the early traditional American singing schools in the original colonies!

• A PBS music station program director, who had accepted the community theater lead in *Man of La Mancha*, needed help when he discovered that time had somehow left his high notes back in his youth (when he had first sung the role). With a series of six lessons, we were able to reestablish a technique whereby he was again comfortable with singing the entire show for several nights running. Now over twenty years later he mentioned in a conversation that he still does those warm-up exercises to keep his voice in shape as he continues his broadcasting career.

• I worked with an equity musical theater actress who spent several summers at the local summer playhouse. She had taken lessons from four teachers throughout her college years, but did not own any music and could not read at all. We spent most of the summers on music reading and vocal technique.

• There was the physician who was a serious opera lover, but regretfully could not carry a tune. His sincere desire was to be able to sing "Happy Birthday" to his children. He started weekly lessons and continued for nearly six months. We started with *the one and only note* he could sing on the syllable "do," and kept working up and down the neighboring syllables in the scale, and in small interval patterns. Once he had mastered a scale, we began little songs so that by the time he had learned "Happy Birthday," he could also sing "Home on the Range," "Joy to the World," and several other familiar one-octave-or-less sing-a-long-type pieces.

• Several men and women came to prepare audition songs for upcoming musical shows. Occasionally I would have to choose a song and perform miracles in two or three lessons.

• There was a lady who merely wanted to pay me to play songs for her that she liked to sing. I soon realized that she was not interested in singing new repertoire, or really learning to sing better. The teacher in me ended this arrangement very quickly.

• I had a "hard rock band" singer come to me who was always hoarse after each evening's performance with her husband's band. After working on breathing, vocal technique, and resonance, and transferring this to my syllable sheets (because she also wanted to learn to read music), she felt she had learned enough to keep vocally healthy. Our paths crossed about a year later, and she still felt good about her vocal health.

• A Greek Orthodox church cantor needed help with tension and high-range issues in his singing. Again, the sessions were all on technique, with applications to the liturgical music he was using.

• It was very satisfying to work with the ballerina who had studied voice very briefly in college. In her time with me following her graduation, she progressed very rapidly. One result was that she had several major musical roles in nearby theater productions—roles that combined her dancing and singing—before she married and left the area.

• A retiree who sang bass in our church choir for ten years began lessons over a year ago. Immediately, I realized that here was a singer who was offering nothing to the bass section but had great potential to boost the tenors. He was thoroughly convinced as we worked through my syllable sheets and claimed that singing was so much easier as he explored his unused upper voice. He progressed so rapidly and discovered a voice he never expected to have and in this time has already sung several solos in our church. He provides a lovely quality to the tenor section.

• Another gentleman, new to our church at the time, brought his ninth grade son to me for lessons and shortly thereafter he decided to also try singing lessons. He had a good vocal sound but could not read music. After concentrating on my syllable sheets and joining the church choir he learned to read enough to definitely add to the bass section sound. We worked primarily on vocal technique and the weekly anthem. Eventually we added some solo songs. When his son was in eleventh grade, I encouraged them to do the Mother's Day Banquet entertainment in our church with solos and several duets. (The son was by now an excellent baritone soloist in high school!) The father, a retired Marine, confessed to his wife that singing these solos in public was more difficult than anything he ever had to do as a 28-year active duty Marine. He really appreciated the singing art in a way he never did before.

• A mother brought her daughter for voice lessons after moving to Carlisle for advanced ballet lessons. After several weeks it was evident that this was not advisable because of the ballet school demands. The mother asked to take her place. You can imagine my utter joy when I discovered that this mother was Richard Rodgers' granddaughter. She was gifted with a rich mezzo voice and we enjoyed a wonderful year and a half together until she moved to San Francisco for her daughter's new ballet experience.

• Then there was the phone call from the Metropolitan Opera singer Julien Robbins, whose mother lived in the area. He wanted coaching on the Mozart opera role he was to sing in Berlin in several weeks. We spent about five glorious sessions where I played and sang all the lead-ins for his rehearsals of the entire role.

LONG-TERM ADULT STUDENTS

The long-term adult student wants to learn all he or she can about singing, and usually has an open-ended time frame. Some adults who come to a private studio may be working professional singers of some accomplishment. On the other hand, very often the adult students never had the opportunity to study due to lack of finances or the demands of a young growing family. Many studied voice in high school and college, but have not seriously sung for a number of years. Some are people who have never studied, but have always had the desire to become better singers, and now find themselves in a position to make this happen. Among such adults are those who are basically interested in the developmental process, those who are pursuing the performance aspect, those who are looking for a new challenge, and those who want to maintain and improve the skills they presently have.

Upon accepting an adult student, I try to find out all about his or her musical background and the main purpose for lessons. A few students, after some fundamental technical review, can pick up where they were as far as repertoire is concerned. I find that most of the students without a specific goal want me to teach them as I would a beginning college student. Several have repertoire requests, such as sacred music only, no languages, or a concentration on Broadway, or opera roles and audition arias. One of my long-term adults worked mainly on the alto part of duets. She sang weekly with her soprano partner at her church. We built a very extensive library of octavo and book duets for them over the years. Periodically, she added some solos.

In most cases, I begin my adult students exactly as I do a beginning teenager. Since I do expect all of my long-term adult students to learn to read music, they tackle my five syllable sheets with the same results as the young people—they breeze through them, or they may struggle for a very long while. I have even had voice graduates with master's degrees in music find this experience very worthwhile when they started with me. Repertoire varies greatly from student to student, as you will see in several of the following examples.

• I once taught a minister who worked primarily on sacred solos. Throughout several years of study, he developed a number of effective "singing" sermons where he used the words of his musical selection as his core text and sang the solo as part of his sermon.

• One student was a lady who worked with the county blind association, and eventually did programs for their groups with taped accompaniments. She had such a wide vibrato that I would not let her sing in public for over a year until she had this problem under control. Later on, she sang solos in church and performed at the local music club.

• There were several women who were church soloists and sang in auditioned chamber groups who wanted to learn the songs in all three of my art song collections (*The First Book of Solos, The First Book of Solos Part II, The Second Book of Solos*). We addressed four languages and various styles of art songs in addition to sacred solos by doing every song in each volume. We also explored other literature to develop a ten to twelve minute group of songs each year to be performed for the local music club. These had a theme that ranged from a single composer, a certain language, a style of music, various pastorals, night songs, four different Ave Marias, etc. Some lesson time was used to perfect any incidental solos these students performed in their chamber groups or their church choirs.

• I once taught a seventy-year-old tenor in our church choir who had never taken a lesson. He was a saxophone player earlier in his life, and started teaching himself the flute when he retired. He was a marvelous student not only because he was retired, but because he could read music, had a high, clear tenor voice, and had all kinds of time to practice when not occupied with his hobby of miniature railroading. It was not long before he became the prominent tenor soloist in our church choir, and regular soloist in the annual *Messiah* presentations. He studied for ten years until he had a second severe heart attack at the age of eighty. The breathing process for singing during ten years of study was a great help in adding longevity to this man's life. The one drawback of lessons was the complaint of his wife that his practicing interfered with his assigned household chores.

• One of my students was a baritone in his seventies who retired in our community and joined our church choir. His vibrato was so wide that he really was a problem in the group, but he was an excellent reader, and had been a prominent soloist with the St. Louis Symphony as a young man in the 1920s. After he had the courage to start lessons with me (and it takes courage for an older adult to start lessons in anything), I would not let him sing solos in public for over a year until we got his technique and vibrato under control. He had given away most of his music twenty years earlier because he thought he was too old to sing. However, he had saved a few favorites that we supplemented with some old and new repertoire. At his first several lessons, he walked in humped over, with low energy, and acting very much like an old man. Soon thereafter he would walk into the studio straight as an arrow before opening his new leather music case, provided by his cellist daughter and her husband. For his eightieth birthday, he gave a memorized recital in four languages to a full house of his family and friends in our church chapel. This baritone encountered some physical problems and had to quit voice lessons at the age of ninety. During the time he studied with me, he spent his summers in New Hampshire. Every spring I would make a cassette of accompaniments for him as a practice aid while on his daily hikes in the White Mountains.

• I have fond memories of the tenor I just mentioned, this baritone, and an elderly bass student when they gave a complete recital at an area college. They called themselves "The Over 65 Trio." They each did several solo groups, and we worked up several sacred trios, adding two fun choreographed and costumed songs, "There Is Nothing Like a Dame" and "The Wild Necktie."

• I have had several accompanists who have studied voice with me to make themselves better performers with singers. Studying breathing, vocal phrasing, and voice technique has made them so much more aware of anticipating the nuances of singing.

• One of my students has been studying with me for over fifty years. Several years ago, I asked her if she didn't want to quit, and she declined, saying she so much enjoyed the variety of music I found for her to sing. For many years, she was the regular soloist on a local religious radio program. She is an area church soloist, sings in large community groups, and has been a regular auditioned soloist in the local community *Messiah* production. For years now, this student has assisted me by recording all my winter and spring studio recitals.

• A bankruptcy attorney has held a paid bass soloist position in a Protestant church for years. He was a student of mine during his senior year of college and three years of law school. At that time, we worked on traditional repertoire with no sacred solos, because he is Jewish. Since his lessons with me were less regular than when he accepted the church position, we worked entirely on building his library of sacred solos for the entire church year.

• Several years ago I started to teach a 35-year-old soprano who moved to our area and joined our church choir. She had a gorgeous solo voice and had taken previous lessons with three reputable teachers. However, she was basically a non-reader. She claimed that the teachers always played or taped the melodies for her. Again, it was a struggle for her to spend so much time on basic fundamentals, but she made constant improvement during her time with me. Later, she moved to another region of the country, where she became the soprano leader of a church choir. She is now a complete singer who can read and teach herself.

• A wonderful student was a young man who never had time in high school to take voice lessons because he was devoted to piano and clarinet lessons, the band, and his other school and musical activities. In college, he was a singer and music arranger for his a cappella group. On several vacation weeks during his years in college and graduate school, he would take a series of daily voice lessons, culminating in the performance of several tenor church solos. Because of his superb musicianship and understanding of the vocal instrument, he was able to accomplish in a few weeks what many students accomplish in a year or two. With graduate degrees in both orchestral and choral conducting, he is presently the resident conductor of the Pittsburgh Symphony Orchestra, and music director of the Pittsburgh Youth Symphony. He is also the director of the Northeastern Pennsylvania Philharmonic.

• For a period of years, I worked with a female minister who could barely carry a tune. She sang each hymn in a key foreign to the one being played and sung by the congregation. Being in seminary with so many male students and being unable to carry a tune, she had settled her voice somewhere in the male range. It was a real struggle as we spent many weeks on first learning to match pitches and bringing her voice up to her natural alto range. Then, we slowly began working through my five syllable sheets (and later repeated them). Later on, in addition to singing a new hymn each week, we worked on portions of the liturgy sung by the minister. She was so pleased the day she sang the liturgy by herself in church for the very first time. We were able to add a few unison sacred solos to her repertoire before she accepted a new church position in another part of the country.

• For a two-year period, one of my students was a Portuguese and Spanish professor at an area college, who had taken ten years of private voice training from various college-level teachers. As a mezzo, she was singing a number of arias, and yet she could not read the alto part of the first line of "America, the Beautiful." She literally spent three to four months on my five syllable sheets before we did any songs. She claimed that none of her teachers would work on music reading since they felt she must enroll in a sight-singing course. She learned by listening to melodies that were played for her on tape. Through our intense reading and technical work, the most gorgeous, deep mezzo voice developed. In her second year with me, she sang solos at churches and in area music programs. She left academia and moved to New York City, where she enrolled in theory and sight-singing courses, and found an excellent voice teacher. She continues to study voice, and in the intervening years, she has given several recitals, performs regularly with the Da Capo opera company of New York, and for several years has been an invited singer for a California Zarzuela Festival. I am quoting from a thank-you note she wrote at the end of our work together to show just what an impact you can have on any one individual adult.

> (Spring, 1996)
> [In] the last two years, I have learned more than I ever thought was possible. It's funny because my last teacher at [name of a university] thought that any progress I made would be in increments so small that it would hardly be noticeable, but the past couple of years proved that wrong! What originally started out as a chore, a frustration, the sight-reading has become a great asset that has opened up a new musical world for me. It's like being deaf for years and then slowly gaining hearing back—each day is a new discovery. The ear is the key to music—which is something you already know, but perhaps not with the same magnitude, since all this is second nature (or first) for you. In your goal to teach all your students to read, you are doing all of them a great service—I know from experience NOW!
>
> (A note received in 2010, fourteen years later.)
> It is so admirable that you still have a busy studio in Carlisle, cranking out the books, traveling, and enjoying life. I have to say that there were times when I just wanted to cry in my voice lessons going over those sight-singing exercises, but you gave me the gift of music. Really, I don't know how I would ever have achieved the things I have done, operas, singing at the MET, Opera Company of Philadelphia, zarzuelas, cantoring, teaching voice to beginners, etc., without you insisting I learn to sight-read and do those exercises!! I know I have said it before, but I'll say it again: THANK YOU, JOAN.

• A radiologist who was involved in barbershop singing and our church choir believed he needed some vocal help. He had some major pitch problems at first, but after some lessons, he discovered he loved singing as much as he loved his many outdoor sports. He was known to take his songs on the long ski lifts in Colorado while on vacation so that he could practice. As it turned out, we decided to try a duet for church and discovered that our voices had a really unique blend. We both enjoyed this singing combination for some twelve years before he moved in 1980. We sang in many area churches, and developed programs for various civic organizations. After several years of not singing, he decided to take lessons again in his new retirement community in the southwest. You can imagine his surprise when his new teacher pulled out my tenor books from her briefcase!

He continued singing in church choirs in Houston, Texas, and Sedona, Arizona, until he moved to Florida in 2013. At age 88, in complete retirement, he sings in both the contemporary and traditional choirs in his church and attends rehearsals two nights a week. He reports that he has restored two notes to his range and he was asked by the director to sing a solo, which he declined. (Proper technique leads to longevity in singing!)

• Currently, I have a student who is in her twenty-fifth year with me. She graduated with a music major from the same college I attended, and studied with my former voice teacher there. This soprano is a fine accompanist, a church organist, and a singer. Each year, in addition to some sacred literature, we delve into a new composer or two, a particular period of song literature, or a language concentration. She is an impeccable musician, and we sing in the same professional summer festival chamber choir of twenty-four voices. We constantly challenge each other to see who will catch the other in a musical mistake. When it happens, we enjoy a good laugh! She came to me having great difficulty with flexibility. As a result, she has gone through almost every exercise book I find worthy of the time. She has now completed for the second time (yes, we do repeat some of these books) the very technically demanding *36 Vocalises* by Bordogni (Kalmus). This is a very comprehensive volume in high and low editions for those who really enjoy very musically challenging vocal etudes that are sometimes seven pages long. Each vocalise is an aria in itself. Each year her singing gets better and better, and her flexibility problems have been almost conquered.

• In 2004, I received a phone call from a woman in Tacoma, Washington, whose husband had just been employed as a radiologist in our local hospital. Her voice teacher, through NATS, referred her to me when she relocated to our area. She has a mezzo voice very similar to mine and is enjoying singing much of the traditional repertoire I had sung in my younger days. In addition, two of her sons, both tenors, began lessons with me starting in ninth grade, and continued throughout high school. Now the third son, also a tenor and in ninth grade has joined my studio. In addition to much solo singing, this mother has joined with another fine adult soprano student to perform almost the entire Pergolesi *Stabat Mater* at our local musical arts club last year.

• A tenor I knew in college, who went on to become an esteemed high school choral director with an outstanding male chorus of over 50 guys, contacted me in the early 1970s and asked me to play for his voice lessons at Indiana University in Bloomington, during summer graduate school. Although I said nothing in my role as accompanist, at the time I was very concerned that he had only very forced high notes and struggled through the passaggio. Thirty years later he called and asked, "Would you consider taking an old geezer of 67 for some voice lessons?" Working with him has proven to be one of the most significant teaching collaborations of my career. The early months were particularly tedious. He clutched his "Linus's blanket" of vocal tension so tightly I did not know if he could ever achieve a totally free sound. With patient work for the first year or two he changed his approach to singing and developed joy in experiencing newfound vocal freedom, and his open-minded ability to change his vocal approach has transformed his retirement life into an exciting venture he never dreamed possible. His range has developed successfully to a high B-flat over the past eight years of study, after previously only being able to sing a very pushed F and G in the past. He performs regularly and has an enthusiastic appetite for exploring diverse literature in multiple languages.

I have taught many school teachers, college and law school professors, music teachers and choir directors, organists and pianists, a pharmacist, a florist, hairdressers, waitresses, salespersons (the Pepperidge Farm representative provided wonderful samples of all the new products), secretaries, nurses, career military officers or their spouses, and individuals from other professions or career specialties. My experience indicates that there is a great need to be flexible with this type of student in both attendance requirements and practice demands. There are many lessons that are supervised practice sessions. With teenagers, I have a very organized agenda to prepare them for college, whether it be in music or other disciplines. With adults, however, the agenda and pace is determined by each individual. This requires insightful help from the teacher.

In dealing with adults, you are often instilling self-confidence, making friends for the arts, and creating more healthy individuals as they pursue this personal interest. In several cases, you may find, as I have, that you are teaching the parent of a future teenager in your studio. By adding adults to your studio, you will be broadening your teaching horizons, dealing with more mature repertoire demands, and filling time slots that may help you to become the full-time voice teacher you desire to be.

There are people in our communities who need what we have to offer as voice teachers to achieve their musical hopes and dreams, whatever they may be. If only we can open ourselves to the possibilities, we can share in some inspiring individual journeys.

CHAPTER 20

I DON'T TEACH CHILDREN…
BUT SOME OF MY FRIENDS DO

Children as Solo Singers, The Voice of Experience,
Further Thoughts on Teaching Voice to Children

Dear Mrs. B.,

I was fascinated when I read about all the adults with different agendas who have come to you for voice lessons. I am going to pursue this aspect of my studio with new excitement and with more confidence that I have something to offer students who are older than I am. But now, I wonder about extending my studio to those at the other end of the age spectrum. I have heard all my life that teaching voice to children can be damaging. I know you do not teach children, but I'm curious about your thoughts concerning formal voice study for students in the elementary grades.

Sincerely,
Nancy

Dear Nancy,

You hear so many people talk about damaging the voice before age sixteen with voice lessons, but these same people say little about damaging the voice by other means, such as yelling at sports events and during child-time play. I have known of younger children who have developed nodes from childhood activities before they attended school. I personally do not teach children, not because I fear damaging their voices, but because my interests are totally directed to the teenage and adult years; however, I could teach them if I had the desire, the time, and if I changed my teaching style. In order to help you, I have contacted a nationally recognized teacher of this younger age, and will share some of his thoughts to supplement my own.

Sincerely,
Mrs. B.

CHILDREN AS SOLO SINGERS

When I heard a concert sung by the treble section of the American Boychoir of Princeton, New Jersey, I witnessed beautiful, pure, tensionless sounds from these boys in grades 5 through 8. After the concert, the associate conductor answered my question, "At what age do you give them voice lessons?" He said that, besides breathing, vowel formation, and resonance help, the boys essentially do not get private voice lessons. He indicated that the boys sing with the sound they use in concert performances quite naturally.

My personal reaction to teaching singing to children is positive if one instills rhythmic concepts, musical phrasing, music reading facility, ear training, resonance, and singing without vocal tension. In other words, we can teach a tremendous amount of "music fundamentals" at this age under the title of voice lessons.

At the same time, many of these same concepts can be learned through piano or other instrumental lessons. If you have a very interested child who is ready for voice instruction, however, what must be taught is clear diction, storytelling through song, and singing with freedom in front of an audience.

I am more comfortable personally, and believe that I can make just as much progress, teaching girls who start in the sixth, seventh and eighth grades and boys who wait until after the voice change. While this is my personal preference, I know other teachers who will wait until a student reaches the age of sixteen. Still others excel at teaching voice to children at young ages. In your case, you need to ask, what are my talents as a teacher, and what are the needs of the singers in my community? If the answer to both those issues includes teaching voice to children, then do it!

I once judged the vocal portion of an arts competition in a rural county in Pennsylvania. One of the singers was a girl in kindergarten, who was physically set in position by her mother. She sang "America" without accompaniment from a laminated sheet that hid her face. Some of the words were changed, and it was called "Sweet America," with the song credited as having been written by this child. I was rather stunned. The next candidate was a seventh grade student who had taken voice lessons for four years. She sang a pop tune by Selena without accompaniment or a starting note. She just stared at me, totally ignoring the audience seated elsewhere in the room. Vocally and rhythmically, she was "all over the place," and showed no expression whatsoever on her face. I could not help but wonder what went on in four years of voice lessons, and how this was a waste of the parents' money.

For a number of summers, I was hired to do a half-hour session daily on voice technique for a church choir of elementary children in a week-long summer workshop at a nearby college. I created a number of child level exercises to deal with each day's subject of Breathing, Phonation, Resonance, Diction, and Expression. I would end each session by relating the subject to one of the choir pieces they were studying for the week. Even though the children were very responsive and I felt my approach was well received, I really did not enjoy the experience as much as I enjoy teaching older students.

THE VOICE OF EXPERIENCE

As I mentioned earlier, there are a number of teachers who are extremely successful teaching the younger age student. Recognition of the validity of teaching children is becoming more widespread, as evidenced in the November 2002 publication from the American Academy of Teachers of Singing, "Teaching Children to Sing." This is a statement of endorsement by over thirty-five teachers of singing.

This pronouncement states that "upon further investigation, no scientific, pedagogical, or physiological evidence indicates that child voice pedagogy is inherently harmful to children's bodies, minds, or spirits."

The Academy recognizes that "well-trained singers of any age are less likely than untrained singers to hurt their vocal instruments or to allow their instruments to be hurt by others."

The Academy recognizes that teachers of children must be sensitive to the fact that the sounds produced are not the full mature sounds of adults. They advise that repertoire must not exceed the intellectual and emotional understanding of the children one teaches. In summary, The American Academy of Teachers of Singing states that "singing can be accomplished on many levels from recreational to professional. At all levels, however, there should be qualified instructors willing and able to help young singers on their musical journey."

Robert Edwin

Robert Edwin is an internationally recognized authority on child voice pedagogy. Over half the students in his independent studio in New Jersey are under the age of eighteen. They range from seasoned professionals on Broadway to raw beginners who are excited about singing. Taking students as young as four years old, he tends to divide the 30-minute lesson in the same way many of us do – 15 minutes on technique and 15 minutes on repertoire. The exercises he uses take advantage of the children's natural desire to play and tell stories. He calls these systematic exercises "the tions" as in body posi<u>tion</u>, respira<u>tion</u>, phona<u>tion</u>, resona<u>tion</u>, articula<u>tion</u>, etc., that cover all the component parts of the singing and speaking system. Robert expects the boys and girls to use their entire voice from bottom to top so that it stays healthy and in balance. That's especially important for kids involved in strong belting shows such as *Annie*, *Matilda*, and *Oliver!*. Robert has produced a vocal pedagogy DVD called *The Kid and the Singing Teacher* (available at www.voiceinsideview.com). This will give you more insight in his method of teaching very young people.

Since his studio includes singers of all genres – from Bach to rock – he needs a great diversity of repertoire. For his young classical singers, he uses my compilation, *36 Solos for Young Singers* and *36 More Solos for Young Singers* (Hal Leonard) as well as several publications edited by Roberta Stephen (Alberta Keys Music Publishing). His favorites are *Songs for In Be Tweens* and Dean Blair's *Six Playful Songs*.

For his theater kids, it's easy to find a plethora of age-appropriate material. In addition to songs from popular Broadway musicals such as *The Sound of Music* and *Les Misérables*, he also suggests less familiar tunes from shows such as *Annie Warbucks*, *Pinkalicious*, *Wonderland*, and *Rags*.

Walt Disney provides Robert's young students with an almost endless supply of repertoire. Old favorites such as "A Dream Is a Wish Your Heart Makes" from *Cinderella* (1950) encourages good classical technique, while "Brand New Day" from *Camp Rock 2* (2010) gives little rock n' rollers a chance to employ their Contemporary Commercial Music skills.

In order to stay on top of current trends in popular vocal music, he suggests listening to the ongoing song compilations called "NOW That's What I Call Music!" to glean songs that might be appropriate for young minds and voices.

Robert published "Vocal Parenting Revisited" in the *Journal of Singing* Volume 70, # 3, January/February 2014. If your personality or your interest leads you to students as young as four through pre-teens, this article definitely is a "must read." For teachers who do not wish to teach this age level of students, it is still important for you to know what is being taught and how it can be very successful.

FURTHER THOUGHTS ON TEACHING VOICE TO CHILDREN

With the growing number of school musical productions at the elementary level, especially with Disney "Junior" shows being performed throughout the country, there are many more students who wish to enjoy the limelight. As talent is recognized at this level, there is an increasing demand for private voice lessons. Other inquiries for lessons will come from parents and participants in the number of children's choruses being formed as outreach organizations of local opera associations and many small choral groups that have sprung up in the last number of years. You may wish to observe teachers working with this age group, even in the public schools, and then decide if you can relate with these students.

If I were teaching children, I would definitely use *36 Solos for Young Singers* and *36 More Solos for Young Singers* (Hal Leonard). These books were compiled especially for students in grades 4, 5, 6, and junior high/middle school. After consulting with several public school teachers of these ages, I settled upon the primary ranges being the octave D to D with several notes above and below added. These volumes include songs suitable for girls and boys, and several songs are very gender determined. Many songs are old time favorites which these singers have never before heard. In addition I would include easy unison, SA, folksongs and sacred octavo selections one can find by researching choral music.

Another group of books I would use are the first four levels of *Resonance – A Comprehensive Voice Series* – developed by The Royal Conservatory Music Development Program and endorsed by NATS (Frederick Harris). This is the fourth edition of this set of books. Personally, even though much less cluttered in this series, I would prefer to stay with our English language for solos at this age because of my training of basic musicianship skills. As a result with the foreign languages listed first, it may be overwhelming to the student learning to read rather than being taught by rote. However, the set includes some very interesting and appropriate songs.

There are many books of Disney songs and Broadway selections for children and upper elementary age. I am including only a partial listing of books that are all very usable. These are all Hal Leonard publications. I have starred several of my favorites.

** *The Great Big Book of Children's Songs* – 77 songs – some easy for small children, fun, sacred, folk, spirituals, TV, movie themes, Broadway, other favorites

Popular Solos for Young Singers – with recorded accompaniments, 22 songs – Sesame Street, Broadway, movies

Kids' Musical Theatre Collection, Vol. 1 – with recorded accompaniments, 29 songs – Broadway, Sesame, films

Kids' Musical Theatre Collection, Vol. 2 – with recorded accompaniments, 30 songs – Broadway, Sesame, films

** *Kids' Musical Theatre Collection*, Complete Vol. 1 and 2 – book only, 59 songs – Broadway, Sesame, films

Kids' Solo Vocal Collection – with recorded accompaniments – 20 songs, many not as familiar

Kids' Musical Theatre Anthology – Lisa DeSpain – with recorded accompaniments, 24 songs – includes show synopsis, audition tips, 16-bar cut suggestions, some more unusual songs

* *Broadway Songs 4 Kids* – with recorded accompaniments, 33 songs – all were sung by children on stage

** *Disney Songs for Singers* – 45 Classic songs – high and low volumes

Disney Collected Kids' Solos – with recorded accompaniments, 38 solos

For those teachers who prefer to have students hear completed performances of the solos, I am including a partial list of books with recorded accompaniments and recorded student performances. (I prefer the students to develop their own character and interpretation and then listen to a performance.)

* *Kids' Musical Theatre Audition* – Michael Dansicker – with recorded accompaniments and performances, 10 songs – Girl's and Boy's editions – interesting, less familiar repertoire

Girl's Songs from Musicals – Louise Lerch – with recorded accompaniments and performances, 10 songs – the singers have all performed on Broadway

Boy's Songs from Musicals – Louise Lerch – with recorded accompaniments and performances, 10 songs – the singers have all performed on Broadway

More Disney Solos for Kids – with recorded accompaniments and performances, 10 songs

Still More Disney Solos for Kids – with recorded accompaniments and performances, 10 songs

Rodgers and Hammerstein Solos for Kids – with recorded accompaniments and performances, 14 songs – the singers have all performed on Broadway

Several Sacred Books

Sacred Vocal Solos for Kids – with recorded accompaniments – 30 easy arrangements including spirituals

Children's Sacred Solos – with recorded accompaniments and performances – 15 easy songs and spirituals

Church Solos for Kids – with recorded accompaniments and performances – 15 well-known church songs

Other recommended volumes

Animal Songs – Richard Carlin (Amsco Publications)

Ready to Sing Folksongs – Jay Althouse (Alfred)

Sesame Street Songbooks – Volumes 1 and 2 – Denes Agay (Warner Publishing)

CHAPTER 21
BUSINESS 101

Raising Lesson Fees, Summer Lessons,
Other Income Producers, Insurance, Retirement

Dear Mrs. B.,

Some of my friends who work in other fields seem to have an easier time than I have when it comes to financial management and planning. They get help from their employers for such things as paying for social security, vacations, sick leave, career development, retirement plans, cost of living adjustments, etc. As a self-employed individual, what can I do to increase my income and plan for my own retirement? I welcome your suggestions for developing a sound financial future for my business.

Sincerely,
Nancy

Dear Nancy,

I understand your frustrations, and know first-hand that private studio work denies one of fringe benefits many friends with employment contracts enjoy. Clearly, the downside of our business means that we may need to work longer hours, raise fees as expenses increase, budget smarter, and plan better to make a comfortable living. The upside can include increased independence, avoidance of institutional politics, flexibility in schedules, and the freedom to teach as long as we wish, given the health and desire to do so. Here are some ideas for your consideration in financial management and planning.

Sincerely,
Mrs. B.

RAISING LESSON FEES

Raising fees is one of the most difficult things I do. I find that it helps to be constantly aware of the fees of the piano teachers, instrumental teachers, and other voice teachers in the area. Voice teachers traditionally command a higher fee than piano teachers, possibly because unless you have a studio accompanist, there is no "dead time." You are "on" every minute of the lesson. Piano and instrumental teachers have more freedom to move around, even while being mentally engaged. (These teachers may disagree with me.)

I usually formulate a letter that I give to my students many months before a fee raise is initiated. I find it better to be short and to the point. You need to list the date the new fees will take effect, and the cost of the new thirty-minute, forty-five-minute, and hour lessons. If you are on the contract system used by many teachers, you need to indicate the new monthly or semester fees, and note when these fees are expected to be paid. I find it better to raise prices at the beginning of a new school year. As part of the letter, I include a statement that says, "If this will cause a hardship in your family, please talk to me privately." Most of the time I have not lost a student. In the case of a needy person, you may wish to negotiate a separate agreement, or a private partial scholarship by giving one free lesson per month to offset the fee increase.

Sometimes I increase adult fees a year or two before doing the same with teenagers. Sometimes the fees are the same for a unit of time. A few times I have raised fees in a staggered fashion. For example, after checking my student roster and finding that I have some adolescent students who have gone through a previous price raise with me, I may decide to keep such students at the old rate until they graduate from high school. In this case, I inform all of my students that the price is changed for all new students and those who were not affected by the last fee change. My method depends upon the economy and the demographics of my studio when I raise my fees.

During a week-long psychology workshop attended by my husband, I arranged to have a private session with a psychology marketing specialist, where I compared my marketing strategies with hers. The main point she stressed to me was that if one has a waiting list, he or she is not charging enough for time and expertise. As much as I believe her, I still cannot bring myself to follow her advice. Were I currently responsible for mortgage payments, saving for children's college educations, repayment of student loans, etc., I'm sure I would be more assertive in raising my fee. While I always have a waiting list, I know there are many good potential students that I will never get because, for them, my fee is too high. Small town private studio teachers, such as me, are often underpaid compared with those who operate in metropolitan areas and nearby affluent suburbs. People will pay a city-based teacher with similar credentials a higher fee, many times without question. After all, there is a higher cost of living in all aspects of city living.

There is the case of a highly qualified piano teacher colleague from the Pennsylvania Music Teachers Association. She moved from a city environment to a small rural community and her fee, although modest at under $20.00 per half hour, seems astronomical where local instructors are still charging under $10.00 per half hour for piano lessons. She is determined to bring about increased standards for the arts in her new location. Meanwhile, she kept her main studio business intact by continuing a long commute.

Since studio teaching is a business and not a hobby, your fee schedule adjustments must be made as economic factors dictate. Some triggers include:

- Social Security, personal tax, and property tax increases
- increased costs of piano tuning, utilities, new music and reference books
- necessary equipment replacement or upgrades
- increases in room rent (for teaching or recitals), printing costs, postage
- registration fees and travel expenses for workshops and conventions
- insurance
- maintenance cost increases for studio and home
- price increases for tickets to concerts, musicals, etc.

The list could be expanded to include general inflation and cost of living factors. You need to cover your expenses and have an income base to support your yearly needs, including the days and weeks you use for vacations.

In summary, delay your adjustments too long, and your cost increases will reduce profit. Raise fees too fast, and you face the possibility of losing income by pricing yourself out of the market.

A few final words are in order before moving to another topic. You need to ask your friends how many hours they work a year, and compare their answers with the total you work. Most full-time wage earners work 40 hours a week for 50 weeks, or approximately 2000 hours per year. Many individuals work many hours beyond that, take work home, are "on call," and/or can be expected to travel or attend extra meetings without reimbursement. You, too, will work many hours for which you won't be paid. The following chart may be helpful in considering what gross annual income can be produced by a given number of billable hours worked in your studio, at given sample rates.

Hrs./Wk.	Wks./Yr.	Billable Hrs.	Fee/Hr.	Gross Income (in thousands)
10	30	300	$30/40/50/60/70	$9/12/15/18/21
10	40	400	$30/40/50/60/70	$12/16/20/24/28
10	50	500	$30/40/50/60/70	$15/20/25/30/35
20	30	600	$30/40/50/60/70	$18/24/30/36/42
20	40	800	$30/40/50/60/70	$24/32/40/48/56
20	50	1000	$30/40/50/60/70	$30/40/50/60/70
30	30	900	$30/40/50/60/70	$27/36/45/54/63
30	40	1200	$30/40/50/60/70	$36/48/60/72/84
30	50	1500	$30/40/50/60/70	$45/60/75/90/105
40	30	1200	$30/40/50/60/70	$36/48/60/72/84
40	40	1600	$30/40/50/60/70	$48/64/80/96/112
40	50	2000	$30/40/50/60/70	$60/80/100/120/140
50	30	1500	$30/40/50/60/70	$45/60/75/90/105
50	40	2000	$30/40/50/60/70	$60/80/100/120/140
50	50	2500	$30/40/50/60/70	$75/100/125/150/175

SUMMER LESSONS

While I realize that many teachers do not teach in the summer and that some teach all year round, I find it preferable to teach either six or seven weeks each summer, depending upon my other commitments. Generally, I end my winter schedule the week after my spring recitals in May, and resume a modified schedule three weeks later. Earlier in my career, I taught more days of the week and more hours per day in the summer than I do now. Currently, I teach only Monday, Tuesday, and Wednesday each week in the summer session from 8:30 to 1:30. I restrict these times for new teenagers, present teens, and college students coming back for the season. The adults have a break until the fall season. With this schedule, I can end before August, when many students go to summer camps for sports or band, or travel on family vacations. You may wish to experiment with several options and find one that works best for your schedule.

OTHER INCOME PRODUCERS

Because the focus of this book is the private studio, I will not elaborate in detail on the many other ways to increase your income by engaging in other pursuits, other than to list some of the obvious opportunities that exist within the music field. Personally, I can list the following as other sources of income during my active career as a musician:

- Public school music teacher (choral, classroom, instrumental)
- College voice instructor
- Summer camp voice teacher
- Vocal recitalist and lecturer
- Master class clinician
- Consultant
- Writer
- Compiler and editor
- Accompanist (vocal and instrumental)
- Opera and musical show rehearsal pianist
- Solo vocal and horn performances
- Choral group performances
- Church soloist
- Church choir director and accompanist (substitute)
- Hornist (orchestra, chamber ensembles, jazz band)
- College horn teacher
- Adjudicator
- Vocal coach
- Church choir clinician

I'm sure you can think of other creative ways to produce income in music areas where you have developed competence and confidence. Very few teachers restrict themselves to studio teaching exclusively throughout their careers, especially in the early years of building studio revenue.

INSURANCE

I previously talked about liability insurance if you teach in your home. This is very important to have as a rider on your general house or apartment insurance. Discuss with your representative the best way to insure your home for complete replacement of the structure and contents. There are various types of policies. You need to make sure that you have adequate coverage.

You will also need to consider other types of insurance. To do so, you may wish to work with local representatives. Another approach is to see what options exist through other business organizations, such as the local Chamber of Commerce or the Small Business Association. A third option is to seek insurance through national organizations. The Music Teachers National Association, of which I am a member, offers to private studio teachers programs of personal coverage for supplemental health insurance, dental insurance, vision insurance, cancer insurance, term life insurance, and a prescription drug program. Additionally, professional policies are offered for liability, instruments, and personal sexual abuse defense coverage. Through MTNA, a variety of investment services are offered that would be similar to those made available by financial planners in most communities.

RETIREMENT

When you have decided to make private teaching your life's career, it is never too early to think about putting some money away for retirement. When I started teaching, junior high school general music plus eight private voice students per week seemed overwhelming, much less thinking of retirement or savings. A guidance counselor at our school tried desperately to talk several of us into investing in mutual funds. None of us did this. Instead, I invested a considerable amount of money per month building my collection of long-playing records. Even though I still have my nineteen linear feet of records, you can guess the value of them today, not to mention the inconvenience of an outdated technology. If I had taken her advice in the 1950s and started an investment program with even a nominal sum, you can imagine how much better off I would be today!

Your first step, however, should be to establish a fund to cover your expenses in the event you should become ill, or for use during non-teaching weeks for vacations and holidays. This money could be put into a dividend earning account for your use at any time with a no-load quality mutual fund company, such as Fidelity, Vanguard, or T. Rowe Price. Certificates of deposit or treasury bills can also be considered for building a cash reserve fund.

As a self-employed person, you must plan for your own retirement. At this writing, you can choose a SEP, KEOGH or SIMPLE plan. Because of its simplicity and requiring the least amount of paper work, the SEP (simplified employee pension) IRA (individual retirement account) is probably the best plan at this time. Once you have chosen a mutual fund for your investment of up to 20% (at the present time) of your net income on Schedule C (after half of your social security is deducted), your dividends and capital gains will grow tax free until withdrawal at age 70 and a half. You may open a SEP IRA as late as April 15 following your tax year. Another advantage of the SEP IRA is that, once you are required to withdraw so much money per the yearly formula, you are allowed to add to it as long as you are still earning at least a matching amount of money. In addition, depending on how much money you will net, you would probably qualify for a Traditional Deductible IRA or a Roth IRA at the same time. *Because the laws change so often, you need to talk to an accountant, lawyer, or financial planner to be certain that you understand all your options.*

A common rule for understanding financial planning is "pay yourself first." With diversification, time, compound interest, and discipline on your side, it is possible to plan for a preferred future of financial security and independence. By careful planning and making appropriate withdrawal decisions, your investments can grow in value even as you use some of your assets for living expenses. The earlier you begin an individual retirement account, the more up to the maximum the law allows each year, the better rate of return you receive, and the smaller the fees associated with maintaining the account are all factors that will impact choices you have later in life as the result of any disciplined saving or investment plan you establish.

If you have knowledge of and interest in the stock market, you can establish your IRA as a "Self-Directed IRA," where you choose individual stocks and trade within the IRA itself, paying only the trading commission. If you are not comfortable in doing this yourself, seek a financial advisor whom you can trust.

I realize that this topic may be totally foreign, confusing, or boring, yet it is important for you to consider once you are earning enough money to be able to take advantage of it. It is to your benefit to be more aware of your financial circumstances at this stage of your life so that you can grow in knowledge and make intelligent decisions later on.

Perhaps the most succinct summary for you is this quote from Lisa Reilly Cullen in the December 1997, (Pg. 81) issue of *Money*:

"Spend less, cut debt, save more, invest smart. That in a nutshell, is all the financial planning you'll ever need."

CHAPTER 22
THE INEVITABLE UNCLE SAM

U.S. Federal Income Taxes, Schedule C, Form 8829, Schedule SE, A Tax Hint for All

Note: This chapter on taxes in the private studio applies only to U.S. citizens and residents. Information presented is current at the time of publication in 2014. Laws can and almost certainly will change regarding taxes. Though thoroughly researched, the information presented here makes no claim to be professional tax advice. Consult proper resources or tax professionals.

Dear Mrs. B.,

Thanks for your earlier tips on keeping records. I definitely want to try several of your ideas. Along these same lines, I feel that I am not taking advantage of the amount of deductions that I am allowed for my federal income tax. Previously, I have used an accountant, but I decided that I am going to tackle the Schedule C form myself. Will you walk me through this form and any others that are necessary for my business?

Sincerely,
Nancy

Dear Nancy,

In addition to using accountants, many people are using the computer software packages which are updated yearly for both the federal and state taxes. I still prefer to do my taxes by hand, because I feel that I understand all aspects of my financial situation better this way. The software programs adjust all figures automatically, and this could lead to the attitude of just punching in the numbers, so that one may not really know how everything fits together. They may be the best option for some, but I am happy to share my approach.

Sincerely,
Mrs. B.

U.S. FEDERAL INCOME TAXES

As a self-employed person who has a private voice studio, you are required to file the Schedule C form with your taxes. If this is also a home-based business, you will need to file a form 8829, or Expenses for Business Use of Your Home. You need to show a profit for three out of the last five years to qualify as a legitimate business and not as a hobby. Therefore, when one starts out, you can use the losses you may incur for the first two years against other household gains. The third year, a profit of even several dollars can keep the business legitimate as you increase your earnings.

Beginning in the tax year 2013, there is a new simplified option for the self-employed person which is known as a "safe harbor home office deduction." Instead of filing Form 8829 – Expenses for the Business Use of your Home, you can use $5 per square foot of your teaching space up to 300 square feet or $1,500. Until you earn enough to take full advantage of Form 8829, which allows more of a deduction, this certainly is more simple. Your mortgage and taxes are fully deductible on Schedule A with the simplified form instead of moving the allocated portion for your studio to Form 8829.

My husband and I kept our separate checking accounts when we got married, but if I were beginning again, I would add a separate account to keep the financial status of my business more defined for tax purposes. In this way, all deposits and expenditures in this special account would be entirely business related.

If your profits and self-employment taxes total more than $1,000 in a calendar year, you are required to pay quarterly estimated taxes April 15, June 15, September 15 and January 15. To avoid a penalty, you need to pay 90% of the current year taxes or 100% to 110% of the past year's taxes as your declaration figure. Since it is very difficult in our business to determine so far ahead, I always use the previous year's figures to make my quarterly payment for the current year.

In the beginning of January, I categorize all my receipts and business expenses, and list them one by one on worksheets. I total each category to transfer to Schedule C. Another worksheet lists my monthly income plus any extra services, such as substitute choir directing, giving a lecture, presenting a master class, accompanying, playing or singing for a wedding, judging a competition, etc. You are paid either by cash or check, and will sometimes receive a 1099 Miscellaneous Income form, which indicates that the IRS expects this income to be reported. One tax guide I recently reviewed stated that because we are self-employed, the IRS tends to audit us four times more than others.

A friend with a private psychology practice was audited several years ago and ended up with a huge sum to pay because he estimated expenses—he had not kept careful records. As a result, his taxes were also audited for several prior years. Keep your records current and document every item. Do not assume that driving to a local concert is not worth logging the mileage. You will be amazed how these seemingly minor sums add up.

For the next three sections, the reader should secure the forms for a fuller understanding of the information provided.

SCHEDULE C

Let us look at the Schedule C. (You may obtain this at the post office, the public library or online from the IRS government website.) In Box B, you need to enter a principal business code. Since there is none that fits us, I use "61000 Educational Services." On line F, most of us will check the box marked "Cash." I make sure that all my accounts are paid in full by the end of the calendar year. On line G, you check "yes" because you do "materially participate" in the business.

Line 1. If I have any 1099 income to report, I write in "1099 Misc." and the total in the upper part of the line, and the total regular earnings in the bottom half. Lines 3, 5, and 7 should each show the combined total from Line 1.

Line 8. You can deduct the cost of studio brochures, patron listings for your studio in school and community programs and shows, and any other form of advertising you use. Publicity photo costs for brochures, recitals and lectures can appear here.

Line 9. Unless your travel for business is extensive, it usually makes sense to use the annual mileage rate, which changes from year to year. For the year 2013 the rate was $.565 per business mile. This figure will include all mileage costs to music stores, competitions for your students, school concerts and musical shows, workshops, trips to the airport for long-distance workshops and conventions, etc. In a previous chapter, I talked about the mileage card list I use so that I do not have to recalculate mileage for places that I frequent. Even if the local music-related places you frequent are only two miles away, keep track of this mileage.

Line 15. If you have a separate liability insurance policy, this is the place to deduct your premiums. Also include any instrument insurance. Ours is combined with our homeowners policy; therefore, I include that portion on form 8829.

Line 17. Tax preparation fees related to only your business are included here, as well as any business attorney fees.

Line 18. This total is a combination of all those little office supplies you need, such as business cards, stationery, envelopes, masking and repair tape, file folders, paper clips, pencils, pens, computer paper, printer cartridges, whiteout, photocopying costs of policy statements, materials for new students, and competition applications.

Line 19. Don't get confused, for this line applies only to people who have associate teachers and pay on plans for them. If you enroll in a SEP, KEOGH, or SIMPLE retirement plan, these contributions are included on Line 28 of your regular 1040 form.

Line 21. This line would include repairs to a piano light, a tape recorder, studio rug replacement, repainting costs for the studio area, and any other repairs that apply to the studio.

Line 23. Generally, the studio percentage of real estate taxes is included on form 8829. If you pay a business license fee, you would include it here.

Line 24. I generally include travel costs in Part V on the other side of the form. However, on line 24b, I write 50% and record all the business meals here.

Line 25. One may *not* deduct routine telephone costs unless you have a separate business line installed. However, all toll calls related to your business are deductible. I write "Toll Calls" after "Utilities" and include the total, after recording each one on a worksheet from the monthly phone bills. Regular utility costs are included on form 8829.

At this point you can move to Part IV and fill out the vehicle questions. Your total business miles should match the total factored in the Line 9 figures. Part V is the section where I use six separate categories. My first is Piano Tuning and Recital Expenses. This includes studio piano tuning, and tuning of the recital piano. Cost of recital hall rental, any reception costs, and all costs of program printing are listed here.

Second, I list Music, CDs, Videos and Books. This includes all such purchases I make for studio use.

My third category is Workshops, Conventions, Competitions and Concerts. Workshops and conventions are usually several days in nature; therefore, you may deduct the cost of the plane, train or bus travel, taxis, airport limousines, rental car expenses, normal hotel costs, dry cleaning and laundry expenses, and tips. If you choose, there are per diem figures listed by the IRS for various sections of the country and certain cities, which means that you do not have to itemize. These figures can be found in some of the large tax guides, such as J.K. Lassers *Your Income Tax*, which is updated every year. I find that keeping receipts sometimes gives you greater deductions. (Some states have other rules. For instance, for Pennsylvania taxes, I am allowed to add back the remaining 50% of meals.) Please note that meals are only deductible if you stay overnight, if you have a business meal with a colleague, or if the meal is totally business in nature. Incidental travel expenses under $75 do not need receipts if they are listed in a diary.

For the fourth line, I list Dues and Donations. This includes all membership dues to NATS, MTNA, NAfME, and other state, chapter or local musical groups. Donations and dues from your business might include the local Chamber of Commerce, your local Friends of the Theater, the Metropolitan Opera and local opera companies, the local PBS television and radio stations, the NATS Foundation, local concert associations, and local chamber or ensemble groups. Routine donations to charities such as the Salvation Army, the United Way, YMCA, or YWCA are not allowed here, since they are not directly related to your business.

My fifth category is Subscriptions and Journals. This includes all music journals, and also magazines selected for the coffee table for students to browse while waiting for lessons. I include financial publications to aid in keeping up on the new tax laws, and to be knowledgeable about retirement investing, since we must make provisions for our own retirement.

On the sixth line I list Postage and Christmas. I include the cost of the boxes of holiday chocolates I give to my students each year, and the cost of the greeting cards I send to all my students. Postage adds to this because I write many thank you notes to students, many professional and business letters, and frequent notes to former students in college or who are now professional musicians. For those using e-mail, these costs will be minimal. It still sets a good example to send personal, written notes for every student gift you receive, regardless of how small.

These six lines are totaled, and the amount listed on Line 27a. The sum of Lines 8 through 27a is listed on Line 28. Line 29 will show your tentative profit or loss.

FORM 8829

This form must also be copied at a public library, tax accountant's office, online or requested from the IRS. For this form you must calculate the amount of space you use regularly and exclusively for your studio business. In my case, I measured the square footage of the rooms and determined what parts of the various rooms are used for an office, music storage, actual teaching area, student waiting area, computer room space, etc. I then came up with a percentage that represents the total area of the house used for business.

This form is used to determine the percentage of your deductible mortgage interest, the real estate taxes (exclude any personal taxes), and heating, water, sewer, electric and trash expenses. If you itemize deductions, the remainder of the taxes are used on Schedule A.

Whether you do or do not depreciate the business portion of your home, you need to be aware that when you sell it, you are liable for taxes on the capital gains realized on that portion that has or has not been depreciated over the years. The final figure from Line 35 is transferred to Schedule C, Line 30, and subtracted from Line 29 to determine your final business profit or loss for the year.

SCHEDULE SE

You now proceed to the schedule that figures your self-employment tax. You will use Section A. After working through the figures, you will have on Line 5 your total self-employment tax, and on Line 6, the portion of this tax that you can take as a credit on Line 27 of your 1040 form.

If you have a separate health policy for yourself or your family taken out in your business name, you are allowed to deduct 100% of the cost on Line 29 of the 1040 form. Verify this on a yearly basis.

Earlier, I described the various retirement plans for which you are eligible as a result of your business. You can establish a SEP, KEOGH, or a SIMPLE plan in addition to a regular IRA or Roth IRA. The SEP, KEOGH or SIMPLE plan payment amount would be included on line 28.

A TAX HINT FOR ALL

Before I close, I want to share a very useful booklet that I recommend for anyone who itemizes deductions. As teachers, we strive to keep up a good appearance, and this means we tend to give away clothes that are wearing out, or the styles have changed, or waistlines somehow increased, and because we are in the public eye. This book, a yearly updated publication for $25.00, is called *Money for Your Used Clothing* by William R. Lewis, CPA, CFP, and Connie Edwards, Tax Auditor. It lists over a thousand clothing and household items generally donated to charity and listed as in "good condition" or "better condition." Each booklet gives you a "registration number" that you can use to request the "audit protection guarantee" and include on tax Form 8283 if claiming goods valued over $500.00. Call 1-866-417-7678, or write to Money – 2013, Certified Use Clothing Values, Inc., 3801 Union Drive, Suite 106, Lincoln, Nebraska 68516, or e-mail www.MFYUC.com. When my husband retired from college teaching, he donated over seventeen cartons of professional books to a fledgling college library, and we used this booklet as the basis for a major deduction. This publication, previously titled *Cash for Your Used Clothing*, has been in existence for more than twenty years and it's deductible. It is worth the investment (which itself is also a yearly deduction). This has been included in some software tax programs.

Don't be afraid to tackle your taxes yourself. You will find ways to increase deductible items as a result, and still be within IRS guidelines. You are operating a legitimate business, and this will help you to really understand its financial structure. Be aware that rules do change every year, and you need to be on the lookout for newspaper and magazine articles that describe these changes as they become known. Each state has its own unique tax structure, which you will need to investigate in order to understand the implications for your tax reporting.

I hope that you find lots of legitimate deductions that you have neglected in the past. Let me end with a quote from a New York accountant that appeared in *The Wall Street Journal*. "The main reason people miss deductions is because they are poor record keepers. The people who are the best record keepers pay the least amount of tax."

CHAPTER 23
NUTS ABOUT NATS

Workshops, Conventions and Conferences, NATS Chapters, Other Professional Organizations and Community Involvement

---

Dear Mrs. B.,

You keep mentioning the National Association of Teachers of Singing. I have definitely decided to make voice teaching my life's work, and I have completed the membership teaching requirement. How have you found NATS to be beneficial to your students and to you? If I should join NATS, will you write a supporting letter for me? What responsibilities and rewards come with membership? What else do you suggest as I expand my involvement in my community as a professional teacher of singing?

Sincerely,
Nancy

Dear Nancy,

Should you join NATS? Absolutely! I consider it to be the most important organization for professional voice teachers. Over half of the more than 6,600 members are teachers in the private sector, so this organization continues to be responsive to the needs and interests of this group. I would be happy to write a letter in support of your application for membership.

Sincerely,
Mrs. B.

I am calling this my "Nuts about NATS" chapter because this organization has influenced my professional life in a way that nothing else has.

In 1962, at Western Michigan University in Kalamazoo, I took some graduate music courses while my husband had a summer fellowship. I spent most of my time in the music library, which was larger than any I had used before. This was where, for example, I found the song lists for adolescent singers compiled by Helen Steen Huls. These, in turn, greatly influenced the creation of *Solo Vocal Repertoire for Young Singers* in 1980, which I compiled and edited for NATS. But I was ecstatic when I found a magazine called The NATS Bulletin representing an organization that was all about the teaching of voice. I wondered if I could ever have the credentials to become a member. Upon investigation, I discovered that both my high school and college teachers were members and could sponsor me. They never mentioned this organization, possibly because it was just formed in 1944, and many early members were city or university based studio teachers. Apparently, my teachers were brand new members when I studied with them.

I'm sure that my 1955-56 Rotary Fellowship in Germany to study voice and horn was influential in getting me accepted as a member, since when I applied I was a high school choral director without a graduate degree, and with only eight private students a year. But I also conducted many group voice classes for members of my choirs during the school week. In addition, I had returned to Germany for the three months during the summer of 1958 to study daily with my voice teacher. I remember distinctly taking her to lunch one day in Munich specifically to discuss with her whether she thought I had the capabilities and the training to become a full-time voice teacher. During the next two summers, I taught voice and horn at Stonegate Music and Arts Camp in the state of New York. I was extremely happy when I received my letter of acceptance into NATS during the presidency of William Vennard in 1964.

Soon after joining, I took advantage of purchasing all the back issues of *The NATS Bulletin* that were still available. This is now the *Journal of Singing*. I spent many months reading these issues and became familiar with the names of some of the well-known teachers in the country. I was particularly interested in any articles about vocal repertoire and the question-and-answer columns that were all about teaching and vocal technique. Until I experienced scientific sessions at conventions and workshops much later, I really did not understand some of the articles. I continue to read every issue of all NATS publications and add them to my reference library.

WORKSHOPS

The first NATS workshop I attended was held at Dartmouth College in 1965. It was a most unusual one, given that it was coordinated with the Dartmouth College summer Arts program. This collaboration with all the instrumentalists gave an emphasis to vocal chamber music. I absorbed the lectures like a sponge, took notes constantly, and was especially excited to be in sessions with Zoltan Kodaly in person, and found the opportunity to accompany Robert Grooters, Temple University Professor of Music, in private lessons with Pierre Bernac was simply awesome. I was in absolute "vocal heaven." I had never been exposed to a solid week of intense vocal classes and day and night performances that all applied to private voice teaching. By meeting many of the 140 persons in attendance, already the seeds of lifelong friendships in NATS were sown. Living together in the dorms, eating in the student cafeteria, and gathering in the downtown nightspots led to many informative conversations about teaching.

In 1967, at the Buffalo workshop, I had the opportunity to sing in a master class for Gerhard Huesch, who was the teacher of one of my friends in Munich the year I studied there. He held my Munich teacher in high esteem, and we established an immediate relationship. As a result, I was invited to accompany in daily private lessons with a singer who came to gain Huesch's thorough knowledge about the repertoire of Kilpinen, the great Finnish composer with whom Huesch collaborated, and whose works he promoted all over the world. A bonus was finding a huge parcel of Kilpinen music as a thank-you from this singer at my doorstep weeks later.

In 2012, I donated all my Kilpinen music to the music library of my alma mater, Indiana University of Pennsylvania, Indiana, Pennsylvania, where my entire music library will eventually reside. The librarian, who is Finnish, was excited to tell me that I presented more vocal copies than the Kilpinen Society had in the United State's archives.

The Murray State University workshop held in Kentucky in 1968 was interesting because the director of the Harrisburg Symphony (in which I played second horn), Edwin McArthur, was a clinician. He was more well-known as the former accompanist for Kirsten Flagstad. Composer Carlisle Floyd and teacher Elena Nikolaidi were also on the staff. My greatest memory was establishing a deep friendship with singer-teacher Carol Notestine, who was a friend of composer John Ness Beck. She brought a manuscript of his newly written song, "Song of Devotion," which together we premiered at the workshop. (This solo is included in *The Second Book of Mezzo-Soprano/Alto Solos*, Part II.)

In 1969, at the Wittenburg University workshop in Ohio, we all worked with Gibner King and went to the Cincinnati Zoo to see the opera Rigoletto, augmented with peacock descants. I had broken my foot, and I still made the plane trip with cane and canvas shoes (at that time, not the trendy code of dress, but good enough for the after-hours room parties with Jean Ludman, a future president of NATS).

At the Salem Academy workshop in 1972, the most memorable sessions were on Purcell and Moravian music. This was my first encounter with a man who became a dear friend, Gordon Myers, who gave several sessions on Moravian music. I had been doing some independent research on Moravian literature, and I remember having the courage to speak up in his session about some Moravian songs he did not know. Harvey Woodruff gave an amazing session on using unison octavo music with young students. This session led me to spend years exploring this vast repertoire, something I continue to do every opportunity I get. Accommodations were memorable, since we were housed on the top floor of the dormitory during an extremely hot week, with no air conditioning. Every night around midnight, my husband and I would carry our pillows into the other part of the building to an air-conditioned mathematics classroom, where we slept on the floor. I mention this because this was all part of the uniqueness of this particular NATS workshop experience. We still meet others who shared the same conditions, and it always brings back memories.

One more example was the Rhode Island workshop in 1975. I did a great deal of singing for Allen Rogers, a prominent Boston voice coach, who was the main clinician. It was a small workshop, and very few had signed up to sing. The intimate nature of these small groups made them very special, as one bonded so quickly with others. The special event of the week was an authentic New England clambake, hosted for us on the beach by one of the English professors from the university.

Later workshops featured the team of Edward Baird and Louise Lerch, who were responsible for presenting new music that had been recently published for all types of teaching situations. This was a wonderful way to enable workshop participants to learn these new pieces in a day or two in order to introduce them to the others. These sessions were extremely valuable for me, both from the standpoint of singing new material, and also for finding teaching gems which I felt safe in ordering for my students.

For many years, the workshops had headliner clinicians, and the subjects of the other sessions were very varied. There were panel discussions, the "quiz cove," and today we often have closing panels by the main clinicians. More recently, the trend has been to have a theme whereby the entire workshop is devoted to the same subject in many forms. At Rutgers University in 1999, we studied all forms of French repertoire and the language. At Miami University in 2000, we spent the entire week on the subject of "belting" and Musical Theatre singing. At Penn State University in 2001, we concentrated on contemporary American music, with solo and chamber opera works.

Some of the more recent workshops included "Tools for Singers – Skill Builders for Teachers and Singers," "From Studio to Stage," "First the Words, Then the Music," and "Opera/Musical Theater in the 21st Century."

Another of my NATS joys was to have the opportunity to present sessions at a number of the workshops. At Connecticut College and Gatlinburg, I presented my "Solo Vocal Repertoire for Young Singers" sessions. At the University of North Carolina at Charlotte, my husband and I gave a joint double session on "Marketing and Management of the Private Voice Studio." At the University of Minnesota, I presented both of these, plus a session on the use of octavos in teaching. I have been greatly enriched by the questions and general feedback from those in attendance.

Even though there are fewer workshops these days, and the number of people attending is larger, the experiences cannot be matched anywhere. So much information is shared as one walks from the dorms to the dining halls, browses the music displays, piles into someone's car to find a late night snack, rides the bus to the mid-week social outing, or grabs a practice room to have another teacher share a vocal technique or piece of music that works. I urge you to attend as many workshops as you can as long as you remain in this profession.

CONVENTIONS AND CONFERENCES

In 1966, I attended my first NATS convention in Washington, D.C. This event left me intimidated as I mingled with many prestigious teachers and personalities from throughout the country. The NATS Artist Awards final competition was an amazing event to me at that time in my life. This is the final round of a professional competition that starts at the regional level earlier in the year. The winner of each region receives a stipend to attend the convention semi-final competition. The actual competition is open to anyone who wishes to listen the day before the convention officially opens. The final competition is one of the convention's main evening events, and is judged by prominent teachers and sometimes celebrity guest artists. All the contestants receive substantial monetary awards. The top winners are awarded additional recital opportunities. To enter, one must be sponsored by a NATS teacher or be a NATS member. A number of our teachers have been finalists and winners in the past. As of 2012 Conference, a second national competition has been started for musical theatre singers.

Although this convention was a totally different atmosphere from the workshop I had attended months earlier, it had a lasting effect on me as I vowed to attend as many future conventions as I could. The music exhibits on display from publishers and music stores was an education in itself. I spent every possible spare minute just trying to look at all the music and books, most of which were new to me. I treasured the lists of music given to us at various sessions, and I still have all of them, as they were a great source in helping me expand my library of music. I had never before been to a business meeting of an organization of this size, and I was happy to be able to put faces with the names I had been reading about in the publications.

Later, I was privileged to be invited to present my vocal repertoire lecture at the Minneapolis and Little Rock conventions, and the marketing and management lecture with my husband at the New Orleans convention. In addition, at the Tampa convention, I was asked to teach three daily live demonstration lessons with a high school volunteer who had had no previous private instruction. These opportunities at the national level led to invitations to lecture and to offer master classes with high school students at workshops and regional and chapter meetings in fifteen states and Calgary, Canada.

In all, I have attended over twenty-five conventions and over twenty workshops. I believe that they have helped to make me the teacher I am today. As one gets to know people more intimately at the workshops, gets the courage to participate in master classes, volunteers to sing and accompany during the new music sessions, and finds a niche to present something of interest to other people, one becomes an integral part of the organization. The workshops are more "hands-on" experiences, while the conferences tend to be more formal, given that several hundred teachers are in attendance. Each convention becomes an opportunity to bond with new groups of people, who over time become close colleagues and friends. As an added benefit, remember that most convention, conference, and workshop expenses are completely deductible items on Schedule C of your income taxes. You can allocate some of your lesson fees to a fund to provide these opportunities for your growth.

There are many opportunities to serve NATS. For instance, I have been the exhibits chairman for two conventions, served for many years on the membership, finance, and ethics committees, and had articles published in the NATS Publications, served as Pennsylvania Governor for two terms, and have presented several sessions for one of the summer intern programs.

Let me mention two incidental happenings at conventions that were extra special for me. At the Dallas convention in 1970, the NATS Artist Award was presented to William Parker. I was really in shock when I remembered that William was just one of the typical students in one of my ninth grade general music classes in 1954 when I student taught in Butler, Pennsylvania. When I congratulated him, he remembered and called me by my maiden name, Miss Frey. At the Boston convention in 1992, someone came up to me in the registration area and asked if I knew her. Standing there was Ellen Chickering, now a professional soprano and professor at the University of Southern Maine. I was her first voice teacher for a summer thirty-two years earlier at Stonegate Music and Arts Camp. What a wonderful reunion we had! It also led to an invitation from her to present a workshop at her institution in Gorham, Maine.

NATS CHAPTERS

If you are fortunate enough to live in an area that sponsors one of the 80 NATS chapters, you have the opportunity to become very active by participating in chapter programs and the student auditions. If there is no chapter, maybe you can round up enough NATS members in the area to start one.

A major advantage of belonging to a chapter is having a wonderful venue to let your better students experience evaluations from other voice teachers. The student evaluations are in levels so that, for example, high school males are judged separately from the females, and each year of college is divided into male and female. There are also divisions for adults, graduate students, advanced singers, and Broadway specialists. Another great advantage of belonging to a chapter is having the opportunity to learn to judge other students at chapter auditions. This is not an easy task, particularly if you are in an independent studio, because you do not get much experience judging. One needs to remain positive, and yet give comments that are constructive for the student and teacher to discuss. Very often you can help a student become a better singer with your comments. I find that often a comment is offered that makes me realize that I have been neglecting a particular part of my student's training. Getting judging experience may lead to opportunities for you to get paid to adjudicate other types of competitions.

I think it is very important for all quality voice teachers to belong to NATS. The publication, *Journal of Singing* (formerly *The NATS Journal* and *The NATS Bulletin*) always has interesting articles that pertain to all levels of teaching. The *InterNos* (a newsletter currently published three times a year) is primarily used to relay association news, news of international happenings, and advance notice of conferences and workshops.

Much more could be said about NATS and its worldwide influence on teachers of singing. Similar organizations have started in other countries, in part with the help of NATS officers, especially Marvin Keenze, International Coordinator. Collaborative efforts with these new associations have led to a regular series of International Voice Teachers Congresses, which are similar in format to NATS conventions. I attended ones that were held in Philadelphia and Vancouver, Canada, and I have many friends who have attended those held in other foreign countries.

OTHER PROFESSIONAL ORGANIZATIONS
AND COMMUNITY INVOLVEMENT

As a professional music teacher, you may wish to search out other groups with which you can identify. One such organization might be the Music Teachers National Association. Whereas NATS is an organization of primarily voice teachers, coaches, music businesses, and related specialties, the majority of MTNA members are piano and instrumental teachers; however, there is a voice division, which is active. This group makes available to its members a variety of insurance plans that may be of interest to the studio teacher. Depending upon where you live, there could be many opportunities for you and your students at either the state level or in local chapters. The chapter I belong to offers recitals and provides chapter scholarships on a competitive basis. This association is especially important if you also teach piano. It is wise to know the qualified piano teachers in the area because they can be a great source for referrals.

NAfMC (National Association for Music Education) is an organization for elementary and secondary school music teachers. Since I started out in the public schools, I am a life member of this and the comparable state organization. I find this to be advantageous to keep abreast of the changes that are taking place in music in our schools. Many college professors of music education also are active in this group.

If there is no music club in your town, you may want to form one. Generally, these groups meet monthly and provide active members with performance opportunities. They may also accept associate members who are lovers of music who participate as listeners, and help in other capacities.

Since 1956, I have been a performing member of the Carlisle Musical Arts Club in my town in Pennsylvania. Many of my adult students are active members and love to prepare a ten to twelve minute group of songs each year for the club. In April, we hold a young artist recital, featuring the top high school juniors and seniors of our teacher members. We sponsor two four-year college scholarships each year. The scholarship money increases each year if the student remains a music major all four years. Scholarship recipients are invited to perform at the June meeting. Even in a small town such as ours, a music club can be a wonderful professional and social experience.

Continuing education is important. You may wish to take additional voice and piano lessons, or participate in master classes, summer courses, and workshops. In addition to NATS workshops, I have participated in four Westminster Choir College Art Song Festival weeks and Master Teachers of Voice workshops. As soon as you are financially able, you may wish to take selected post-master's degree courses that will augment your present understanding of vocal pedagogy and literature. I was so thankful that I was able to complete thirty credits beyond my master's at Indiana University in Bloomington, in such studies as private voice, piano accompanying, four separate vocal literature courses, and vocal pedagogy.

If you wish to perform more, you can let it be known that you are available for mini-recitals or will sing special music for celebrations and certain community events. You can audition for the area opera company and the local chamber choir. You may wish to form a chorus that has the potential to grow, for example, into an established thirty-voice adult group.

It is important to get to know the church choir directors and school music teachers in your community. Be a paid patron for the school musical. Attend public concerts and recitals. Arrange to go out to lunch or breakfast with someone from the community with whom you can relate musically.

If you live near an established voice teacher, and you are in the early stages of your teaching career, you might seek permission to observe lessons, or even attempt to be mentored by a willing teacher you respect. As a result of a lecture I gave to a NATS chapter in a neighboring state, one of the young teachers came for an overnight stay to observe some of my summer teaching. Another teacher began to correspond with me as a result of using my song volumes. She has traveled four hours several times to observe some of my studio lessons. A university professor who was close to retirement wanted to move and start a private studio. She asked to observe the "grass roots" type of studio. Another retired college professor has written me a number of letters with questions about beginning a studio with students of an age level he has never taught before. Norman Spivey observed me as part of research he was doing on comparative vocal pedagogies of eleven area teachers.

I cannot imagine how limited my teaching might have been were it not for all the additional graduate work I have had with some wonderful and innovative professors, and the many additional inspirational experiences I have had as a result of belonging to NATS. Resolve to deepen your background, to extend your connection to a larger musical community and to participate in musical ensembles and performances. The most important lesson for any teacher is still the most obvious one: always remain a student yourself.

CHAPTER 24

THOU SHALT NOT PHOTOCOPY!
And Other Ethical Issues

Illegal Photocopying Practices, The Value of Building a
Music Collection, Out of Print Does Not Mean Out of Copyright,
Cost, Value, and Publisher Relationship with Teachers, Ignorance of the
Law Is No Excuse, Code of Ethics, Other Ethical Concerns

Dear Mrs. B.,

What do you do when you get a student from another teacher who comes with only photocopied music? Do guidelines exist for helping me understand the copyright law? Does NATS have a Code of Ethics? If so, can you explain how it applies to us as private teachers?

Sincerely,
Nancy

Dear Nancy,

You have really brought up a topic that puts me on my "soap box" every chance I get. Because of the widespread use of photocopied songs, many items go out of existence every year. If every studio teacher required all students to purchase all the music they sing in the studio and for performance, most (but not all) issues regarding the copyright law compliance in the studio would disappear. Every professional organization has a Code of Ethics which is the expected standard of conduct and moral judgment for its members, NATS included.

Sincerely,
Mrs. B.

ILLEGAL PHOTOCOPYING PRACTICES

When students come into my studio with illegal photocopies, *I refuse to use them.* I make a big point of explaining why it is illegal, and emphasize that the practice has led to many wonderful pieces of music going out of print permanently, and to the increase in costs of music remaining in print. I explain that under U.S. law, the Public Domain cutoff date has been frozen by Congress to remain at 1922 (1923 or beyond being protected) as the law now stands. Music published before 1923 may be copied only if it is the original edition. Newly edited, copyrighted editions of music composed before 1923 are fully protected, however. Laws differ in Europe and other areas of the world. I refuse to accompany from photocopies unless it is an emergency, as described in the guidelines provided by the Music Publisher's Association, found later in Appendix IV.

Let me share some of my experiences so you will realize why this is such a major issue. I had a female high school student who had taken two years of lessons with an opera singer. This girl owned a John Jacob Niles book and the rest of her music consisted of photocopies. A student came to me after studying for six years with a NATS member teacher. This girl owned the Zaninelli *5 Folk Songs* book and the rest of her music was photocopies. I had a law student who had studied for three years in college, again with a NATS member teacher, and she had only photocopies. Her excuse was, "Well, I was not a voice major." I had another law student who was a voice minor in college. She owned only the *24 Italian Songs and Arias* and my *Second Book of Soprano Solos*. The rest of her music had been borrowed from (and since returned to) her teacher and her roommate. One of my own students, who purchased all her own music for five years of lessons with me, was a voice major for two years in a reputable college. When she returned for summer lessons following her sophomore year, she had only photocopies from her college experience. She stated, "They did not want us to have to spend money on music." Needless to say, I was very upset that she did not fight the system, but I realize such students are under grade pressure and may be afraid to speak up. A young baritone student who purchased his music for four years with me was not a music major, but took voice lessons all four years of college. He came back after college with only photocopies from his college work. His teacher's view was, "You've spent enough coming here." Again, the student knew better, but was reluctant to take on the teacher's unfounded and illegal attitude.

Another student came with four years of voice lessons and only owned the familiar G. Schirmer Italian book. She auditioned on a photocopied Russian song by Tchaikovsky, which is still available in print. Despite all these lessons, she was totally unaware where middle C was located on the keyboard.

An adult male I referred to a former student of mine for lessons bought one of my books for male voice in a local music store. He reported to me that he was happy to say that this teacher liked the songs so well she copied some of them for her use.

I'm not saying that all voice teachers are unethical in directing the use of illegal photocopying, but this abuse is definitely out there. Do we as teachers really have to be reminded that we are setting an example to students? Do we really want to work in a profession where day in and day out we are in ethical and legal conflict by using photocopies in the studio? If you heard of someone in another field who admitted that something essential to the work they do every day was willfully stolen, and that they encouraged the continual stealing to impressionable students, what would you think of them? The rationalizations and the ignorant assumptions about "fair use" litter our profession and drag it down. Music teachers need to clean up their act! Would you like to read more?

Four high school students recently transferred to my studio. One was a baritone who had only music from his "soprano" days, and only photocopies from his years as a baritone student. The soprano, from another state, had two quality Italian books, and the rest were photocopies. The third student, a soprano, had three years of training and arrived with only a notebook of photocopies, and some of these were traditional men's songs. Another soprano had sung only Broadway music for an entire year while studying with an opera singer. She pleaded with me not to do any more Broadway. Again, most of her songs were photocopies.

Other excuses I get are, "I used my teacher's music mainly, and I had to give it back," or, "My teacher always had us photocopy music from books," or, "My teacher always gave us photocopies from her music for us to use." I know a piano teacher who uses only photocopies and admits her guilt by warning her students not to tell anybody about this practice!

The cost of music cannot be used to justify photocopying. I do not believe that music is a proportionately expensive purchase. But what if it were? Do we steal cars because they are too expensive? Do we steal groceries and feel justified when the prices go up? I've heard teachers say that they cannot bear to ask their students to spend money on music. If the student or parent is not willing or able to pay the cost of study, which includes purchasing music, then the answer surely is not to resort to the illegal action of photocopying. The solution is for a teacher to clarify the situation, making the costs clear, and possibly finding a way of financing the purchases for those truly in need. If it is not a question of financial ability to pay, but an unwillingness to pay for music, then the student should not be taking lessons in the first place. It would be like signing up for scuba lessons and then not to be willing to rent or buy the oxygen tank and wet suit, but assuming that the equipment would be somehow stolen instead. Do you see how ridiculous our assumptions about photocopying have become?

I certainly hope that these examples make you reflect on what is the prevalent practice of too many teachers. Share the "soapbox" with me!

THE VALUE OF BUILDING A MUSIC COLLECTION

Many times in my lectures, I have contrasted irrational excuses about photocopying music with my experiences in taking oil and watercolor painting classes. My fellow students and I *never used our teachers' materials*! We were always expected to purchase our own brushes, canvas, watercolor blocks, paints, and other materials that were needed. In fact, this was so logical and implicit that no teacher or student probably even consciously thought of any other option. When we painted our pictures, we certainly did not give them back to the teacher.

When the approximate fee for new music purchases for the upcoming term or year is included in a studio policy statement (see Chapter 4), or at least is discussed at the outset, then there is never a question about music costs. When put into context, if a student goes to a movie and has a soda and popcorn, it is all gone the next day. In 2013, many movie theaters sell tickets for $10.00. Many teens will also buy a large popcorn and a large soda for an additional $10.00 or more. The very same amount of money can be invested purchasing a lovely book of music that will last a lifetime. Now, how many times a year does this student go to the movies, purchase a ticket to a rock concert, or go to an amusement park? How many times do we purchase CDs that we listen to only once or a few times? Even if a music book, which may be comparably priced, is only used for a few songs, the amount of time spent actively using it adds up to many hours. I'm sure you get my point and can come up with other examples.

A textbook in college for just one class can easily cost over $100. A great deal of music can be purchased for that amount. A former student, the orchestral conductor about whom I wrote, paid over $500 for scores for just one class at Yale University, and these were not the more expensive editions.

Some localities have music stores where students can buy music. Some will even stock your most-used items. But a lack of a local music store is no excuse for becoming your own illegal music publisher. There are any number of places that specialize in vocal music, and with a phone call or an internet order, the music is sent within days. Sometimes you can get discounted music for your students at conventions, at workshops, and from large music retailers. Occasionally, I have received boxes of old music (some of it to be tossed, of course) from retirees and former students to use with needy students. Many of my students have benefited from this generosity. I also have people who will underwrite music costs for a student in need.

Students need to learn to build a library of music of their own and to value it as an important resource. Each selection or volume added to the singer's "tool box" enhances his or her ability to make music for a lifetime. One concept I wish more NATS chapters would consider to encourage the building of student libraries is used by the Allegheny Chapter (Central Pennsylvania). Instead of money awards for student auditions, the winners get vouchers for the purchase of music from the vendor that comes to the site to display vocal collections or who arranges to supply all the winners with their individual orders of music by mail. The student has several weeks to confer with the teacher before ordering this music. Some of my students have received useful supplemental volumes as a result of this wonderful practice.

OUT OF PRINT DOES NOT MEAN OUT OF COPYRIGHT

NATS has prepared a form for use in seeking permission from publishers to make legal photocopies of out-of-print material. I have included a copy for your use in Appendix V. Being out of print, however, does not give you the right to make illegal photocopies. I have used this form a number of times. In some cases, the publishers will charge you for the actual copies they make for you, and others will charge a flat fee that will allow you to make a certain number of copies on your own. Others will refer you to the original composer, who may now own the copyright. Remember, the publisher owns the material if it is in copyright protection. Even if a publisher does not respond to your inquiry, you are committing an illegal act by taking matters into your own hands by making photocopies without permission.

COST, VALUE AND PUBLISHER RELATIONSHIP WITH TEACHERS

At the 1989 NATS convention in Los Angeles, I attended a late afternoon session that featured a panel of publishers and composers. The discussion centered around the industry dilemma of photocopying, and its effects on composers and businesses dealing with printed music. I stood up and explained that I *always* have my students purchase every piece of music they study. I continued to say that I was a horn player, and that if I were to replace my Alexander horn that day, it would cost me at least $3,000. In 2013, that would cost $6,000. Also, I purchased all the music I played on that horn as a private student and solo performer. *Since all singers and voice teachers have been given their instrument entirely free of charge, I offered that I couldn't understand why some are not willing to spend a few thousand dollars for music during their lifetime.* These remarks that day led to my first acquaintance with Richard Walters, my editor at Hal Leonard Corporation (he wanted to meet the lady who championed such a cause), and to a professional relationship that ultimately gave birth to the many affordable volumes I have compiled for students to use. Even the very book you are reading is an eventual result of my remarks that day.

The major music publishing firms make an effort to present music in books that are reasonably priced for students. The cost of a single song sheet starts at $3.95 to $10.00 or beyond at this time; therefore, any book for $10.00 to $30.00 with five to eight usable songs is quite a bargain. Most books contain twenty to forty songs for teacher/student consideration, and some large collections have even more than that. Even if only selected songs are sung and studied, the book is a good value. How can we expect composers and music publishers, which are comprised of individuals and families relying on the corporate income for their living, to continue to meet music teachers' needs if we dishonor the work they do by stealing it in photocopying?

There are two enlightening articles which I absolutely recommend that you download and read concerning publishers and music teachers. They are written by Ted Piechocinski, who is a former band director, music publishing executive and music/copyright attorney and consultant. They are titled "Relationship Building Between Music Publishers and Music Teachers Through Understanding of Business Realities." Part I is from the *American Music Teacher*, Vol. 61, #3, February/March, 2012, and Part II is from the *American Music Teacher*, Vol. 61, #4, April/May, 2012.

IGNORANCE OF THE LAW IS NO EXCUSE

Would you operate any business without knowing the applicable laws that effect your pursuits? Music teachers are no exception. I want you to promise to take time to read *Copying Under Copyright: A Practical Guide*, made available by the Music Publisher's Association, and included for your reference as Appendix IV with "permission to copy this book of guidelines for distribution." If you read it, you will see:

• Printed music comes from a collaboration of composers and arrangers, publishers, and local music retailers and that, whenever printed music is copied without permission, "you are STEALING from composers/arrangers, publishers, and music businesses."

• Some acts are expressly prohibited.

• Some acts can be carried out without having secured previous permission.

• Penalties can be steep in cost, and may lead to possible imprisonment.

• Photocopies force the price of legal editions higher.

Most people understand that plagiarism is a blatantly illegal and immoral act, yet they fail to see that the same laws that protect music and other intellectual property from plagiarism also protect it from illegal duplication and use, whether it be in print, on recording or on the Internet. And why do musicians and music teachers, who should value the existence and publishing of music, need persuasion on the validity of the protection of intellectual property, which includes music?

CODE OF ETHICS

Ethical behavior in the voice studio goes far beyond the willful resistance to illegal photocopying. The Code of Ethics of the National Association of Teachers of Singing is reproduced in full in Appendix VI. Here I would like to give some examples that are covered in the code.

• It is not ethical to make any false claims about yourself or your students. For example, if you sang occasionally in a U.S. Army Chapel in Germany, you cannot claim you sang all over Europe, as someone I have known has claimed.

• It is not ethical to tell students that you will make them into stars, particularly if the talent is not there.

• Scholarships for lessons may be given, but it is unethical to advertise this fact because it is unfair competition with other teachers. Along with many other teachers, I do give scholarships at times. Sometimes a student pays for every other lesson, sometimes he or she pays for one lesson per month, sometimes I give a scholarship covering all music costs, and sometimes I will give a fee reduction, as in a case where I taught mother, father, son, and two daughters. In all cases, the parents and the student understand that this arrangement is totally confidential and cannot be made public. I sometimes have people who are willing to completely underwrite a needy student's lessons while remaining anonymous.

• It is not ethical to criticize the work of fellow teachers unless substantiated with proof. If, for instance, students come to me after several years of lessons with only photocopies, I feel I am justified in telling them that this is an illegal practice, since the copies themselves are the proof.

• It is not ethical to try to steal students from other teachers after hearing them perform, or as a result of any other circumstance. Another teacher approached one of my adults after a concert in which she was a featured soloist. This teacher suggested that she could "do better" if she would switch to him. Was this ethical?

• If a student is a transfer, the credit must be shared with the previous teacher until eight consecutive months of lessons have passed.

• It is not ethical for teachers to offer less than the best instruction of which they are capable. A teacher must give the instruction, the attention, and the full amount of time agreed upon.

• It is not ethical to ask a student to photocopy songs from your music or any other copyrighted music.

OTHER ETHICAL CONCERNS

Although the Code of Ethics covers other issues, I wish to add some personal ideas for your consideration of behaviors I believe are unacceptable, if not necessarily unethical.

I do not think that a teacher should reduce fees for a student who recommends a new student; however, a thank-you note would be in order.

I do not believe it is appropriate to teach a student who is already studying with another teacher, unless that teacher has given specific instructions to seek out one's advice for several lessons. For instance, if you teach primarily females and you have a particular technique problem you do not quite understand with a male student, this could lead to a referral for one or two sessions. Even if a student wishes to make a permanent switch, I want a complete break from the previous teacher for several months before I will accept the student. An exception is if the parents have talked to the teacher, and the teacher gives a verbal release for the immediate change, or the family or student moves from one geographical area to another. Another might be if a teacher announces he or she is closing a studio for personal reasons, such as moving from the area or accepting full-time employment, and suggests that students explore other study opportunities in the studios where openings exist. In the case of college students coming back home during summer breaks, I have found that many college teachers encourage their students to resume study with their previous teacher for the summer when possible. Some of my students even have specific repertoire they are asked to learn. Some college teachers have requested that I pick new music for their students for the next term! If college teachers do not wish their students to study with former teachers, their wishes must be respected.

I do not think it is ethical to waste the student's time during a lesson by conducting lengthy telephone conversations, or in telling self-glorifying stories. (Once in a while I will get a business call that demands my immediate attention. I always apologize to the student and schedule a session to make up the lost time at no additional cost to the student.)

I know I discussed earlier the topic of making physical contact with a student, but it is becoming a very serious issue. A cantor was recently convicted in our area because of touching two girls inappropriately while teaching them to breathe correctly when singing. At a master class, I even asked the student's permission to touch his hand while checking breathing. At that point, I spoke to the teachers present about the seriousness of touching students in any way these days. Afterward, one of the teachers who worked with him all week at this voice camp said, "Oh my goodness, I had my hands all over that young man this week." Of course, this was in checking posture and breathing. She was so thankful that I talked about the subject, and she vowed to rethink what she would do with students in the future.

In my opinion, it is inappropriate to teach while also attempting to supervise one's own small children. One must have someone to take care of them so they do not constantly interrupt the lesson. A teacher should not expect a student's parent to do this chore. I also believe that a teacher who is nursing an infant should not carry out this function while teaching anyone, especially young students. (All of these things have been reported as personal experiences encountered in other studios by students who later started lessons with me.)

As part of the current application process for NATS membership, applicants affirm that they have read the Code of Ethics and "hereby pledge my adherence to all its provisions." I encourage those who qualify for, or are current members of NATS, to review this code regularly. Those who cannot or will not accept these standards probably will find a reason to drop their membership or avoid joining in the first place. But the fact remains: there are standards professional teachers of singing must uphold, if we are not to be subjected to governmental regulations and/or scandals that have unfolded in other professions and businesses in recent years.

I could summarize the serious nature of the topics of this chapter in two sentences:

1. Buy the music and use it properly.

2. Respect both colleagues and students.

CHAPTER 25

CHAPTER 25
PICK-ME-UPS
AND PARTING THOUGHTS

Dear Mrs. B.,

I want to thank you for all the ideas you have shared with me (and perhaps others) throughout my voice teaching "incubation period." One final question, if I may, Mrs. B. While I try to be an upbeat person, there are times when I get discouraged and wonder if it is worth the effort to strive to do my best as a voice teacher. Do you have any quotations or stories from students that I might file away for reference when I need a pick-me-up? Thanks again! If and when we meet in person, I'll buy lunch!

Sincerely,
Nancy

Dear Nancy,

It has been my pleasure to guide you along as you determined that you wish to devote your career to that of being a voice teacher. Let me share a few stories and quotations that give me a lift from time to time. Maybe we can exchange others when we meet for lunch.

Sincerely,
Mrs. B.

When a voice teacher gets discouraged, it is time to reflect on your successes and to seek out inspirational comments from those who have gained insights through their own teaching. Once I received a note from a former student who was in college. He wrote, "Thank you for your passion to teach music, and the love you showed us and show us through insisting on excellence. . .not only in sound, but in musicianship." This is what it's all about! What could be more gratifying than knowing you've helped another student get a good start in life through the influence of musical training? All teachers sincerely committed to their profession receive occasional "pats on the back" like this. Save them and treasure them.

A number of years ago, another young baritone who was a high school senior decided to write an essay for his college applications about "Captain Boytim." He shared it with me after he graduated from college. He wrote, "Former students call her 'Captain Boytim,' but Mrs. Joan Boytim would have it no other way. There has been no teacher in my career as a student who has had a greater impact on my life than Mrs. Boytim. From her, I've learned the meaning of the word discipline, as well as that of mastery and expression."

I include such a statement not as a testament to myself, but as an example of the kind of inspiration that can come in hearing from former students. Some students go on to other things, and I rarely hear about them again. Others stay in touch. When they leave my studio, I simply tell them that if they'd like to write to me, I will always be happy to hear from them about how they're doing and will write back.

When we are just starting out in our profession we do not even imagine the tremendous influence we have on our students. For a student to experience the "one on one" closeness with a teacher of any kind is a rarity these days when so much is always group-oriented. To have such a relationship through the gift of music, using the most special of instruments, the human voice, is too often taken for granted.

I would like to share some examples of the gratitude I have received from students, which I'm sure have a counterpart in the life of any longtime teacher. These are the very best pick-me-ups.

A young baritone who had tremendous problems learning to read music and words, who worked twice as long on school work as his peers, wrote me long letters each Christmas the four years he studied with me. (In retrospect, he probably had Scotopic Sensitivity Syndrome, but at the time I did not know anything about that condition.) An excerpt from a letter he wrote to me in twelfth grade reads

> You and I know that excellence comes to those who always strive beyond the unattainable. This is the time of the year when I look back on my progress in voice (over the previous year and the past). What I see is indescribable. This year we have done so much with working on a better quality (more steadiness in pitch), posture and relaxation (which has improved immensely), and musicology. I have seen obvious results in each of these areas. Each piece of music I pick up becomes a little easier to read, each song I sing sounds a little more pure to pitch and quality, and each time I perform my head and face relax more and more… This is progress! We have created something — an instrument! You build voices like an expert woodsman makes a violin.

This was an unusually diligent and articulate student. As a college freshman this young man was chosen as the baritone soloist for a large choral work, and many thought he was a "professional."

This next letter excerpt comes from an extremely talented tenor who reacted so positively to my strict type of structure with weekly lessons for his last two years of high school. He wrote the following to me.

> When I came to your studio two years ago, I was kind of a mess. My vocal technique was less than optimal and I had a repertoire list that wouldn't have filled a blank page. I was also completely unconfident in myself as a singer, and although I asserted myself and tried to come off as strong as possible, my self-critical nature was beating myself down inside. I needed a teacher that would force me to work to get better, a teacher that would enforce essential practicing habits for success in the music field. Thankfully, you just about fit the bill where that's concerned…
>
> Ultimately, I have you to thank for my success in the arts in high school. Your infamous dedication to helping your students reach their full potential proved true especially with me. I surpassed what I thought my potential was, and now I will be attending one of the best music theatre schools in the country. I know that any challenge I face will be surmountable; if I can make myself sound decent singing French, there's hope for anything! I know that this is possible through the self-assurance and work ethic you gave me. Thank you for helping me mature over these past two years, and I only hope I

had some impact on your life, however small. It was a pleasure being part of your studio, and I know that this will not be the last time our paths cross.

The article "Gratitude Is Good for You" by Lynn Brinckmeyer in the *Music Educator's Journal* (September, 2006) points out that living in a state of gratitude for former mentors and people who care makes life more enjoyable. A teacher's successes far outweigh the frustrations periodically faced. Have you ever thanked some of the influential teachers who were so important in your life?

Sometimes as teachers of young students we have an important impact on future teachers. My last example is a letter excerpt from a former student I began teaching in seventh grade who got her doctorate in voice and is on the faculty of a Colorado college.

> Thank you, Mrs. Boytim, for teaching me in a way that has profoundly affected my life as a singer and inspired me to teach the way I do today. You always emphasized technical accuracy, learning efficiency, inherent musicality, and genuine expression. I speak of you daily to my students and feel so blessed to have you as my teacher and mentor.

What teacher wouldn't be inspired by such beautiful words? I want to emphasize that the grass roots independent teacher, such as myself, can have as great an influence on students of all ages as those teachers at the top institutions and those teaching the top performing artists. There is a time and purpose for each of us to give important input, depending on the student and the circumstances. A teacher can make a difference in a person's life, no matter where the teacher is encountered or at what time of life. We really do change the world, one student at a time. And when students are aware of our influence and are grateful to us for it, we are all the more grateful for the privilege it is to be a teacher.

Many years ago, in *The NATS Bulletin* of May 1958, Vol. 14, No. 4, was an article called "Unseen Harvests," rewritten from a presentation of a keynote address at the Kansas City convention by Gertrude Tingley of Boston. She said, "I am a 'run of the mill' teacher of 'run of the mill' students. I am most sincere when I say it is in my work with them that I have found my deepest satisfaction and richest rewards as a teacher. What are the people of medium or slight talent really seeking?" She then speculates that these students want a means of expression, to be part of a great chorus, to sing to the "glory of God" in church, or they merely want the confidence to sing using the language of music. She continues, "We hold youth in our hands, youth in the making, and we may experience the incomparable happiness of helping create a human being."

My husband Jim wrote an interesting commentary on the average studio student that I have used in lectures throughout the country, and I want to share it with you:

> Many teachers deal with pre-professional or young professional singers, but the typical community studio instructor will have all types of students. Some of these people will not become professional musicians, yet they have other personal needs met in coming to your studio. The purchase of voice lessons for such individuals may parallel what I once read about persons who purchase toothpaste, a drill, a video game, or an automobile. When one buys toothpaste, he or she may be seeking decay prevention, a pleasant taste, or bright teeth. When buying a drill, one might want holes, reliable delivery, quality, or safe operation. A person buying a video game may be looking for personal entertainment, a chance for family togetherness, or development of hand-eye coordination. The purchaser of an automobile may see it as an outlet for showing wealth or as a reflection of lifestyle. So when a person uses discretionary funds on music lessons, what can a student get from

voice instruction other than improved musicianship, a wider repertoire, better breath support, proper technique, and a smoother line?

When people come to us for voice lessons, most of the time they get much more for their money. Sometimes it is confidence, sometimes it is a new artistic outlet, sometimes it is a re-affirmation of youth, sometimes it is in the finding of someone who cares enough to trust in them, and sometimes it is personal encouragement. The side effects of studying voice with a professionally qualified instructor can be enormous.

On the other hand, what do we as teachers gain? Carl Rogers, a writer, psychologist, counselor, and group facilitator, authored the article "In Retrospect: Forty-Six Years," in the February 1974 issue of *American Psychologist*, Vol. 29, No. 2. He compared his work with his hobby as a gardener. Since I spend many hours outside caring for and harvesting flowers, vegetables, and berries, his words also remind me of the rewards in my profession. After describing his disappointment when he could not spend time in his garden, and reflecting on the effective conditions for growth, Rogers spoke for me as he noted, "And when, through patient, intelligent, and understanding care, I have provided the conditions that result in the production of a rare or glorious bloom, I feel the same kind of satisfaction that I have felt in the facilitation of growth in a person or in a group of persons."

While I could share many inspirational pieces I have collected over the years, perhaps the two that follow will renew your energies when you need a boost. The first is a short piece of writing by the famous "author unknown" that has been reprinted many times in the Pennsylvania Music Educators Association newsletter:

THAT IS WHY WE TEACH MUSIC

Not because we expect you to major in music
Not because we expect you to play or sing all your life Not so you can relax
Not so you can have fun
BUT— so you will be human
        so you will recognize beauty
        so you will be sensitive
        so you will be closer to an infinite beyond this world
        so you will have something to cling to
so you will have more love, more compassion, more gentleness, more good—
        in short, more life.
Of what value will it be to make a prosperous living unless you know how to live?
THAT IS WHY WE TEACH MUSIC

The second piece I would encourage you to review from time to time was in a newsletter my piano tuner published (without citation) several years ago:

A SUCCESSFUL TEACHER NEEDS. . .

. . .the education of a college president
. . .the executive ability of a financier
. . .the humility of a deacon
. . .the adaptability of a chameleon
. . .the hope of an optimist
. . .the courage of a hero
. . .the wisdom of a serpent
. . .the gentleness of a dove
. . .the patience of Job
. . .the grace of God, and
. . .the persistence of the devil.

As this revised edition is being published, I note that I am 81 years old, have been married for 52 years, and still teach 30 teenage and adult students on a weekly basis in my independent studio.

When I was awarded a "Distinguished Alumni Award" in 2007 from Indiana University of Pennsylvania, I closed my acceptance speech with this motto – I *aspire* to *inspire* until I *expire*!

And finally, I will quote Plato: "Those having torches will pass them on to others." Now it's your turn to CARRY THE FIRE!

APPENDICES

APPENDIX I

I suggest every teacher have a ready resumé of qualifications. Here is mine as an example.

EDUCATION

B.S. in Music Education, 1955, Indiana University of Pennsylvania

Academic year 1955-56 – voice and French horn major at Staatliche Hochschule für Musik, Munich, Germany, with an International Rotary Fellowship

Summer 1958 – Three months daily lessons with my voice teacher in Munich, Germany

M. Ed. in Music Education with Graduate Voice Recital, 1964, Indiana University of Pennsylvania

Additional summer graduate work – 1962 at Western Michigan University (6 credits); 1967, 1970, 1971 at Indiana University, Bloomington (30 credits in voice pedagogy, vocal literature and private voice)

National Association of Teachers of Singing weeklong workshops – active participant

1965 – Dartmouth College	1984 – Connecticut College
1967 – U. of New York at Buffalo	1985 – U. of North Carolina at Charlotte
1968 – Murray State U., Kentucky	1986 – Arizona State U., Phoenix
1969 – Wittenburg U., Ohio	1988 – Gatlinburg, Tennessee
1972 – Salem Academy, N. Carolina	1993 – U. of North Texas, Denton
1974 – Indiana U., Bloomington	1995 – Las Vegas
1974 – U. of Maryland	1997 – U. of Minnesota, Minneapolis
1975 – U. of Rhode Island	1999 – Rutgers University
1976 – Glassboro State College	2000 – Miami U., Florida
1978 – U. of Maryland	2001 – Penn State University
1981 – Old Dominium U., Virginia	

Westminster Choir College weeklong workshops and festivals – active participant

1975 – Art Song Festival	1977 – Art Song Festival
1976 – Master Teachers of Voice	1978 – Art Song Festival

Total years of private study – Voice – 15   French Horn – 10   Organ – 2
Piano – 16   Violin – 3

Voice teachers: Ernestine Hohl Williams, Allentown, Pa.
Gladys Dunkelberger, Indiana, Pa.
Anna Kayssler-Beblo, Munich, Germany
Elizabeth Mannion, Bloomington, Indiana

Coaching sessions and master classes with: Hans Altman, Allan Rogers, Gerhard Huesch, Gibner King, Paul Sperry, Phyllis Curtain, Todd Duncan, Pierre Bernac, Evelyn Lear, Terry Decima, John Alexander, Horst Günter, Phyllis Bryn-Julson

TEACHING AND PROFESSIONAL EXPERIENCE

Nine years public school vocal teaching – Carlisle Junior High – 3, Carlisle Senior High – 6

Two summers – head of voice department – Stonegate Music and Art Camp, Long Lake, New York

58 years of private voice teaching

Four years part-time voice faculty – Messiah College

Currently active as a vocal soloist, recitalist, piano accompanist, and hornist

Presented 15 recitals, including lecture recitals on the vocal works of Alan Hovhaness, Vincent Persichetti, Amy Beach, Dominick Argento, and Daniel Pinkham.

Soloist with Shippensburg University Choral Groups, Potomac Symphony, St. Cecilia Choral Society in Hagerstown, West Shore Symphony, Harrisburg Opera Company, Harrisburg Choral Society, Gettysburg Community Chorus, Hagerstown Bach Festivals, Dickinson College Choir and Orchestra, Allison United Methodist Church.

Since 1970, I have presented 70 voice-related lectures to local, state, and national groups at Minneapolis, Mason City, Cincinnati, Connecticut College, Gatlinburg, Little Rock, New Orleans, Wichita, Charlotte, NC, Reading, Hershey, Philadelphia, Eastern Kentucky U., Michigan State U., Columbia College, SC, Calgary, Canada, Salisbury, MD, Gainesville, FL, Ohio State U., Bucknell U., Rutgers U., Orlando, FL, Gorham, ME, Seattle, WA, Lincoln, NE, Penn State U., Bloomington, IL, Westfield, MA, Salt Lake City, and Vancouver, Canada.

Since 1984, I have been a master class clinician at Eastern Kentucky U., Calgary, Canada, Columbia, College, SC, Hammond, LA, Wichita, KS, Orlando, FL, Gorham, ME, Jackson, MS, Seattle, WA, Lincoln, NE, Reading, PA, and Dickinson College.

In December, 1993, I taught three demonstration lessons on three consecutive days to a new student at the National Association of Teachers of Singing Convention in Tampa, Florida.

Articles published:

> "Why Neglect the Sacred Solo Duet?" – *NATS Journal*, February, 1972
> "Cooperation Instead of Conflict" – *Music Educator's Journal*, March 1975
> "Duet Literature for the Christmas Season" – *NATS Journal*, October, 1976

In May, 1980, I compiled and edited a 124-page Bibliography entitled *Solo Vocal Repertoire for Young Singers* which was published by the National Association of Teachers of Singing and reprinted in 1982, 1986, and 1988.

In 1990, I compiled a First Book Series of four vocal song anthologies for Soprano, Mezzo/Alto, Tenor, Baritone/Bass, which were published by G. Schirmer in June, 1991. The First Book – Part 2 for each voice was published in December, 1993, and The Second Book for each voice was published in December, 1994.

In 1997, I compiled a First Book Series of Broadway anthologies for Soprano, Mezzo/Alto, Tenor, Baritone/Bass, published by Hal Leonard Corporation, followed by Part II for all voices in 2007.

In 2000, I compiled a set of four song anthologies for Soprano, Alto, Tenor, and Bass called *Easy Songs for Beginning Singers*, and also published in 2001, a single volume entitled *36 Solos for Young Singers*, and *Christmas Solos for All Ages* published in high, medium, and low voice editions.

In 2002, I compiled the anthologies *Sacred Solos for All Ages* in high, medium, and low editions. In addition, I wrote *The Private Voice Studio Handbook: A Practical Guide to All Aspects of Teaching* (Published 2003).

In 2003, I compiled the anthologies, *Daffodils, Violets and Snowflakes* for junior high school girls in both high and low voices, and *Lovers, Lasses and Spring* for high school sopranos, and also published in 2004, *The Second Book of Solos* – Part II for all four voices. In 2005, I compiled *The First Book Series* – Part III for all four voices, and in 2006, published, *Easy Songs for Beginning Singers* – Part II for all four voices.

In 2008, I compiled *Roses, Laughter and Lullabies* for high school mezzos and *Young Ladies, Shipmates and Journeys* for high school tenors and basses.

In 2010, I compiled two duet books – *Easy Classical Duets* and *Traditional Sacred Duets* for high and low voices.

In 2012, I compiled *36 More Solos for Young Singers*.

I was awarded a Distinguished Alumni Award for Service in 2007 from Indiana University of Pennsylvania. Listed in *Who's Who in the East*, 21st Edition – 1986-87, *Who's Who of American Women*, 17th and 18th Edition – 1991-92; 1992-93, *Who's Who in Entertainment*, 2nd and 3rd Edition – 1992-93; 1998-99, and *International Who's Who of Professional and Business Women*, 10th Edition – 2008.

Joan Frey Boytim – Winter, 2014

APPENDIX II
WARM-UP EXERCISES

Joan Boytim

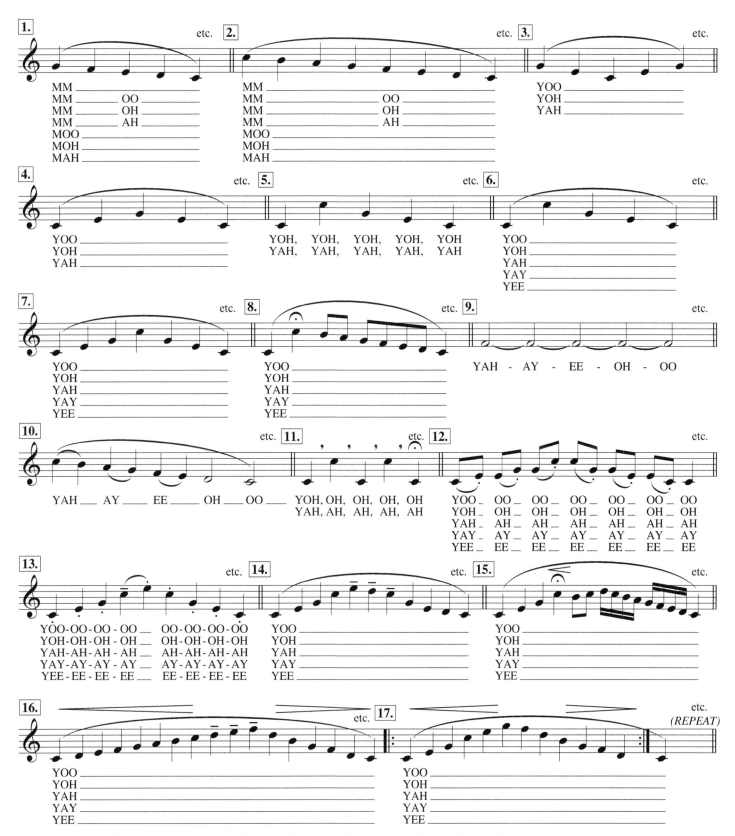

APPENDIX III
SOLFEGGIO SYLLABLE SHEETS
Introduction to Music Reading

Ever since I have given workshops on various aspects of private voice teaching, I have been asked for a set of my syllable sheets that I use with every student—beginner, intermediate or advanced—before going on to songs. I have even used these sheets with adults who had earned masters degrees in voice, with surprising results. This was the only aspect of my teaching with which I refused to part because I felt that all teachers were capable of developing their own sheets unique to their own studios. I sometimes indicated that someday I might write a book. At that time, I remarked, I would include all my melodic drills for teachers to use with their students, if they were inclined to use them to teach music reading, or refresh the reading process.

The main purpose of these sheets is to make certain that the students learn the basic fundamentals of music reading that leads to the increased ability to sightread. The fact that these exercises are practiced makes them studies in reading, not sight-singing. In addition, the use of the syllables strengthens proper vowel formation, vocal line balance and musical phrasing without the distraction of text and interpretation considerations. Some students can possibly read better with the neutral syllable "la," but I believe that much can be learned with the use of the "movable do" solfeggio system. I was trained on the "fixed do" system and I found it frustrating because I was one of those students who could read naturally at sight, and the syllable intervals did not feel right. Over the years I have found that the "movable do" system is a great help to the majority of students who come to the studio without the ability to read music.

Even though I improvise frequently when accompanying the following melodic passages, I have included a sample of the chords and rhythms I use in working with these drills. Teachers can compare my accompaniment interpretation with their own. The variations you can make are endless. In Chapter 7, I referred to these drills as a "cram course" in music reading to purposely help my students become more independent readers as quickly as possible.

These exercises are mostly homemade melodic patterns I developed for my first junior high school chorus and then used again with senior high school choral groups. I revised them and added many more melodies for private voice students over the years. Personally, I do not know how I would successfully teach a beginning student if I did not have these five sheets as my bridge to songs. It is so much easier developing beginning vocal techniques, understanding the particular personality traits of the student, and predicting the tessitura and range of the voice using these simple tonal patterns. Please refer to Chapter 7 on the first lesson and Chapter 9 on reading techniques for discussions on the use and benefits of this teaching approach.

I encourage students to sing with a full voice. If mistakes are made, they need to be strong sounds so the student can tell the difference when the correct note is produced. Only when a student can hear or feel that he or she is not accurate can the student make a positive change. This sometimes takes weeks of experimentation.

At a NATS workshop in Gatlinburg, Tennessee, in a late, after hours "extra" session, several of us learned about color sensitivity and color dominance. This disorder is Scotopic

Sensitivity Syndrome or also known as Irlen Syndrome, named after psychologist Helen Irlen of the Irlen Institute in California, who authored a related book, *Reading By the Colors*. When I encounter a severe problem, I ask the student to choose his or her favorite color, either pink, red, blue, green or yellow. Previously I used a plastic overlay of this color and placed it over the sheet of music. In some cases, it transforms everything from jumbled signs to orderly notes. The students have a much easier time decoding the music. Now I use sunglasses with lenses in five colors for the studio and I find them easier for the student to use to check if this helps the situation. I have several students who have purchased their own colored glasses and they use them for lessons, lesson practice and school homework reading assignments with much success. Students with severe problems can be referred to a certified Irlen screener for professional diagnosis and prescription colored glasses. The colored glasses or overlays do not work in every case, but when they do, the results are very worthwhile.

In researching Scotopic Sensitivity Syndrome you will find that this is a form of dyslexia with light sensitivity, a sensory perception disorder. Some signals from the eye are not reaching the brain in time or intact. This causes a double exposed view with sometimes making the word and note images to be moving or blurred or even showing space gaps at wrong places. This causes exhaustion because the brain has to constantly adjust.

Those of my students who have this problem have a great difficulty with recognizing patterns within what looks like jumbled notes and words. They are likely "word readers" instead of "phrase readers" and have always had difficulty but this was not detected in elementary school. They often have more problems with pattern glare, busy note patterns, black print on white or glossy paper, seeing part but not the whole, losing part and seeing rivers of white space.

As a response to this topic on the Internet, a woman writes about her amazing struggle with trying to cope with this disability. She relates that she played violin for four years and memorized everything because she could not read the notes. She actually figured that everyone saw the notes dancing around like ants and the corresponding white pulsing spaces were normal. She wondered why everyone else could read the dancing ants, while she could not. She also found out that fluorescent lights made all the distortions worse. She concludes describing how she has overcome many of the problems.

As voice teachers teaching one on one, we are in a better position to recognize this problem in our students before they become adults. My most recent discovery led to a complete diagnosis of my student with a physician who found ADHD in addition to this syndrome. My use of the colored glasses was encouraged in addition to medication which addressed the severe migraines, also an effect of this syndrome. She now notices big differences, although she realizes she will always have some difficulty reading music.

Once I taught a successful lawyer whose overlay of blue made the difference between a jumble and an organized page to his sight. Another student, a girl with a gorgeous voice, struggled so much that I called her piano teacher several times and found out she was just as frustrated as I was. We both then used a yellow overlay with much success.

By the way, this student's father had been a non-reader in school and had his grandmother do all his homework. I had known him from my teaching days in high school because I gave his sister voice lessons. One night he asked to try the yellow overlay his daughter had been using on the newspaper that he really couldn't read. He called me the next day, totally elated that for the first time he actually could read parts of the newspaper. You can imagine that the tears came to my eyes hearing this.

Another technique I learned at the same NATS workshop had to do with physical movement while singing. It sometimes helps for the student continually to swing an arm in a circle while singing. However, I find that using motion to place the notes on an imaginary vertical keyboard seems to substitute for the circle movement with as much success.

Continuing the reading process, the students learn time and key signatures as well as note values in the process of using the solfeggio syllable sheets. You may need to create a note value chart to use in explaining to a non-music reader the essentials before beginning the first syllable sheet. I have taught students with as many as four years of piano lessons who could not correctly identify the note values. When teaching dotted notes, I stress pulsating the three sub-beats. You will notice that I make a special point of emphasizing that in my sample accompaniments.

I *always* give the starting note and will often rapidly play the scale up and down in the key I have chosen before we begin. I constantly transpose the keys to fit the student's comfortable range, although the student sings from the one printed key. This is not a problem unless you have a student who has perfect pitch, a very rare phenomenon. (For those teachers who need it, you may wish to write out several accompaniment transpositions for each exercise.) Then, as the lessons progress, I gradually transpose the exercises further to increase the student's vocal range. I *never* play the melodic line, even though occasionally a melody note appears in my accompaniment. When a student makes a mistake, we go back to the scale or the second and third exercise to find the correct interval. Sometimes students will have an exercise (for example, #4 on page 1) for three or four weeks without passing it because they consistently sing the "pitch" re for the first note mi in the third measure with my chord structure. He or she must hear or feel this difference. Eventually the student understands how to practice and by the time he or she gets through the second sheet, things begin to make more sense.

Musical phrasing is also developed at this stage. I do not tell the student where to breathe. If the student breathes anywhere other than at a phrase or sub-phrase ending, I make her or him go back and find the logical place for the breath. Sometimes I make up and sing little word phrases to fit the melody, and the student immediately senses the phrases. Students learn to feel pick-up notes to phrases and sometimes they will experience alternate phrase possibilities. At that point, we discuss why one choice is stronger than the other. They are taught that when we work with songs, the words dictate the phrase endings. This way the student has a sense of musicality before encountering the first song. These students learn to see the notes as groups to detect the rhythmic structure. They also learn to see the melodic line in interval patterns and learn to compare where they are starting and where they will end the phrase to experience tonal similarities and possible tonal landing places in between. At first, to a non-reader, none of these things make any sense whatsoever. If the students continue to learn these patterns by someone playing them, it will still make no sense six months later.

Here are samples of my students' comments after the five sheets are completed:

- "These are fun."
- "They are painful, but so helpful."
- "I never worked so hard at anything before."
- "I can really see such a difference in school choir—I can actually read."
- "I don't want to pass this exercise off until I can really do it correctly."
- "I never even looked at the notes in my choir music before. Now they are starting to make sense."
- "I don't mind that you are being hard on me because I want to learn to read."
- "You know, I really think I should review all five sheets before you put me into an exercise book."
- "My friend's voice teacher only has her singing songs, but she's really missing so much."
- "I'm glad you moved so fast since those sheets were easy for me."
- "I am embarrassed. I thought I really could read music better than this."
- "You are doing all your students a big favor by requiring this discipline from the very beginning."

- "I can't believe how much I learned by struggling with these five syllable sheets."
- "I had a party when I finally finished these sheets!"

Of course, you do not have to use my exercises. You can make up your own set of drills. If you have never used anything like this in the first number of lessons with your students, it is certainly worth a try. When you accept a student and use this approach, you should explain that songs will not be used for a certain number of weeks. You must have a great deal of patience and not give in by playing the notes for the student. If a student has not completed these sheets in eight to nine weeks, I will add a few songs. When I do this, these drills still remain the focus for at least half of the lesson time. On a rare occasion, if a student has had extensive problems, I will review the set before assigning a formal exercise book such as *School of Sight-Singing* by Concone. By doing so, they can really see how much progress they have made. It is so much easier the second time around. With most students, as a result of this preliminary training, I rarely have to play notes of song melody lines. Of course, there are always a few students who need occasional special help.

To those of you who try this approach, I will be very interested in hearing about the results in your studio.

SOLFEGGIO SYLLABLE SHEETS
Set 1

Joan Boytim

(This page is left intentionally blank. The previous page may be carefully removed from the book.)

SOLFEGGIO SYLLABLE SHEETS
Set 2

Joan Boytim

(This page is left intentionally blank. The previous page may be carefully removed from the book.)

SOLFEGGIO SYLLABLE SHEETS
Set 3

Joan Boytim

Copyright © 2003 by HAL LEONARD CORPORATION
International Copyright Secured. All Rights Reserved.

(This page is left intentionally blank. The previous page may be carefully removed from the book.)

SOLFEGGIO SYLLABLE SHEETS
Set 4

Joan Boytim

(This page is left intentionally blank. The previous page may be carefully removed from the book.)

SOLFEGGIO SYLLABLE SHEETS
Set 5

Joan Boytim

(This page is left intentionally blank. The previous page may be carefully removed from the book.)

Accompaniments for Set 1

Joan Boytim

For exercises 1-3 move up or down by half-step *ad lib.* on repeat
The chord for the new key may be played before each transposition.

Set 1, continued

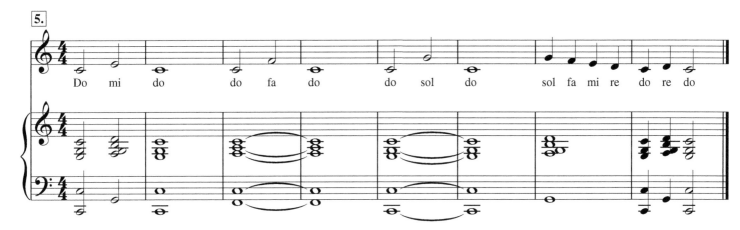

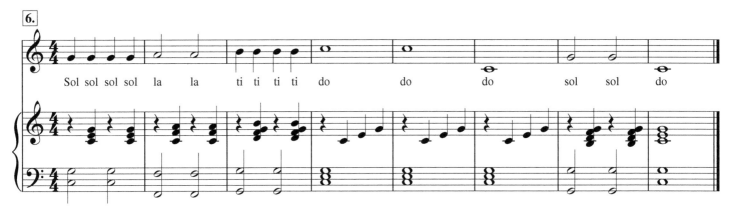

Set 1, continued

12.

Do re mi re mi fa mi fa sol fa sol la sol la ti la ti do ti do re do

Do ti la ti la sol la sol fa sol fa mi fa mi re mi re do re do ti do

Accompaniments for Set 2

Joan Boytim

Set 2, continued

5.

Do do re mi re re mi fa mi re do re sol mi mi fa sol re re mi fa mi fa mi re do re do

6.

Do do do do do do mi mi mi re re re re re re fa fa sol sol sol sol mi re do

7.

Sol sol la ti do do do sol sol mi mi do fa fa sol ti ti do sol ti do

8.

Do re mi do fa mi mi re do fa mi mi re do mi fa sol la ti do

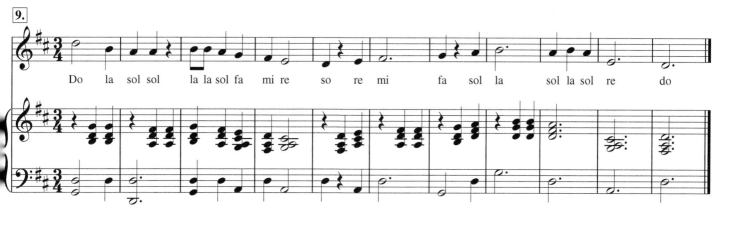

Accompaniments for Set 3

Joan Boytim

(etc.)

1.

Do mi sol do   do fa la do   do mi sol do sol mi do   do fa sol do

2.

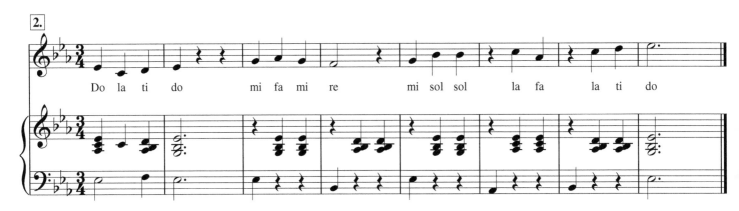

Do la ti do   mi fa mi re   mi sol sol   la fa   la ti do

3.

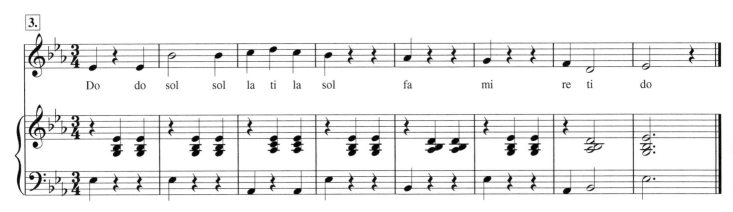

Do do sol sol   la ti la sol   fa   mi   re ti   do

4.

Mi sol mi fa   fa mi re   mi do re   re   do mi sol fa   mi re do   re   mi do

5.

Mi sol la sol mi do re mi fa re mi fa sol fa mi re la sol fa mi fa mi do

6.

Do re mi mi fa sol sol do sol do mi mi mi mi fa mi re ti do

7.

(etc.)

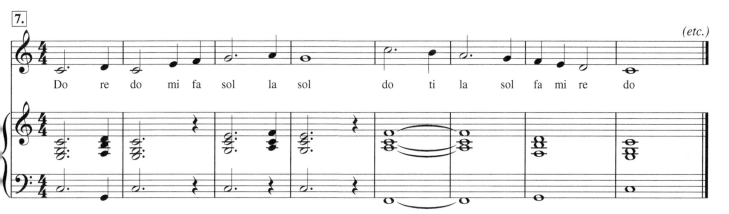

Do re do mi fa sol la sol do ti la sol fa mi re do

8.

Do do sol la sol fa mi mi re do sol sol fa mi mi re sol fa mi

Set 3, continued

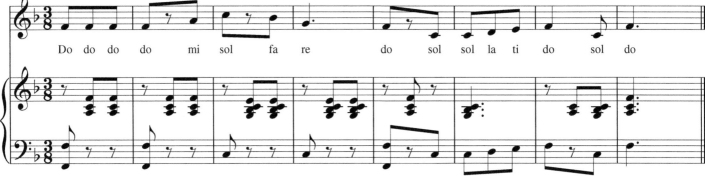

Accompaniments for Set 4

Joan Boytim

Set 4, continued

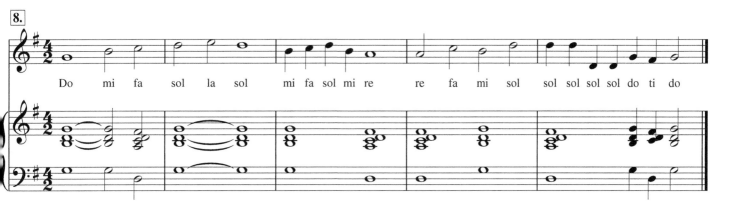

Accompaniments for Set 4

Joan Boytim

1.

Do do re mi mi fa sol do ti la sol fa mi do do ti re re mi sol do do do sol do

2.

Do do do ti do do mi sol sol fa re mi sol do ti la sol fa mi fa mi re ti do

3.

Mi mi re do fa fa mi re mi fa sol ti do la sol sol la sol mi re fa mi re do do

4.

Do ti la sol fa mi re mi fa mi do re mi do mi do re do ti re do

Set 5, continued

APPENDIX IV
COPYING UNDER COPYRIGHT

A Practical Guide

Dos and Don'ts about the U.S. Copyright Law

Published by the Music Publishers' Association (www.mpa.org). Visit the MPA website for more information on music publishing and copyright protection.

Reprinted here by permission.

AN OUTLINE FOR THE CORRECT USE OF COPYRIGHTED PRINTED MUSIC

This outline is intended to be a guide to the major requirements of the Copyright Law as they apply to users of printed music, to inform them so that they may maintain proper standards of ethics, and help protect themselves, their schools, colleges and organizations from incurring liability or subjecting themselves to the possibility of being sued.

This outline does NOT presume to be a comprehensive summary of the United States Copyright Act. It does NOT attempt to deal with all the issues covered by the legislation, nor does it provide answers to many of the legal questions. The purpose of this outline is to inform all users of printed music of the relevant basic provisions of the statute.

CONTENTS

- COPYRIGHT--What Does It Mean?
- THE RIGHTS OF OTHERS
- WHAT YOU MUST NOT DO!
- WHAT YOU CAN DO!
- PENALTIES FOR INFRINGEMENT
- OUT-OF-PRINT MUSIC
- THE MOST FREQUENTLY ASKED QUESTIONS

COPYRIGHT—WHAT DOES IT MEAN?

Under the U.S. Copyright Law, copyright owners have the exclusive right to print, publish, copy, and sell their protected works. The copyright owners of the books and music you purchase usually are indicated on those publications.

The printed music you use reaches you as a result of the collaboration of a number of people:

- the composer or arranger who devotes her or his time and creative effort

- the publisher who invests time and money

- your local music retailer who supplies your musical needs.

Whenever printed music is copied without permission, you are STEALING from

- composers/arrangers

- publishers

- music retailers

THE RIGHTS OF OTHERS

The U.S. Copyright Law is designed to encourage the development of the arts and sciences by protecting the work of the creative individuals in our society: composers, authors, poets, dramatists, choreographers and others.

It is essential to the future of printed music that the Copyright Law be upheld by all. Composers, arrangers, publishers and dealers are losing a significant percentage of their income because of illegal photocopying. This loss of revenue ultimately means that less and less printed music is available on sale, short print runs mean higher prices for what is available, and dealers are no longer able to afford to carry large stocks of sheet music.

Copyright owners have every right to prosecute offenders under the U.S. Copyright Law. To date, there have been a notable number of court decisions against individuals, churches, colleges, and other institutions for violations of the Copyright Law--some involving substantial fines.

WHAT YOU MUST NOT DO!

The following are expressly prohibited:

- Copying to avoid purchase
- Copying music for any kind of performance (note emergency exception below)
- Copying without including copyright notice
- Copying to create anthologies or compilations
- Reproducing material designed to be consumable such as workbooks, standardized tests and answer sheets
- Charging students beyond the actual cost involved in making copies as permitted

WHAT YOU CAN DO!

What you can do without having secured prior permission:

- Emergency copying to replace purchased copies which for any reason are not available for an imminent performance *provided purchased replacement copies shall be substituted in due course.*

- For academic purposes other than performance, multiple copies of excerpts of works may be made, provided that the excerpts do not comprise a part of the whole which would constitute a performable unit such as a section, movement, or aria but in no case more than 10% of the whole work. The number of copies shall not exceed one copy per pupil.

- Printed copies which have been purchased may be edited OR simplified provided that the fundamental character of the work is not distorted or the lyrics, if any, altered or lyrics added if none exist.

- A single copy of recordings of performance by students may be made for evaluation or rehearsal purposes and may be retained by the educational institution or individual teacher.

- A single copy of a sound recording (such as a tape, disc or cassette) of copyrighted music may be made from sound recordings owned by an educational institution or an individual teacher for the purpose of constructing aural exercises or examinations and may be retained by the educational institution or individual teacher. (This pertains only to the copyright of the music itself and not to any copyright which may exist in the sound recording.)

PENALTIES FOR INFRINGEMENT

The remedies provided by the law to a copyright owner mean that anyone found making illegal copies, or otherwise infringing, could face:

1. Statutory damages of from $750 to $30,000 and, if the court finds willfulness, up to $150,000; and

2. If willful infringement for commercial advantage and private financial gain is proved, fines of up to $250,000 and/or five years' imprisonment, or both.
   (as of March 1, 1989)

OUT-OF-PRINT MUSIC

Sometimes, music may be erroneously reported to be out-of-print. If you are in doubt and it is vital that you obtain the music, write directly to the publisher. Only the publisher or copyright owner has the right to confirm that a title is out-of-print. If a title is out of print, many publishers will make arrangements for you to obtain a copy.

THE MOST FREQUENTLY ASKED QUESTIONS

Why can't I copy anthing I want?

It's against the law, other than in very specific circumstances, to make unauthorized copies of copyrighted materials.

What if I am faced with a special situation?

If you want to include copyrighted lyrics in a song sheet--arrange a copyrighted song for four baritones and kazoo--or make any special use of copyrighted music which the publisher cannot supply in regular published form, the magic word is...ASK. You may or may not receive permission, but when you use someone else's property, you must have the property owner's permission.

What if there's not time to ask?

That makes no difference. Think of copyrighted music as a piece of property, and you'll be on the right track. Plan ahead.

What about photocopies that are now in our church/school/library?

Destroy any unauthorized photocopies immediately. Replace them with legal editions.

Can I make copies of copyrighted music first and then ask permission?

No. Permission must be secured prior to any duplication.

What if I can't find the owner of a copyrighted song? Can I go ahead and copy it without permission?

No. You must have the permission of the copyright owner. Check the copyright notice on the work, and/or check with the publisher of the collection in which the work appears. Once you have this information, write to the copyright owner.

As a soloist, is it permissable for me to make a photocopy of a copyrighted work for my accompanist?

No. Permission for duplication, for any purpose whatsoever, must be secured from the copyright owner.

Is it permissable to print words only on a one-time basis, such as in a concert program?

No. Permission must be secured prior to any duplication. Using "just the words" makes no difference.

But what about items that are out of print?

Most publishers are agreeable, under special circumstances, to allow reproducing out-of-print items, but again, permission must be secured from the copyright owner prior to any duplication.

Can I make a transparency of a copyrighted song for use by overhead projector?

No. The making of a transparency is a duplication, and permission must be secured from the copyright owner.

Can I make a record or tape using a prerecorded instrumental accompaniment track?
> Two permissions are necessary here. One is from the copyright owner of the selection to be recorded, and the second is from the producer/manufacturer of the original record.

Can I make a band arrangement of a copyrighted piano solo? Can I make a flute arrangement of a copyrighted work for clarinet?
> No. Making any arrangement is a duplication, and permission must be obtained from the copyright owner.

What about the photocopiers who don't "get caught?"
> They force the price of legal editions higher. They enrich the manufacturers of copying machines at the expense of composers, authors, publishers and music retailers. They risk embarrassment from professional colleagues who understand the law; and they risk fines and jail sentences if taken to court. Frankly, we cannot imagine what kind of school, church or professional musician would derive satisfaction from being a thief.

Remember, any use of a copyrighted work for any purpose—

> for church
> for school
> for a non-profit organization
> to be sold, to be rented
> "just for our church"
> words only
> "we're not selling copies"
> emergency use
> failure to locate the owner

or any other reason or justification, requires permission **BEFORE** any duplication or copies can be made.

FORM OF INQUIRY ON OUT OF PRINT COPYRIGHTED MATERIAL
(This form may be freely reproduced.)

Date_____

Prepare 2 completed copies of this form to send to a publisher for each inquiry, and mail or fax both forms to the publisher. Current publisher addresses may be confirmed by consulting a music retailer.

To (name of publisher):_____

address:_____

_____

I wish to procure _____ copies of your copyrighted publication:

Title _____

Composer _____Arranger/editor_____

Arrangement (i.e., high voice & piano)_____

If the above is in print, please indicate; or if available in a collection, please give the publication title.

_____

If the above is out of print, do you have plans for reprinting? If so, please give information.

_____

If there are no immediate plans for reprinting the above, I request your permission to have a non-exclusive right to

reproduce by photocopy _____ copies for this stated use:_____

If you require a fee for your permission to do so, I agree to pay you $_____ (amount to be filled in by the publisher) in advance of making the copy (copies).

Any copies made with your permission will be identical to your publication, including the copyright notice. The following will be legibly included on the first page of each copy of our reproduction:

This reproduction is made with the express consent of
_____(copyright owner's name) _____
in accordance with the provisions of the United States
Copyright Law.

I acknowledge that I am granted no right to sell, loan, or otherwise distribute reproduced copies of the publication other than for the use set down above. No other rights of any kind for any other use are included in this permission.

If you do not grant the above permission, will you supply me with _____ photocopies of the requested title?

If so, fill in the amount to submit to your company for this purpose. $_____

Requested by (please type or print): _____

Address:_____

Accepted and agreed to (on behalf of the copyright owner)_____

Date_____

(This page is left intentionally blank. The previous page may be carefully removed from the book.)

APPENDIX VI

CODE OF ETHICS
of the
NATIONAL ASSOCIATION OF TEACHERS OF SINGING, INC.

Used by permission.

This Code of Ethics is established by NATS in order that its members may understand more clearly their ethical duties and obligations to their students, other teachers, and the general public, as well as to promote cooperation and good fellowship among the members.

I. Personal Ethical Standards

1. Members will strive to teach with competence through study of voice pedagogy, musicianship, and performance skills.
2. Members will present themselves honestly, in a dignified manner, and with documented qualifications: academic degrees, professional experience, or a combination of both.
3. Members will faithfully support the Association and are encouraged to participate in its activities.

II. Ethical Standards Relating to Students

1. Members will respect the personal integrity and privacy of students unless the legal or academic system requires disclosure.
2. Members will treat each student in a dignified and impartial manner.
3. Members will clearly communicate all expectations of their studios including financial arrangements.
4. Members will respect the student's right to obtain instruction from the teacher of his/her choice.
5. Members will offer their best voice and music instruction and career advice to all students under their instruction. They will complete the full number of lessons and amount of time paid for by each student in accordance with studio policies.
6. Members will not make false or misleading statements regarding a student's hopes for a career or guarantees of performances or favorable contracts.

III. Ethical Standards Relating to Colleagues

1. Members will refrain from making false claims regarding themselves or their students and from making false or malicious statements about colleagues or their students.

2. Members will render honest and impartial adjudication at NATS auditions and/or NATS competitions and students will not be requested to disclose names of present or former teachers until after the event.

3. Members will disclose at NATS events the name of a student's previous voice teacher if the student has studied with the current teacher for less than eight months.

4. When a member's expertise warrants collaboration, members will work collegially with other professionals (i.e., voice therapists, speech pathologists, and medical practitioners).

5. Rules and regulations of any accredited academic institution take precedence over the NATS Code of Ethics, should there be a conflict.

APPENDIX VII
COMPLETE BOYTIM PUBLICATIONS
AND TABLE OF CONTENTS

Books are generally listed in order of difficulty level.

36 SOLOS FOR YOUNG SINGERS

For upper elementary to mid-teens
(Hal Leonard)

April Fool (Gartlan)
The Blue Bells of Scotland (Traditional)
Country Gardens (Traditional English)
Cradle Song (prev. attributed to
    Mozart)
Cuckoo (Shaw)
Dancing (arr. Culli)
Dandelions Gold and Green
    (Icelandic Folk)
The Desperado (arr. Culli)
Didn't My Lord Deliver Daniel?
    (arr. Jackson)
The Generous Fiddler (arr. Culli)
Git Along, Little Dogies (arr. Culli)
He's Got the Whole World in His
    Hands (Spiritual)
Home on the Range (Traditional)
I Know Where I'm Goin' (arr. Hughes)
A Jolly Good Laugh (Thomas)
The Keys of Heaven
    (Traditional English)
Little David, Play on Your Harp
    (arr. Burleigh)
Longing for Spring (Mozart)
McNamara's Band (O'Conner)
Old Dog Tray (Foster)
Old King Cole (English Song)
Peace of the River (Wood)
The Quest (Bohemian Folksong)
Red River Valley (arr. Culli)
The Sea Breeze (Folksong)
Sidewalks of New York
    (Lawlor and Blake)
Sit Down, Sister (arr. Culli)
Skip to My Lou (American Folksong)
Sleep, Baby, Sleep (Folksong)
Softly Sleeping (Schubert)
Some Folks (Foster)
Spinning Song (German Folksong)
Sweet and Low (Barnby)
Tell Me Why (arr. Culli)
Toyland (Herbert)
The Weather (arr. Culli)

36 MORE SOLOS FOR YOUNG SINGERS

For upper elementary to mid-teens
(Hal Leonard)

Alpine Song (Ireland)
The Band Played On (Ward)
Buffalo Gals (Cool White)
Bury Me Not on the Lone Prairie
    (arr. Clemens)
Cradle Song (Taubert)
For Me and My Gal (Meyer)
Four-Leaf Clover (Brownell)
Gently, Johnny, My Jingalo (Sharp)
The Glendy Burk (Foster)
Grandfather's Clock (Work)
Hey! Pretty Lady (Boulter)
His Favorite Flower (Lowitz)
I Heard You Go By (Wood)
I'm Forever Blowing Bubbles (Kellette)
Ja-Da (Carleton)
Listen to the Mocking Bird (Milburn)
Love's Wondrous Garden (Lewis)
Memories (Alstyne)
My Old Friend John (arr. Manney)
My Soldier (German Folksong)
The Night Wind (Ball)
O No, John! (Sharp)
Oh, Charlie Is My Darling
    (Traditional Scottish)
The Old Woman and the Peddler
    (English Folksong)
Peace of Night (Reinecke)
Ragtime Cowboy Joe
    (Muir, Clarke, Abrahams)
Ring the Bluebell (Bunning)
Rowing (Guglielmo)
Shenandoah (American Folksong)
Smilin' Through (Penn)
Spring (Ireland)
There stands a little man
    (Humperdinck)
This Little Light of Mine (Spiritual)
The Train for Poppyland (Wilson)
Wait for the Wagon (arr. Knauff)
The World Is Waiting for the Sunrise
    (Seitz)

DAFFODILS, VIOLETS AND SNOWFLAKES

24 Classical Songs for Young Women
Ages Ten to Mid-Teens
High Voice & Low Voice editions
(Hal Leonard)

An April Girl (Fairlamb)
Boats of Mine (Miller)
Care Flies from the Lad That Is Merry
    (Arne)
Daddy's Sweetheart (Lehmann)
Does He Love Me or Love Me Not?
    (Sterling)
The Fairy Pipers (Brewer)
Four and Twenty Snowflakes (Stickles)
Heigh-Ho! The Sunshine (Phillips)
Her Dream (Waller)
Ho! Mr. Piper (Curran)
Kitty of Coleraine (Irish Folksong)
The Leaves and the Wind (Leoni)
The Linnet's Secret (Rowley)
Little Maid of Arcadee (Sullivan)
The Minuet (Mosenthal)
Molly Malone (Irish Folksong)
My Daffodils (Berwald)
Nursery Rhymes (Curran)
The Secret (Speaks)
'Tis Spring (Ware)
To My First Love (Löhr)
Violets (Woodman)
The Wind (Spross)
You'd Better Ask Me (Löhr)

EASY SONGS FOR THE BEGINNING SOPRANO

(G. Schirmer)

Alice Blue Gown (Tierney)
April Showers (Silvers)
Butterflies (Schulz)
Cradle Song (Brahms)
Evening Prayer from *Hansel and Gretel*
    (Humperdinck)
The False Prophet (Scott)
Florian's Song (Godard)
Golden Slumbers (arr. Vincent)
It Was a Lover and His Lass (Austin)
Ladybird (Schumann)
The Lilac Tree (Gartlan)
The Little Sandman (arr. Brahms)
My Little Heart (Weckerlin)
The Nightingale (Alabieff)
Oh! Dear, What Can the Matter Be?

(English, 16th century)
Oh, Pretty Birds (Riegel)
The Rosebush (Himmel)
The Sweetest Flower that Blows
  (Hawley)
Two Marionettes (Cooke)
The Willow Song (English, 16th
  century)
The Willow Tree (arr. Reimann)
The Winter It Is Past (arr. Hopekirk)

**EASY SONGS FOR THE BEGIN-
NING SOPRANO – PART II**
(G. Schirmer)

April (Quilter)
Because (d'Hardelot)
The Bells of St. Mary's (Adams)
By the Waters of Minnetonka
  (Lieurance)
Cradle Song (De Koven)
Fairy Lullaby (Beach)
From the Land of Sky-blue Water
  (Cadman)
Glow Worm (Lincke)
He Stole My Tender Heart Away
  (Endicott)
Hedge-Roses (Schubert)
In the Woods (Franz)
A Kiss in the Dark (Herbert)
A Little Bit of Heaven (Brennen)
The Little Red Lark (arr. Fisher)
One Spring Morning (Nevin)
The Rose Has Charmed the Nightingale
  (Rimsky-Korsakov)
Song of Love (Romberg)
Stars with Golden Sandals (Franz)
Trees (Rasbach)
Wake Up! (Phillips)

**EASY SONGS FOR
THE BEGINNING
MEZZO-SOPRANO/ALTO**
(G. Schirmer)

At Parting (Rogers)
Early One Morning (arr. Williams)
Ev'ry Time I Feel the Spirit
  (arr. Jackson)
The First Primrose (Grieg)
Gently, Johnny, My Jingalo (arr. Sharp)
If No One Ever Marries Me (Lehmann)
It Was a Lover and His Lass (Morley)
Last Night (Kjerulf)
Little Wild Rose (Schubert)
Long, Long Ago (Bayly)
The Lotus Flower (Schumann)
The Maiden's Wish (Chopin)
Mother, Oh Sing Me to Rest (Franz)
Now is the Month of Maying (Morley)

Oh, Come Again, Beautiful Spring
  (Weckerlin)
Shepherd, Play a Little Air! (Stickles)
Sing Me to Sleep (Greene)
Snowbells (Schumann)
That's an Irish Lullaby (Too-ra-loo-ra-
  loo-ral) (Shannon)
There are Plenty of Fish in the Sea
  (Foster)
Vienna, My City of Dreams (Sieczynski)
Who'll Buy My Lavender? (German)
You are Free (Love Is Just a Game)
  (Jacobi)

**EASY SONGS FOR
THE BEGINNING MEZZO-
SOPRANO/ALTO – PART II**
(G. Schirmer)

The Bonney Lighter-Boy (arr. Sharp)
Cradle Song (Arensky)
Go From My Window, Go (arr.
  Somervell)
Johnny Has Gone for a Soldier
  (arr. Walters)
Just for This (Beach)
Kiss Me Again (Herbert)
Little Boy Blue (Nevin)
Love's Own Sweet Song (Kálmán)
The Mission of a Rose (Cowen)
My Days Have Been So Wondrous Free
  (Hopkinson)
Philosophy (Emmell)
Second Hand Rose (Hanley)
Soft-footed Snow (Lie)
Soldier, Soldier Will You Marry Me?
  (arr. Dean)
Somewhere a Voice Is Calling (Tate)
Spring Sorrow (Ireland)
The Stranger-Man (Chadwick)
A Swan (Grieg)
'Twas in the Lovely Month of May
  (Schumann)

**EASY SONGS FOR THE
BEGINNING TENOR**
(G. Schirmer)

The Ash Grove (Welsh Folksong)
By the Light of the Silvery Moon
  (Edwards)
Come, Aurora (arr. Lange)
Drink to Me Only with Thine Eyes
  (Old English Air)
A Fable (Arensky)
Flow Gently, Sweet Afton (Spilman)
Hark! Hark! The Lark (Schubert)
If You've Got a Mustache (Foster)
I'm Always Chasing Rainbows (Carroll)
Katy Bell (Foster)

The Little Irish Girl (Löhr)
My Wild Irish Rose (Olcott)
Passing By (Purcell)
A Pretty Girl is Like a Melody (Berlin)
Requiem (Homer)
Rock-A-My-Soul (arr. Jackson)
The Rose of Allandale (Nelson)
The Rose of Tralee (Glover)
Santa Lucia (Cottrau)
Scarborough Fair (arr. Sharp)
Standin' in the Need of Prayer
  (arr. Jackson)
Steal Away (arr. Jackson)
When Irish Eyes are Smiling (Ball)

**EASY SONGS FOR THE
BEGINNING TENOR – PART II**
(G. Schirmer)

Believe Me, If All Those Endearing
  Young Charms (Moore)
Bendemeer's Stream (Irish Folk Melody)
Bill Groggin's Goat (Southern
  Appalachian Folksong)
A Blackbird Singing (Head)
Greensleeves (arr. Stanley)
Harrigan (Cohan)
How Can I Keep From Singing
  (arr. Ruck)
I Love a Piano (Berlin)
I Want a Girl (Von Tilzer)
The Lark in the Morn
  (English Folksong)
My Love's an Arbutus (arr. Stanford)
O Heart of Mine (Clough-Leighter)
Passing By (Purcell)
A Sailor Loved a Lass (arr. Wilson)
Thine Alone (Herbert)
Twenty, Eighteen (arr. Taylor)
The Wind Speaks (Grant-Schaefer)
Yankee Doodle Boy (Cohan)

**EASY SONGS FOR THE
BEGINNING BARITONE/BASS**
(G. Schirmer)

Aura Lee (Poulton)
Beautiful Dreamer (Foster)
The Erie Canal (New York Worksong)
Foolish Questions (arr. Culli)
Funiculi, Funicula (Denza)
Go Down, Moses (arr. Culli)
I Wish I Was Single Again (Beckel)
If You Were the Only Girl in the World
  (Ayer)
The Jolly Miller (arr. Manney)
Joshua Fit the Battle of Jericho
  (arr. Jackson)
The Lark in the Morn (Sharp)
The Lost Chord (Sullivan)

The Minstrel Boy (arr. Weckerlin)
Mrs. Murphy's Chowder (arr. Culli)
Out of My Soul's Great Sadness (Franz)
Request (Franz)
Simple Gifts (Traditional Shaker Song)
Smick, Smack, Smuck (Sousa)
Sometimes I Feel Like a Motherless
    Child (arr. Burleigh)
The Story of a Tack (Parks)
Swing Low, Sweet Chariot (arr. Jackson)
Where Did You Get That Hat?
    (J. Sullivan)
While Strolling Through the Park One
    Day (Haley/Keiser)
You'll Miss Lots of Fun When You're
    Married (Sousa)

EASY SONGS FOR THE BEGINNING BARITONE/BASS – PART II
(G. Schirmer)

Autumn (Alison-Crompton)
Colorado Trail (arr. Dougherty)
Farewell (Franz)
For Me and My Gal (Meyer)
Give My Regards to Broadway (Cohan)
Gypsy Love Song (Herbert)
The Happy Lover (arr. Wilson)
He'd Have to Get Under – Get Out and
    Get Under (Abrahams)
Her Rose (Coombs)
Hey, Ho, the Wind and the Rain
    (Quilter)
It Was a Lover and His Lass (Barton)
Kashmiri Song (Woodforde-Finden)
The Man Who Broke the Bank at
    Monte Carlo (Gilbert)
Red River Valley (arr. Dougherty)
The Road to Paradise (Romberg)
The Sailor's Life (arr. Wilson)
Soft Dews from Heaven Falling
    (W.F. Bach)
Sylvia (Speaks)
The Water is Wide (arr. Ruck)

THE FIRST BOOK OF BROADWAY SOLOS SOPRANO
(Hal Leonard)

All the Things You Are (*Very Warm for May*)
And This Is My Beloved (*Kismet*)
Can't Help Lovin' Dat Man (*Show Boat*)
Climb Ev'ry Mountain (*The Sound of Music*)
Goodnight, My Someone (*The Music Man*)
Hello, Young Lovers (*The King and I*)

I Could Have Danced All Night (*My Fair Lady*)
I Have Dreamed (*The King and I*)
I'll Know (*Guys and Dolls*)
It's a Grand Night for Singing (*State Fair*)
Just Imagine (*Good News*)
Look for the Silver Lining (*Sally*)
Look to the Rainbow (*Finian's Rainbow*)
Make Believe (*Show Boat*)
Many a New Day (*Oklahoma!*)
Once You Lose Your Heart (*Me and My Girl*)
Out of My Dreams (*Oklahoma!*)
The Simple Joys of Maidenhood (*Camelot*)
The Sound of Music (*The Sound of Music*)
Till There Was You (*The Music Man*)
Why Do I Love You? (*Show Boat*)
With a Song in My Heart (*Spring Is Here*)
Wouldn't It Be Lovely? (*My Fair Lady*)
You'll Never Walk Alone (*Carousel*)

THE FIRST BOOK OF BROADWAY SOLOS – PART II SOPRANO
(Hal Leonard)

Before I Gaze at You Again (*Camelot*)
Bewitched (*Pal Joey*)
Carousel in the Park (*Up in Central Park*)
Come Home (*Allegro*)
Everything Beautiful Happens at Night (*110 in the Shade*)
Far From the Home I Love (*Fiddler on the Roof*)
Home (*Beauty and the Beast*)
I Didn't Know What Time It Was (*Too Many Girls*)
In My Life (*Les Misérables*)
It's a Most Unusual Day (*A Date with Judy*)
A Lovely Night (*Cinderella*)
Love, Look Away (*Flower Drum Song*)
Mister Snow (*Carousel*)
Much More (*The Fantasticks*)
No Other Love (*Me and Juliet*)
One Boy (*Bye Bye Birdie*)
Show Me (*My Fair Lady*)
So in Love (*Kiss Me, Kate*)
Strange Music (*Song of Norway*)
Ten Minutes Ago (*Cinderella*)
Think of Me (*The Phantom of the Opera*)
Wishing You Were Somehow Here Again (*The Phantom of the Opera*)

THE FIRST BOOK OF BROADWAY SOLOS MEZZO-SOPRANO
(Hal Leonard)

As Long as He Needs Me (*Oliver!*)
Bali Ha'i (*South Pacific*)
A Cock-Eyed Optimist (*South Pacific*)
The Earth and Other Minor Things (*Gigi*)
Falling in Love with Love (*The Boys from Syracuse*)
Getting to Know You (*The King and I*)
I Enjoy Being a Girl (*Flower Drum Song*)
I Love Paris (*Can-Can*)
If I Ruled the World (*Pickwick*)
In My Own Little Corner (*Cinderella*)
It Might as Well Be Spring (*State Fair*)
Maria (*The Sound of Music*)
My Favorite Things (*The Sound of Music*)
My Funny Valentine (*Babes in Arms*)
On My Own (*Les Misérables*)
People (*Funny Girl*)
Simple Little Things (*110 in the Shade*)
Something Wonderful (*The King and I*)
The Song Is You (*Music in the Air*)
What's the Use of Wond'rin' (*Carousel*)
Where or When (*Babes in Arms*)
A Wonderful Guy (*South Pacific*)

THE FIRST BOOK OF BROADWAY SOLOS – PART II MEZZO-SOPRANO
(Hal Leonard)

Beauty and the Beast (*Beauty and the Beast*)
Bill (*Show Boat*)
Castle on a Cloud (*Les Misérables*)
Feed the Birds (*Mary Poppins*)
How Are Things in Glocca Morra (*Finian's Rainbow*)
I Cain't Say No (*Oklahoma!*)
I Got the Sun in the Morning (*Annie Get Your Gun*)
I've Never Been in Love Before (*Guys and Dolls*)
I Loved You Once in Silence (*Camelot*)
I Never Knew His Name (*The Civil War*)
In the Still of the Night (*Rosalie*)
Is It Really Me? (*110 in the Shade*)
Lazy Afternoon (*The Golden Apple*)
Love, Don't Turn Away (*110 in the Shade*)
Matchmaker (*Fiddler on the Roof*)
Memory (*Cats*)
Once Upon a Dream (*Jekyll and Hyde*)
Shall We Dance? (*The King and I*)
Stepsister's Lament (*Cinderella*)

Sympathy, Tenderness (*Jekyll and Hyde*)
They Say It's Wonderful (*Annie Get Your Gun*)
Violets and Silverbells (*Shenandoah*)
What I Did for Love (*A Chorus Line*)
Whistle Down the Wind (*Whistle Down the Wind*)

THE FIRST BOOK OF BROADWAY SOLOS TENOR
(Hal Leonard)

Bring Him Home (*Les Misérables*)
I Believe in You (*How to Succeed in Business Without Really Trying*)
I Could Write a Book (*Pal Joey*)
I Do Not Know a Day I Did Not Love You (*Two by Two*)
Kansas City (*Oklahoma!*)
A Man and a Woman (*110 in the Shade*)
Me and My Girl (*Me and My Girl*)
My Heart Stood Still (*A Connecticut Yankee*)
My Romance (*Jumbo*)
Oh, What a Beautiful Mornin' (*Oklahoma!*)
Old Devil Moon (*Finian's Rainbow*)
On the Street Where You Live (*My Fair Lady*)
Once in Love with Amy (*Where's Charley?*)
The Only Home I Know (*Shenandoah*)
Plant a Radish (*The Fantasticks*)
Stranger in Paradise (*Kismet*)
That's the Way It Happens (*Me and Juliet*)
Very Soft Shoes (*Once Upon a Mattress*)
We Kiss in a Shadow (*The King and I*)
When the Children Are Asleep (*Carousel*)
A Wonderful Day Like Today (*The Roar of the Greasepaint—The Smell of the Crowd*)
You've Got to Be Carefully Taught (*South Pacific*)
Younger than Springtime (*South Pacific*)

THE FIRST BOOK OF BROADWAY SOLOS – PART II TENOR
(Hal Leonard)

Any Dream Will Do (*Joseph and the Amazing Technicolor® Dreamcoat*)
Anyone Can Whistle (*Anyone Can Whistle*)
The Big Black Giant (*Me and Juliet*)
Close Every Door (*Joseph and the Amazing Technicolor® Dreamcoat*)
Do I Love You Because You're Beautiful (*Cinderella*)

Follow me (*Camelot*)
I, Huckleberry, Me (*Big River*)
It Only Takes a Moment (*Hello, Dolly!*)
If I Loved You (*Carousel*)
A Lot of Livin' to Do (*Bye Bye Birdie*)
Love Changes Everything (*Aspects of Love*)
Little Red Hat (*110 in the Shade*)
Lucky in Love (*Good News*)
Manhattan (*Garrick Gaeties*)
Miracle of Miracles (*Fiddler on the Roof*)
The Most Beautiful Girl in the World (*Jumbo*)
One Alone (*The Desert Song*)
Passegiatta (*The Light in the Piazza*)
Sarah (*The Civil War*)
That Great Come and Get It Day (*Finian's Rainbow*)
The Tree (*The Me Nobody Knows*)
You Are Beautiful (*Flower Drum Song*)
You Are Love (*Show Boat*)

THE FIRST BOOK OF BROADWAY SOLOS BARITONE/BASS
(Hal Leonard)

Comedy Tonight (*A Funny Thing Happened on the Way to the Forum*)
Edelweiss (*The Sound of Music*)
Get Me to the Church on Time (*My Fair Lady*)
The Girl That I Marry (*Annie Get Your Gun*)
Gonna Be Another Hot Day (*110 in the Shade*)
How to Handle a Woman (*Camelot*)
I Talk to the Trees (*Paint Your Wagon*)
I've Grown Accustomed to Her Face (*My Fair Lady*)
If Ever I Would Leave You (*Camelot*)
The Impossible Dream (*Man of La Mancha*)
Just in Time (*Bells Are Ringing*)
Leaning on a Lamp-Post (*Me and My Girl*)
My Cup Runneth Over (*I Do! I Do!*)
My Defenses Are Down (*Annie Get Your Gun*)
Oklahoma (*Oklahoma!*)
Some Enchanted Evening (*South Pacific*)
Soon It's Gonna Rain (*The Fantasticks*)
The Surrey with the Fringe on Top (*Oklahoma!*)
There Is Nothin' Like a Dame (*South Pacific*)
They Call the Wind Maria (*Paint Your Wagon*)
This Nearly Was Mine (*South Pacific*)
Try to Remember (*The Fantasticks*)
Wunderbar (*Kiss Me, Kate*)

THE FIRST BOOK OF BROADWAY SOLOS – PART II BARITONE/BASS
(Hal Leonard)

Anyone Would Love You (*Destry Rides Again*)
Brother, My Brother (*The Civil War*)
Camelot (*Camelot*)
C'est moi (*Camelot*)
The Crossing (*Big River*)
The Desert Song (*The Desert Song*)
Dulcinea (*Man of La Mancha*)
A Fellow Needs a Girl (*Allegro*)
Guys and Dolls (*Guys and Dolls*)
I Do, I Do (*I Do, I Do!*)
If I Were a Rich Man (*Fiddler on the Roof*)
London Bridge (*The Prince and the Pauper*)
Luck Be a Lady (*Guys and Dolls*)
Man of La Mancha (*Man of La Mancha*)
More I Cannot Wish You (*Guys and Dolls*)
My Time of Day (*Guys and Dolls*)
Never Say No (*The Fantasticks*)
Other Pleasures (*Aspects of Love*)
Put on a Happy Face (*Bye Bye Birdie*)
The Sun Has Got His Hat On (*Me and My Girl*)
This Can't Be Love (*The Boys from Syracuse*)
Waitin' for the Light to Shine (*Big River*)
Wand'rin Star (*Paint Your Wagon*)
Were Thine That Special Face (*Kiss Me, Kate*)

THE FIRST BOOK OF SOPRANO SOLOS
(G. Schirmer)

The Beatitudes (Malotte)
Bel Piacere (Handel)
Bonne Nuit (Massenet)
The Crucifixion (Barber)
El Majo Discreto (Granados)
El tra la la y el punteado (Granados)
Everywhere I Look! (Carew)
The Green Dog (Kingsley)
Have You See But a White Lily Grow (Anon.)
Hear My Cry, O God (Franck)
Heffle Cuckoo Fair (Shaw)
I Love All Graceful Things (Thiman)
Into the Night (Edwards)
The K'e (Dougherty)
Let My Song Fill Your Heart (Charles)
Let Us Dance, Let Us Sing (Purcell)
Lied der Mignon (Schubert)
A Little China Figure (Leoni)

Little Elegy (Duke)
Love Has Eyes (Bishop)
Lullaby (Scott)
The Mermaid's Song (Haydn)
Minnelied (Mendelssohn)
My Johann (Grieg)
Night is Falling (Haydn)
O Peace, Thou Fairest Child of Heaven (Arne)
Oh, What a Beautiful City! (arr. Boatner)
Piercing Eyes (Haydn)
Rose Softly Blooming (Spohr)
Si mes vers avaient des ailes! (Hahn)
Waldensamkeit (Reger)
Water Parted from the Sea (Arne)
When I Have Sung My Songs (Charles)

THE FIRST BOOK OF SOPRANO SOLOS – PART II
(G. Schirmer)

Animal Crackers (Hageman)
Andenken (Beethoven)
Ave Maria (Abt)
Charmant Papillon (Campra)
Come and Trip It (Handel)
Come to the Fair (Martin)
The Crying of Water (Cambell-Tipton)
Drift Down, Drift Down (Ronald)
Gesù Bambino (Yon)
Grandma (Chanler)
Here Amid the Shady Woods (Handel)
L'heure exquise (Hahn)
How Lovely Are Thy Dwellings (Liddle)
Ich liebe Dich (Beethoven)
Intorno all'idol mio (Cesti)
Lachen und Weinen (Schubert)
No Flower that Blows (Linley)
The Last Rose of Summer (Miliken)
A Nun Takes the Veil (Barber)
Nur wer die sehnsucht kennt (Tchaikovsky)
O Saviour, Hear Me! (Gluck)
Orpheus with His Lute (Schuman)
La Pastorella (Schubert)
Per non penar (d'Astorga)
Petit Noël (Louis)
Romance (Debussy)
Seligkeit (Schubert)
Solvejg's Song (Grieg)
A Spirit Flower (Cambell-Tipton)
To a Wild Rose (MacDowell)
When Daisies Pied (Arne)
When I Was Seventeen (Swedish Folksong)

THE FIRST BOOK OF SOPRANO SOLOS – PART III
(G. Schirmer)

Art thou Troubled? (Handel)
Bluebird (Schirmer)
A Brown Bird Singing (Wood)
For My Soul Thirsteth for God (Mendelssohn)
The Green Cathedral (Hahn)
I Will Lay Me Down in Peace (Greene)
I Will Sing of Thy Great Mercies (Mendelssohn)
In meinem Garten die Nelken (Franz)
Love Among the Daffodils (Coates)
Maman, dites-moi (arr. Weckerlin)
May-Day Carol (arr. Taylor)
The Merry Widow Waltz (Lehár, arr. Higgs)
Mother Sorrow (Grieg)
My Mother Bids Me Bind My Hair (Haydn)
Il neige (Bemberg)
Nuit d'étoiles (Debussy)
The Pool of Quietness (Cator)
Praise (Dyson)
Ridente la calma (Mozart)
Der Sandmann (Schumann)
Se meritar potessi (Bruni)
Sound the Flute! (Dougherty)
Spleen (Poldowski)
Star vicino (Anonymous, attr. Rosa)
Sur la terrasse de Saint Germain (Fourdrain)
The Time for Making Songs has Come (Rogers)
To a Little Child (Edwards)
Under the Greenwood Tree (Arne)
La vezzosa pastorella (Bruni)
Vilia (Lehár, arr. Higgs)
Waters Ripple and Flow (Czecho-Slovak Folksong, arr. Taylor)
Welcome, Pretty Primrose (Pinsuti)
When Jesus Walked on Galilee (Edwards)
The Willow Song (Coleridge-Taylor)

THE SECOND BOOK OF SOPRANO SOLOS
(G. Schirmer)

Art is Calling for Me (Herbert)
Bescheidene Liebe (Wolf)
Les Cloches (Debussy)
Die Nacht (Strauss)
Down in the Forest (Ronald)
Fiocca la neve (Cimara)
Hark! The Echoing Air (Purcell)
Hear My Prayer, O Lord (Dvořák)
Love's Philosophy (Quilter)
Mein Gläubiges Herze (Bach)

Un moto di gioja (Mozart)
My Heart is Like a Singing Bird (Parry)
O Divine Redeemer (Gounod)
Oh! Had I Jubal's Lyre (Handel)
A Pastoral (Veracini)
Shepherd! Thy Demeanour Vary (Brown/Wilson)
Sleep, Gentle Cherub, Sleep Descend (Arne)
Song of the Blackbird (Quilter)
A Spring Morning (Carey)
The Sun Shall Be No More Thy Light (Greene)
The Sun Whose Rays Are All Ablaze (Sullivan)
Take, O Take Those Lips Away (Beach)
These Are They Which Came (Gaul)
To the Birds (A des Oiseaux) (Hüe)
Vergebliches Ständchen (Brahms)
Villanelle (Dell'Acqua)
Das verlassene Mägdlein (Wolf)
Vieille Chanson (Bizet)
La Zingara (Donizetti)

THE SECOND BOOK OF SOPRANO SOLOS – PART II
(G. Schirmer)

Alleluja (Mozart)
Als Luise die Briefe ihres ungetreuen (Mozart)
Après un rêve (Fauré)
La belle au bois dormant (Fourdrain)
The Bird (Duke)
Care selve (Handel)
Chanson Norvégienne (Fourdrain)
Clavelitos (Valverde)
Crabbed Age and Youth (Parry)
Domine Deus (Vivaldi)
The Fields are Full (Gibbs)
I Mourn as a Dove (Benedict)
Il mio ben quando verrà (Paisiello)
J'ai pleuré en rêve (Hüe)
The Lord's Name is Praised (Greene)
Love is a Plaintive Song (Sullivan)
Mandoline (Fauré)
Mausfallen-Sprüchlein (Wolf)
Mondnacht (Schumann)
My Sweetheart and I (Beach)
Niemand hat's Geseh'n (Loewe)
Non ti fidar (Handel)
Quel ruscelletto (Paradies)
Le rossignol des lilas (Hahn)
Sorry Her Lot Who Loves Too Well (Sullivan)
Spring (Gurney)
Ständchen (Brahms)
Sure on This Shining Night (Barber)
That's Life (Sacco)
Think on These Things (Kirlin)

To One Who Passed Whistling Through
  the Night (Gibbs)
The White Peace (Bax)
Wind (Chanler)

THE FIRST BOOK OF MEZZO-
SOPRANO/ALTO SOLOS
(G. Schirmer)

American Lullaby (Rich)
L'anneau d'argent (Chaminade)
Die Bekehrte (Stange)
Der Blumenstrauss (Mendelssohn)
The Cherry Tree (Gibbs)
Chi vuol la zingarella (Paisiello)
Christopher Robin Is Saying His Prayers
  (Fraser-Simson)
Cloud-Shadows (Rogers)
Crabbed Age and Youth (White)
Crucifixion (arr. Payne)
El majo timido (Granados)
Evensong (Lehmann)
Go 'way from My Window (Niles)
Ici-bas! (Fauré)
Jesus Walked This Lonesome Valley (arr.
  Myers)
The Lamb (Chanler)
The Lass from the Low Countree
  (Niles)
The Lord is My Shepherd
  (Tchaikovsky)
Loveliest of Trees (Duke)
Morning (Speaks)
O Rest in the Lord (Mendelssohn)
Oh Sleep, Why Dost Thou Leave Me?
  (Handel)
Open Our Eyes (Macfarlane)
Prayer (Guion)
Pregúntale a las estrellas (arr. Kilenyi)
Silent Noon (Vaughan Williams)
Der Schwur (Meyer-Helmund)
The Sky Above the Roof (Vaughan
  Williams)
The Statue at Czarskoe-Selo (Cui)
This Little Rose (Roy)
Turn Then Thine Eyes (Purcell)
Volksliedchen (Schumann)
Wie Melodien zieht es mir (Brahms)
Wind of the Western Sea (Peel)

THE FIRST BOOK OF MEZZO-
SOPRANO/ALTO SOLOS – PART II
(G. Schirmer)

Ah! Mio Cor (Handel)
As I Went A-Roaming (Brahe)
Auf dem Meere (Franz)
Ave Verum (Mozart)
Beneath a Weeping Willow's Shade
  (Hopkinson)

Bist du bei mir (Stölzel)
The Blue-Bell (MacDowell)
Carmeña (Wilson)
The Carol of the Birds (Niles)
C'est mon ami (arr. Crist)
Clouds (Charles)
Come Ye Blessed (Gaul)
Crépuscule (Massenet)
Danny Boy (Old Irish Air)
Dream Valley (Quilter)
Elégie (Massenet)
Das erste Veilchen (Mendelssohn)
Es muss ein wunderbares sein (Liszt)
Gott im Frühling (Schubert)
Keine Sorg' um den weg (Raff)
A Legend (Tchaikovsky)
The Lovely Song My Heart is Singing
  (Goulding) Mariä Wiegenlied (Reger)
Mystery's Song (Purcell)
Nymphs and Shepherds (Purcell)
Rend'il sereno al ciglio (Handel)
Separzione (Sgambati)
Sérénade (Gounod)
The Sleep That Flits on Baby's Eyes
  (Carpenter) Spring Is at the Door
  (Quilter)
Die Stille (Schumann)
Die stille Wasserrose (Fielitz)
Te Deum (Handel)
Weep No More (Handel)
When I Have Often Heard Young
  Maids Complaining (Purcell)
The Willow Song (Sullivan)
Wind of the Wheat (Phillips)

THE FIRST BOOK OF
MEZZO-SOPRANO/ALTO SOLOS
– PART III
(G. Schirmer)

At the Zoo (Kramer)
Beau soir (Debussy)
The Bubble Song (Shaw)
But the Lord is Mindful of His Own
  (Mendelssohn)
By Dimpled Brook (Arne)
Clair de lune (Fauré)
Corals (Treharne)
Dolce scherza (Perti)
Evening Song (Edwards)
I Walked Today Where Jesus Walked
  (O'Hara)
Ich liebe dich (Grieg)
If There Were Dreams to Sell (Ireland)
Landscape (Griffes)
The Lark Now Leaves His Watery Nest
  (Parker)
The Little Old Lady in Lavender Silk
  (Vinmont)
Lord, How Long Wilt Thou Forget Me?
  (Ranzzini)

The Lotus Bloom (Niles)
Menuet d'Exaudet (Exaudet)
Mit einer Wasserlilie (Grieg)
Morgen! (R. Strauss)
Morgen-Hymne (Henschel)
My Lover is a Fisherman (Strickland)
Der Nußbaum (Schumann)
O Lovely Peace (Handel)
O Praise the Lord (Greene)
Over the Land is April (Quilter)
Prayer of the Norwegian Child
  (Kountz)
Première Danse (Massenet)
Sapphische Ode (Brahms)
Since First I Met Thee (Rubinstein)
Slumber Song (Gretchaninoff)
Spiagge amate (Gluck)
Still wie die Nacht (Böhm)
To Come, O Lord, to Thee (Stickles)
Un cor da voi ferito (Scarlatti)

THE SECOND BOOK OF
MEZZO-SOPRANO/ALTO SOLOS
(G. Schirmer)

An die Musik (Schubert)
An die Nachtigall (Brahms)
Au bord de l'eau (Fauré)
Les berceaux (Fauré)
Un certo no so che (Vivaldi)
Con rauco mormorio (Handel)
Du bist die Ruh' (Schubert)
Eye Hath Not Seen (Gaul)
Great Peace Have They Which Love
  Thy Law (Rogers)
Heard Ye His Voice? (Rubinstein)
Hushed the Song of the Nightingale
  (Gretchaninoff)
I Sought the Lord (Stevenson)
Im Herbst (Franz)
The Jolly Jolly Breeze (Eccles)
Kind Fortune Smiles (Purcell)
Lilacs (Rachmaninoff)
Little Buttercup (Sullivan)
Love, I Have Won You (Ronald)
A Lullaby (Harty)
Orpheus with His Lute (Sullivan)
Pastorale (Bizet)
Patiently Have I Waited (Saint-Saëns)
Pleasure's Gentle Zephyrs Play (Handel)
Silver'd Is the Raven Hair (Sullivan)
The Smiling Hours (Handel)
Te souviens-tu? (Godard)
Thou shalt bring them in (Handel)
To the Children (Rachmaninoff)
Varren (Grieg)
Verborgenheit (Wolf)
We Sing to Him (Purcell)
Where Corals Lie (Elgar)

THE SECOND BOOK OF MEZZO-SOPRANO/ALTO SOLOS – PART II
(G. Schirmer)

Affanni del pensier (Handel)
Ah, Love, but a Day! (Beach)
All mein Gedanken (Strauss)
Allerseelen (Strauss)
As thou wilt father (Williams)
Au jardin de mon pére (Viardot)
Avril (Delibes)
The Awakening (Coates)
Before My Window (Rachmaninoff)
Chanson Triste (Duparc)
Cherry Valley (Quilter)
Du meines Herzen's Krönelein (Strauss)
Du Ring an meinem Finger (Schumann)
Et exultavit spiritus meus (Bach)
Immer leiser wird mein Schlummer (Brahms)
L'heure exquise (Poldowski)
Lord, Lead Me in Thy Righteousness (Cherubini)
Lord to Thee, Each Night and Day (Handel)
Lungi da te (Bononcini)
Die Mainacht (Brahms)
Mon jardin (Fourdrain)
Nebbie (Respighi)
Qui sedes (Vivaldi)
Se tu della mia morte (Scarlatti)
Serenity (Ives)
Song of Devotion (Beck)
Song of the Open (La Forge)
La speranza é giunta (Handel)
Tears (Griffes)
The Twenty-Third Psalm (Malotte)
When a Merry Maiden Marries (Sullivan)
When Frederic Was a Little Lad (Sullivan)
Where the Music Comes From (Hoiby)

THE FIRST BOOK OF TENOR SOLOS
(G. Schirmer)

All Day on the Prairie (Guion)
All Through the Night (Old Welsh Air)
At the Ball (Tchaikovsky)
The Black Dress (Niles)
Black is the Color of My True Love's Hair (Niles)
Brother Will, Brother John (Sacco)
By Mendip Side (Coates)
Come Again, Sweet Love (Dowland)
The Daisies (Barber)
Ein Jüngling liebt ein Mädchen (Schumann)

Go, Lovely Rose (Quilter)
He That Keepeth Israel (Schlösser)
I Attempt from Love's Sickness to Fly (Purcell)
I Love and I Must (Purcell)
Jesu, the Very Thought of Thee (Wesley)
Loch Lomond (arr. Deis)
The Lord is My Light (Speaks)
Lydia (Fauré)
Mailied (Beethoven)
Mistress Mine (Walthew)
Der Mond (Mendelssohn)
My Lady Walks in Loveliness (Charles)
My Lord, What a Mornin' (arr. Johnson)
Der Neugierige (Schubert)
Noche serena (arr. Kilenyi)
Ol' Jim (Edwards)
Orpheus with His Lute (Coates)
Religion is a Fortune (Johnson)
Rio Grande (arr. Dougherty)
La Seña (arr. Kilenyi)
Sento nel core (Scarlatti)
Silent Worship (Handel)
Ständchen (Schubert)
Wayfaring Stranger (Niles)
What Shall I Do to Show How Much I Love Her? (Purcell)

THE FIRST BOOK OF TENOR SOLOS – PART II
(G. Schirmer)

Adieu (Fauré)
An die Geliebte (Beethoven)
Ave Maria (Saint-Saëns)
The Birthday of a King (Neidlinger)
Bonjour, Suzon! (Delibes)
The Cloths of Heaven (Dunhill)
Un doux lien (Delbruck)
Down by the Sally Gardens (arr. Hughes)
Du bist wie eine Blume (Rubinstein)
Every Day is Ladies' Day with Me (Herbert)
Fame's an Echo (Arne)
Forget Me Not (Bach)
Das Fischermädchen (Schubert)
In der Fremde (Schumann)
Incline Thine Ear (Charles)
It Was a Lover and His Lass (Coates)
A Kingdom by the Sea (Somervell)
Linden Lea (Vaughan Williams)
Love Quickly is Pall'd (Purcell)
My Lovely Celia (Monro)
Nobody Knows the Trouble I've Seen (arr. Burleigh)
O Come, O Come, My Dearest (Arne)
O del mio amato ben (Donaudy)

On Richmond Hill There Lives a Lass (Hook)
Panis Angelicus (Franck)
Phillis Has Such Charming Graces (Young)
Russian Picnic (Enders)
Sea Fever (Ireland)
Sonntag (Brahms)
Stille Sicherheit (Franz)
El trobador (arr. Kilenyi)
Wanderers Nachtlied (Schubert)
Weep You No More (Quilter)
What Songs Were Sung (Niles)
Where'er You Walk (Handel)
Who is Sylvia? (Coates)

THE FIRST BOOK OF TENOR SOLOS – PART III
(G. Schirmer)

Arise, O Lord (Hoffmeister)
Auf Flügeln des Gesanges (Mendelssohn)
Behold, What Manner of Love (Humphreys)
Bon jour, ma belle! (Behrend)
The Children (Chanler)
Come, Fair Rosina (Hopkinson)
Douce dame jolie (Machaut)
Down by the Riverside (Old English Folksong, arr. Manning)
I Hear You Calling Me (Marshall)
J'ai tant de choses à vous dire (Ferrari)
Kitty, My Love, Will You Marry Me? (Old Ulster Song, arr. Hughes)
Der Kuß (Beethoven)
The Lark in Clear Air (Irish Air, arr. Fisher)
Der Leiermann (Schubert)
Let the Heavens Rejoice (La Forge)
Mädchen sind wie der Wind (Loewe)
Now Sleeps the Crimson Petal (Quilter)
'O sole mio! (di Capua)
Peace I Leave with You (Roberts)
Sailor's Song (Haydn)
A Seasonal Thanksgiving (Thiman)
Seek Ye the Lord (Roberts)
Selve amiche, ombrose piante (Caldara)
Shady Grove (American Folksong, arr. Dougherty)
Shoes (Manning)
Sing a Song of Sixpence (Hughes)
The Sleigh (Kountz)
Sonnet d'amour (Thomé)
Ständchen (Franz)
Torna a Surriento (de Curtis)
Trade Winds (Keel)
Wehmut (Schumann)
When I Think upon the Maidens (Head)

THE SECOND BOOK OF TENOR SOLOS
(G. Schirmer)

Alleluia! (17th century)
Autumn Evening (Quilter)
Be Thou Faithful Unto Death
  (Mendelssohn)
The Call (Vaughan Williams)
Christkind (Cornelius)
Dein Angesicht (Schumann)
Der Gang zum Liebchen (Brahms)
Die Forelle (Schubert)
Dream-Land (Vaughan Williams)
Fair House of Joy (Quilter)
Free from His Fetters (Sullivan)
Frühlingsträum (Schubert)
The Green Hills o' Somerset (Coates)
I'll Sail Upon the Dog Star (Purcell)
Long Ago (MacDowell)
The Lord is My Shepherd (Liddle)
Mit einem gemalten Band (Beethoven)
My Life's Delight (Quilter)
Nature Beyond Art (Arne)
O Thou Billowy Harvest-Field!
  (Rachmaninoff)
Orpheus with His Lute (Vaughan
  Williams)
Ouvre tes yeux bleus (Massenet)
The Plague of Love (Arne)
Polly Willis (Arne)
Rose Chérie, Aimable Fleur (Grétry)
Le soir (Thomas)
Spirate pur, spirate (Donaudy)
Total Eclipse (Handel)
Turn Thee to Me (Dvořák)
Vaghissima sembianza (Donaudy)
When First My Old (Sullivan)
Whither Must I Wander? (Vaughan
  Williams)

THE SECOND BOOK OF TENOR SOLOS – PART II
(G. Schirmer)

À Chloris (Hahn)
As Ever I Saw (Warlock)
By the Sea (Quilter)
Cabin (Bowles)
Canzonette (Loewe)
Cieco si finse amor (Pignatta)
Le Colibri (Chausson)
Delizie contente, che l'alma beate
  (Cavalli)
He Counteth All Your Sorrows
  (Mendelssohn)
In der Fremde (Schumann)
Let's Take a Walk (Thomson)
Mein schöner Stern! (Schumann)
My Songs Shall Arise (La Forge)

Nell (Fauré)
O Lord, Thou Hast Searched Me
  (Lekberg)
O Waly, Waly (Dougherty)
Oh Gentlemen, Listen, I Pray (Sullivan)
Le papillon (Fourdrain)
Per formare la betta (Scarlatti)
Piggesnie (Warlock)
The Poet's Life (Elgar)
En prière (Fauré)
Reward (Niles)
Schäfers Klagelied (Schubert)
Silver (Gibbs)
Strictly Germ-Proof (Sacco)
Strings in the Earth and Air (Barber)
Then Shall the Righteous Shine Forth
  (Mendelssohn)
Under the Greenwood Tree (Quilter)
Vedi quel ruscelletto (Marcello)
Viens, Aurore (A.L.)
Widmung (Schumann)
Youth (Warlock)

THE FIRST BOOK OF BARITONE/ BASS SOLOS
(G. Schirmer)

Across the Western Ocean (arr.
  Dougherty)
The Bells of Clermont Town
  (Goodhart)
The Blind Ploughman (Clarke)
Blow, Blow, Thou Winter Wind
  (Quilter)
Blow High, Blow Low (Dibdin)
Create In Me a Clean Heart (Mueller)
Encantadora Maria (arr. Kilenyi)
False Phillis (Old English Melody)
The Friar of Orders Gray (Shield)
Hör' ich das Liedchen klingen
  (Schumann)
Intermezzo (Schumann)
Jagdlied (Mendelssohn)
The Jolly Roger (Robertson)
The King of Love My Shepherd Is
  (Gounod)
Leave Me, Loathsome Light (Handel)
Let Us Break Bread Together (arr.
  Myers)
Lord, I Want to Be a Christian (arr.
  Payne)
Lungi dal caro bene (Sarti)
Next, Winter Comes Slowly (Purcell)
O Mistress Mine (Quilter)
On the Road to Mandalay (Speaks)
La paloma blanca (arr. Kilenyi)
The Rovin' Gambler (Niles)
The Sea (MacDowell)
Sea Moods (Tyson)
Le secret (Fauré)
Shenandoah (arr. Dougherty)

The Splendour Falls (Walthew)
Tally-Ho! (Leoni)
There Was a Mighty Monarch
  (Beethoven)
Why So Pale and Wan (Arne)
Widmung (Franz)

THE FIRST BOOK OF BARITONE/ BASS SOLOS – PART II
(G. Schirmer)

L'amour de moi (15th century)
Blow, Blow, Thou Winter Wind (Arne)
Blow, Ye Winds (arr. Dougherty)
Bois épais (Lully)
Bright Is the Ring of Words (Vaughan
  Williams)
Build Thee More Stately Mansions
  (Andrews)
Deep River (arr. Burleigh)
Down Harley Street (Kingsford)
Du bist wie eine Blume (Liszt)
Du bist wie eine Blume (Schumann)
Ein Ton (Cornelius)
Eldorado (Walthew)
The First Concert (Mana-Zucca)
Give a Man a Horse He Can Ride
  (O'Hara)
God is My Shepherd (Dvořák)
The Heart Worships (Holst)
I Wonder as I Wander (Niles)
In einem kühlen Grunde (German
  Folksong)
Jesus, Fount of Consolation (Bach)
Die Könige (Cornelius)
Le miroir (Ferrari)
O'er the Hills (Hopkinson)
Os tormentos de amor (arr. Kilenyi)
Pilgrim's Song (Tchaikovsky)
Pretty As a Picture (Herbert)
The Pretty Creature (Storace)
The Roadside Fire (Vaughan Williams)
Rolling Down to Rio (German)
Sea Fever (Andrews)
The Slighted Swain (arr. Wilson)
The Song of Momus to Mars (Boyce)
Toglietemi la vita ancor (Scarlatti)
Verrathene Liebe (Schumann)
Was ist Sylvia? (Schubert)
Die Wetterfahne (Schubert)

THE FIRST BOOK OF BARITONE/ BASS SOLOS – PART III
(G. Schirmer)

The Beggar's Song (Leveridge)
Bergère légère (arr. Weckerlin)
Blue Are Her Eyes (Watts)
Captain Mac (Sanderson)

Come, O Come, My Life's Delight
(Parker)
The Complacent Lover (Parker)
Consecration (Franz)
Evening (Niles)
Five Eyes (Gibbs)
Geheimes (Schubert)
God So Loved the World (Stainer,
arr. Stickles)
How Long Wilt Thou Forget Me
(Speaks)
In the Luxembourg Gardens (Manning)
Invictus (Huhn)
Io so che pria mi moro (Aniello)
It Was a Lover and His Lass (Quilter)
Let Not Your Heart Be Troubled
(Speaks)
La maison grise (Messager)
Morir voglio (D'Astorga)
Der Musikant (Wolf)
Once I Loved a Maiden Fair (Parker)
The Pasture (Naginski)
Que l'heure est donc brève (Massenet)
River-Boats (Manning)
Die Rose, die Lilie (Franz)
Der Schnee ist zergangen (Franz)
The Sea-Bird (Quilter)
The Ships of Arcady (Head)
The Skipper (Jude)
Song of the Armourer (Nevin)
Spirit of God (Neidlinger)
The Tinker's Song (Dibdin)
Trusting in Thee (Fichthorn)
When All Night Long a Chap Remains
(Sullivan)
When Big Profundo Sang Low "C"
(Botsford)
When I Was One-And-Twenty
(Somervell)

THE SECOND BOOK OF
BARITONE/BASS SOLOS
(G. Schirmer)

Ah! Willow (arr. Wilson)
Annie Laurie (Scott)
Arise, Ye Subterranean Winds (Purcell)
Arm, Arm, Ye Brave (Handel)
Le charme (Chausson)
Child of the Flowing Tide (Shaw)
Come, Ye Blessed (Scott)
Gefror'ne Thränen (Schubert)
Die Hirten (Cornelius)
I Will Sing New Songs (Dvořák)
The Island (Rachmaninoff)
Let Each Gallant Heart (Purcell)
Like the Shadow (Handel)
Der Lindenbaum (Schubert)
Lord God of Abraham (Mendelssohn)
Love Is a Bable (Parry)
Mattinata (Leoncavallo)

Memory (Ireland)
More Sweet is That Name (Handel)
Nature's Adoration (Beethoven)
Più vage e vezzosetta (Bononcini)
Plaisir d'amour (Martini)
The Policeman's Song (Sullivan)
Die Post (Schubert)
Les roses d'Ispahan (Fauré)
Salvation Belongeth Unto the Lord
(Greene)
Si, tra I ceppi (Handel)
Since From My Dear (Purcell)
The Vagabond (Vaughan Williams)
Der Wanderer (Schubert)
When I Was a Lad I Served a Term
(Sullivan)

THE SECOND BOOK OF
BARITONE/BASS SOLOS – PART II
(G. Schirmer)

All'acquisto di gloria (Scarlatti)
An Chloe (Mozart)
Art Thou the Christ? (O'Hara)
Auf dem Kirchhofe (Brahms)
Ave Maria (Luzzi)
Die beiden Grenadiere (Schumann)
The Bird and the Beast (Dougherty)
La chanson du pêcheur (Fauré)
Le Cor (Flégier)
Heavenly Grass (Bowles)
Honor and Arms (Handel)
If You Give Me Your Attention
(Sullivan)
Madrigal (Sandoval)
My Boy, You May Take It from Me
(Sullivan)
My Soul Is Athirst for God (Stickles)
Nel riposo e nel contento (Handel)
Nocturne (Fauré)
Non è ver! (Mattei)
Obstination (Fontenailles)
Revenge, Timotheus Cries (Handel)
Silver (Duke)
Sleep (Gurney)
Son tutta duolo (Scarlatti)
Take, O Take Those Lips Away
(Quilter)
Three for Jack (Squire)
The Topsails Shiver in the Wind (Arne)
Traum durch die Dämmerung (Strauss)
Va per lo mare (Scarlatti)
Zueignung (Strauss)

THE FIRST BOOK OF SOPRANO
SOLOS COMPLETE –
PARTS I, II, AND III COMBINED
(G. Schirmer)

See above for contents of individual
volumes.

THE FIRST BOOK OF MEZZO-
SOPRANO/ALTO SOLOS
COMPLETE – PARTS I, II, AND III
COMBINED
(G. Schirmer)

See above for contents of individual
volumes.

THE FIRST BOOK OF TENOR
SOLOS COMPLETE –
PARTS I, II, AND III COMBINED
(G. Schirmer)

See above for contents of individual
volumes.

THE FIRST BOOK OF BARITONE/
BASS SOLOS COMPLETE – PARTS
I, II, AND III COMBINED
(G. Schirmer)

See above for contents of individual
volumes.

LOVERS, LASSES AND SPRING
*14 Classical Songs for Soprano, Ages
Mid-Teens and Up*
(Hal Leonard)

*For teaching beginning coloratura
(to be used generally as a supplement to
The First Book of Soprano Solos Parts I,
II and III)*

Be Still, Blackbird (Sanderson)
Charming Chloe (German)
Cherry Ripe (Horn)
A Heart That's Free (Robyn)
It Was a Lover and His Lass (German)
The Kerry Dance (Molloy)
The Lass with the Delicate Air (M.
Arne)
The Little Damozel (Novello)
The Little Shepherd's Song (Watts)
Love's a Merchant (Carew)
The Piper of Love (Carew)
The Smile of Spring (Fletcher)
When Love Is Kind (arr. A.L.)
Woodland Sketches (Godfrey)

ROSES, LAUGHTER AND LULLABIES
18 Classical Songs for Mezzo-Soprano
(Hal Leonard)

Birds in the Night (Sullivan)
Cradle Song (Schubert)
The Forsaken Maid (Smart)
Hymn to the Night (Campbell-Tipton)
I Have Twelve Oxen (Ireland)
It Was a Lover and His Lass (Clough-Leitner)
I Will Go With My Father A-Ploughing (Quilter)
Jeanette and Her Little Wooden Shoes (Herbert)
Love Is a Sickness Full of Woes (Parker)
O Bid Your Faithful Ariel Fly (Linley)
Should He Upbraid (Bishop)
Spring Comes Laughing (Carew)
Tears (Tchaikovsky)
Two Roses (Gilberté)
Under the Greenwood Tree (Buzzi-Peccia)
The Valley of Laughter (Sanderson)
The Winds are Calling (Ronald)
Without Thee (Gounod)

YOUNG LADIES, SHIPMATES AND JOURNEYS
21 Classical Songs for Young Men
Tenor & Baritone/Bass editions
(Hal Leonard)

Barbara Allen (Quilter)
The Bay of Biscay (Davy)
Blackbirds and Thrushes (Sharp)
The Coasts of High Barbary (Sharp)
Come Let's Be Merry (Wilson)
The Duke of Bedford (Sharp)
Farewell, Nancy (Sharp)
Gentle Annie (Foster)
I Am a Pirate King (Sullivan)
I Want What I Want When I Want It (Herbert)
Nothing But a Plain Old Soldier (Foster)
The Law is the True Embodiment (Sullivan)
The Midshipmite (Adams)
My Generous Heart Disdains (Hopkinson)
The Old Road (Scott)
Punchinello (Molloy)
The Rambling Sailor (Sharp)
Shipmates of Mine (Sanderson)
The Song of Brother Hilario (Cox)
Three Poor Mariners (Quilter)
While the Foaming Billows Roll (Linley)

CHRISTMAS SOLOS FOR ALL AGES
45 Songs
High Voice, Medium Voice, & Low Voice editions
(Hal Leonard)

Carol Arrangements
As Lately We Watched (19th century Austrian)
Bells Over Bethlehem (Traditional Andalucian)
Carol of the Birds (Traditional Andalucian)
Caroling, Caroling (Burt)
The Darkness Is Falling (Austrian)
Fum, Fum, Fum (Traditional Catalonian)
Go, Tell It on the Mountain (African-American Spiritual)
He Is Born, The Divine Christ Child (18th century French)
Lo, How a Rose E'er Blooming (Alte Catholische Geistliche Kirchengesäng)
Mary Had a Baby (African-American Spiritual)
O Come Away, Ye Shepherds (18th century French)
O Hearken Ye (Burt)
On Christmas Night (Sussex)
Rise Up, Shepherd, and Follow (African-American Spiritual)
The Sleep of the Child Jesus (Geveart)
The Snow Lay on the Ground (Traditional Irish-English)
Some Children See Him (Burt)
The Star Carol (Burt)
Still, Still, Still (Traditional Austrian)
This Is Christmas (Burt)

Art Songs/Traditional Songs
The Birthday of a King (Neidlinger)
Christmas Candle (Warren)
A Christmas Carol (Dello Joio)
A Christmas Cradle Song (Hamblen)
Come to the Stable with Jesus (O'Hara)
Gesù Bambino (Yon)
The Holy Infant's Lullaby (Dello Joio)
O Holy Night (Adam)
In the Bleak Midwinter (Caldwell)
Love Came Down at Christmas (Thiman)
O Savior Sweet (Bach)
The Kings (Cornelius)
Little Noel (Louis)
Mary's Slumber Song (Hamblen)
The Shepherds (Cornelius)
Shepherd's Cradle Song (C.D. Schubert)

A Slumber Song of the Madonna (Head)
There's a Song in the Air (Speaks)
The Virgin at the Manger (Périlhou)
The Virgin's Slumber Song (Reger)
Voices of the Sky (Matthews)
What Songs Were Sung? (Niles)

Popular Songs
The Christmas Song (Torme/Wells)
Do You Hear What I Hear? (Shayne)
White Christmas (Berlin)

SACRED SOLOS FOR ALL AGES
43 Songs
High Voice, Medium Voice, & Low Voice editions
(Hal Leonard)

All in the April Evening (Diack)
Alleluia! (Hummel)
Alleluia! (O'Conner-Morris)
Ave Maria (O Lord, Most Holy) (Abt)
Ave Maria (Gounod)
Ave Maria (Schubert)
Ave verum (Mozart)
Before the Crucifix (La Forge)
The Call (Vaughan Williams)
Come Unto Him (Dunn)
Come, Ye Blessed (Scott)
The Cross of Calvary (Ave Maria) (Gounod)
David's Prayer (Costa)
The Earth is the Lord's (Lynes)
Gethsemane (Salter)
God is My Shepherd (Dvořák)
Great Peace Have They Which Love Thy Law (Rogers)
Hear My Cry, O God (Franck)
The Heart Worships (Holst)
The Holy City (Weatherly and Adams)
How Lovely Are Thy Dwellings (Liddle)
Hymn of Thanks (Kremser)
I Sought the Lord (Stevenson)
If God So Clothe the Grass (Bischoff)
The King of Love My Shepherd Is (Gounod)
Like as the Hart (Liddle)
Light of the World (Hatton)
The Lord is My Light (Allitsen)
The Lord is My Light (Speaks)
The Lord is My Shepherd (Liddle)
Love Ye the Lord (Largo) (Handel)
Not a Sparrow Falleth (Abt)
O Lord, Be Merciful (Bartlett)
The Palms (Fauré)
Panis angelicus (O Lord Most Holy) (Franck)
Prayer (Guion)

The Publican (van de Water)
Thanks Be to God (Dickson)
This Joyful Eastertide (Somervell)
Thou Wilt Keep Him in Perfect Peace
  (Speaks)
Vouchsafe, O Lord (Te Deum)
  (Handel)
When I Think Upon Thy Goodness
  (Haydn)
With Thee There is Forgiveness
  (Cowen)

EASY CLASSICAL DUETS
18 Duets for Student Singers
High Voice, Low Voice, and Piano
(Hal Leonard)

About Katy (Wilson)
All Through the Night (Welsh Melody)
Come to the Fair (Martin)
The Day Is Fair (Strickland)
From Far Away (Caracciolo)
In Springtime (Newton)
Let Us Wander (Purcell)
May Day Carol (Essex County Air)
Morning (Grieg)
Nearest and Dearest (Caracciolo)
Only to Thee (Saint-Saëns)
A Poor Soul Sat Sighing (Carmichael)
Spring-Song (Lassen)
The Time of Youth (Pinsuti)
Trip It in a Ring (Purcell)
When Twilight Weaves (Beethoven)
Who Is Sylvia? (Coates)

TRADITIONAL SACRED DUETS
18 Songs
High Voice, Low Voice, and Piano
(Hal Leonard)

As the Hart Panteth (Marcello)
Come, Blessed Savior (Ave, Maria)
  (Saint-Saëns)
Come, Let Us All Rejoicing (Warhurst)
Give Ear Unto Me (Marcello)
God Is a Spirit (Bennett)
Hear Us, O Savior (Ave, Maria)
  (Rameau)
Is It Nothing to You? (Foster)
I Waited for the Lord (Mendelssohn)
Jesus, Savior (Ave, Verum) (Mozart)
The King of Love My Shepherd Is
  (Shelley)
Like As the Hart (Novello)
Lord, Speak to Me (Roberts)
O, Divine Redeemer (Parce, Domine)
  (Gounod)
O How Amiable Are Thy Dwellings
  (Maunder)
O Lovely Peace (Handel)
Savior, Like a Shepherd Lead Us
  (Jones)
Songs of Praise the Angels Sang
  (Attwood)